APTITUDES FOR GROWTH ATTITUDES FOR SUCCESS

KIMBERLY HENSLEY

© 2010 by Kimberly Hensley. All rights reserved.

WinePress Publishing (PO Box 428, Enumclaw, WA 98022) functions only as book publisher. As such, the ultimate design, content, editorial accuracy, and views expressed or implied in this work are those of the author.

No part of this publication may be reproduced, stored in a retrieval system, or transmitted in any way by any means—electronic, mechanical, photocopy, recording, or otherwise—without the prior permission of the copyright holder, except as provided by USA copyright law.

Unless otherwise indicated, all Scriptures are taken from *The Living Bible*, © 1971 owned by assignment by Illinois Regional Bank N.A. (as trustee). Used by permission of Tyndale House Publishers, Inc., Wheaton, Illinois 60189. All rights reserved.

Scripture references marked MESSAGE are taken from *The Message Bible* © 1993 by Eugene N. Peterson, NavPress, PO Box 35001, Colorado Springs, CO 80935, 4th printing in USA 1994. Published in association with the literary agency—Alive Comm. PO Box 49068, Colorado Springs, CO 80949. Used by permission.

Scripture references marked NKJV are taken from the *New King James Version*, © 1979, 1980, 1982 by Thomas Nelson, Inc., Publishers. Used by permission.

Scripture references marked AMP are taken from *The Amplified Bible, Old Testament*, © 1965 and 1987 by The Zondervan Corporation, and from *The Amplified New Testament*, © 1954, 1958, 1987 by The Lockman Foundation. Used by permission.

Scripture references marked KJV are taken from the *King James Version* of the Bible.

Also used The Life Recovery Bible and The Archaeological Study Bible

ISBN 13: 978-1-4141-1732-4
ISBN 10: 1-4141-1732-9
Library of Congress Catalog Card Number: 2010902672

APTITUDES FOR GROWTH
ATTITUDES FOR SUCCESS

*To Carole,
the most cordial
person I know.
God bless you,
Kimberly Klmdy*

DISCLAIMER

This book at its core is unapologetically a work concerned with the ultimate message Jesus Christ came to give—that through believing in Him we shall be saved. I believe the Bible is God's inspired Word.

I have chosen to use the empirically supported research surrounding positive psychology to undergird my discussion of the importance of character strengths, social support, and work in a fulfilled life.

Let me be perfectly clear: Positive psychology is religion-neutral and absolutely does not endorse any religious beliefs beyond the findings that indicate people with spirituality in their lives are happier than those who lack this quality.

I hope positive psychologists who might read this work would do so with a mind open to experimentation and the testing of various formats for the presentation of positive psychology's important and relevant findings.

Some of the personal stories in this book are composites of individuals. Names were changed to protect their privacy.

This book is dedicated to the memory of my father,
Rev. William E. Mittendorf, a great man.

CONTENTS

Foreword..................................... xi

PART 1: CHARACTER STRENGTHS
1. God Has Something Special in Mind for You 1
2. Faith: Believing Every Promise for Your Life
   (a study of Abraham) 11
3. Optimism: Yes, We Can! (a study of Joshua and Caleb)........ 23
4. Forgiveness: Let Go and Be Free (a study of Joseph) 35
5. Courage: I Come to You in the Name of the Lord
   (a study of David) 47
6. Perseverance: Never Give Up (a study of Nehemiah).......... 65
7. Patience: I Will Wait Upon the Lord (a study of Job).......... 77
8. Wisdom: Mining For Gold (a study of Solomon).............. 93
9. Peace: Being a Mary in a Herod-ruled World
   (a study of Mary, Jesus' mother) 105
10. Enthusiasm and Commitment: With All His Heart;
    With All Your Heart (a study of Simon Peter) 113
11. Gratitude: Mary Magdalene Washes Feet and the
    Cleansed Leper Gives Thanks (a study of Mary
    Magdalene and a leper) 121
12. Happiness: Found on a Road and
    Up a Tree (a study of Paul and Zacchaeus) 131
13. Using Your Strengths for Growth and Success 143

PART 2: BUILDING A SUPPORT NETWORK
14. The Gift of Support．．．．．．．．．．．．．．．．．．．．．．．．．．．．．．157
15. Friendship: People Need People．．．．．．．．．．．．．．．．．．．．165

PART 3: DISCOVERING AND EMBRACING YOUR CALLING
16. Daring to Honor Your Deepest Desires．．．．．．．．．．．．．．．．177
17. Committing Yourself to Your Life's Work．．．．．．．．．．．．．．．187

PART 4: EMPOWERED BY OUR TRIUNE GOD
18. The Holy Spirit: Source of Self-Control．．．．．．．．．．．．．．．．197
19. Jesus: Hope in a Manger, Hope on a Cross．．．．．．．．．．．．．．213
20. God: An Everlasting Love．．．．．．．．．．．．．．．．．．．．．．．．．．221

Endnotes．．227

FOREWORD

THIS BOOK EXAMINES various Bible characters' lives for their aptitudes and attitudes. In the process of digesting this book, you will be able to explore your strengths and talents and compare them to those of the Bible characters. You will explore how to use your aptitudes and attitudes to deal triumphantly with whatever challenges you face.

You will understand the importance of a strong support system in overcoming those challenges and gain clues about your calling and ultimate purpose. Each chapter is designed to help you grow spiritually and live more successfully. Ultimately, of course, we must place all our trust and dependence on the Lord. If all else goes by the wayside, He will still be there for you and me. If you ask Him, He will help you find your calling, as well as great purpose in your life.

You will learn how to use positive psychology to move beyond survival and actually thrive in your life's work. You will understand that you have God-given strengths that the world very much needs.

It is my fervent desire that the stories in this book will inspire you to learn more about the stories in the Bible. After all, the Bible is the only book filled with truth, life, and power.

APTITUDES FOR GROWTH; ATTITUDES FOR SUCCESS

I hope and pray that as you read this book you will become aware of your character strengths and use them fully in service to Christ Jesus.

PART 1
CHARACTER STRENGTHS

CHAPTER 1

GOD HAS SOMETHING SPECIAL IN MIND FOR YOU

> Every time we think of you, we thank God for you. Day and night you're in our prayers as we call to mind your work of faith, your labor of love, and your patience of hope in following our Master, Jesus Christ, before God our Father. It is clear to us, friends, that God not only loves you very much but also has put his hand on you for something special.
>
> (1 Thess. 1:2–4 MESSAGE)

THIS IS A book about possibility—the possibility that you might reach your God-given potential and fulfill your calling. I wrote it to encourage you in your trials and challenges. Even more, I wrote it to help you discover your strengths and put them to work on behalf of others in ways that will glorify God. I assure you God has put His hand on you to accomplish something special.

This book takes a serious look into the Bible, the most important book ever written. It is the only text that is active and alive, because the Holy Spirit breathed out its words. The Holy Spirit will help you obey the Bible and live in a way that pleases the Lord and gives you peace of mind.

As you read about important Bible characters, you will have the opportunity to explore the various aptitudes and attitudes that caused them to grow and lead successful lives. What you learn about God's work in their lives will inspire you to develop similar traits.

Picture this: You can become a positive force in the world. Briefly stated, here's how. You can read the Bible, memorize it, and quote it aloud. Because God's Word is active and very powerful, your level of consciousness can improve as you read it and quote it aloud. Tap into the supernatural realm of absolute truth, absolute purity, and absolute goodness. You will learn who you really are and perceive that God loves you absolutely. Through consistent interaction with the Bible, you can wrap a robe of righteousness around yourself and allow the deep-level healing of being in Christ to germinate and grow.

You have a distinct and important purpose for living. One of the main tenets of this book is to make you aware that you have specific strengths that God can use to further the work of His kingdom. I hope you will take the time to visit the www.authentichappiness.com website, where you will find an assessment to assist you in discovering your top five strengths. It is called the VIA (Values in Action) Signature Strengths Questionnaire. It measures twenty-four individual character strengths.[1] You cannot fail this computerized test; and I know you will find your results both stunning and enlightening. This assessment is part of a new field of study called *positive psychology*.

Along with the biblical character studies in this book, I have included ideas from the emerging scientific domain of positive psychology. Using rigorous research methods, positive psychology confirms that morals and character do matter. It shows how human strengths and virtues enable people to thrive. It also seeks to nurture talent and to make normal life more fulfilling.

Dr. Martin Seligman, director of Positive Psychology at the University of Pennsylvania, is the founder of positive psychology. This academic discipline focuses on the empirical study of such things as positive emotions, strengths-based character, and healthy institutions. Seligman's research has demonstrated that it is possible to be happier—to feel more satisfied, to be more engaged with life, and to find more meaning in all you do. According to the research, counting your blessings, practicing kindness, savoring life's joys, thanking a mentor, learning to forgive, investing time and energy in friends and family, taking care of your body, and developing strategies to cope with stress and hardships can help you lead a more significant and purposeful life.[2]

Positive psychology has emerged as a viable pursuit. The International Positive Psychology Association, born in 2007, offers members the latest research and happenings in the field as well as seminars via computer led by Seligman and other pioneers. Positive psychology in science and practice can help researchers continue to expand understanding of the impact of focusing on strength, virtue, and wellbeing.[3]

It is interesting how Seligman came to create the field of positive psychology. While spending time with his daughter Nikki in their garden, he had an epiphany. In a speech he delivered in 1999, he recounted the experience that changed his view of parenting and psychology. He said even though he writes books about children, his goal-oriented and time-urgent personality can limit his effectiveness with kids.[4]

He recalled a garden scene. He was intent on weeding the garden, and Nikki was throwing around weeds while singing and dancing. He admonished his daughter about her apparent frivolity.

Nikki responded with a serious look, "Daddy, I want to talk to you."

"Yes, Nikki?"

"Daddy, do you remember before my fifth birthday? From the time I was three to the time I was five, I was a whiner. I whined every day. When I turned five, I decided not to whine anymore. That was the hardest thing I've ever done. And if I can stop whining, you can stop being such a grouch."[5]

Seligman concluded that raising Nikki would not be about correcting her whining. Obviously, she had done that herself. Rather, it would be about taking the strength she had just shown, and using it to help her build her life around it. She could use it as a buffer against her weaknesses.

In that moment, Seligman learned that the psychology to which he had dedicated his life was "half-baked."[6] The field has learned a lot about repairing mental illness. But the other side of the spectrum, the side of strength, the side of what people are good at, had been sorely neglected.

That other side, this approach of looking at health and optimum functioning, is what positive psychology is all about. It is the scientific pursuit of optimal human functioning and the construction of a field focusing on human strength and virtue. It builds on the bench science and research methods that shed light on the "dark side" of human functioning, and it opens the door to understanding prevention and health promotion.[7]

Researcher Shane Lopez explained, "We have discovered that there is a set of human strengths that are the most likely buffers against mental illness: courage, optimism, interpersonal skill, work ethic, hope, honesty, and perseverance. Much of the task of prevention will be to create a science of human strength whose mission will be to foster these virtues in young people"[8]

Perhaps today you are facing a formidable challenge. It could be that you are worried about family issues, frazzled by job stress, or weakened by chronic illness. In his seminal work, *Learned Optimism*, published originally in 1990, Seligman recounted his research with dogs and the phenomenon of learned helplessness. He discovered that a dog strapped into a cage and shocked many times would eventually give up and not try to escape even if an eventual escape became available. He compared what happened with dogs to the explosion of depression in our society. Its prevalence has skyrocketed, and it continues to afflict people at younger and younger ages.[9]

Seligman's research revolutionized the way researchers thought about behavior. They discovered a greater complexity was at work beyond the influences of rewards or punishments on behavior. This is the central message that this emerging field of cognitive psychology touted: It is what you are thinking that determines your behavior, not just whether that behavior is rewarded or punished.[10]

Depressed individuals learn to be helpless by their illogical thought patterns. They feel as though their lives are futile and they have no control over them. They tend to look at unfortunate incidents in their lives more pessimistically than someone who is not depressed.

Learned helplessness explained a lot, but then researchers began to find exceptions— people who did not get depressed, even after many bad life experiences. This is the resilient group of people that was flourishing despite rough circumstances.[11]

I want to encourage you—there is an antidote to despondency in your life. The answer is found in following the Master, Jesus Christ.

How can you follow the Master? By heeding the example of the Thessalonians referenced in the Scripture passage at the beginning of this chapter. They lived faithfully, labored lovingly, and hoped patiently. Through God's power, you can become a strong believer. Through His grace, you can work diligently out of love for Him, others, and yourself. Through Christ's example, you can become patient and hopeful.

Think of the suffering and pain Jesus endured. He fulfilled His glorious purpose through blood, sweat, and tears. Should we, mere humans, expect to get through our lives without trials? No. Quite the contrary! But as we grow through our pain, we can move beyond simply surviving and begin to thrive.

Beethoven composed some of his finest scores after he had become totally deaf. Paul Pearsall's book, *The Beethoven Factor*, points out that people often learn their greatest lessons through hardship. Some people come through adversity with more meaning and purpose in their lives. Such people are called "thrivers."[12]

Pearsall describes thriving as "a renewal of faith, energy, trust, hope, and connection just when doubt, cynicism, fear, fatigue, and alienation seem at their worst. It is not just bouncing back, but up and beyond. It is the emergence of a new creative spirit through and because of the darkest times, a spirit that can guide us to the Beethoven factor so we, too, can creatively conduct our lives as an ode to joy."[13]

APTITUDES FOR GROWTH; ATTITUDES FOR SUCCESS

"Thriving" is a condition described in Jeremiah 17:7–8: "Blessed is the man who trusts in the Lord and has made the Lord his hope and confidence. He is like a tree planted along a riverbank with its roots reaching deep into the water—a tree not bothered by the heat nor worried by long months of drought. Its leaves stay green and it goes right on producing its luscious fruit."

I want to produce healthy fruit like that tree, don't you? Well, the good news we read in 1 Thessalonians affirms that God not only loves us but also has something very special for each of us to do. Can you even take in the wonder of it? You are designed to bear wonderful fruit—service you offer based on your distinct character strengths and talents.

With the right attitude and dependence on God, you have the capacity to stay supple mentally and physically and keep right on producing throughout your life. When we wait upon the Lord, He will renew us in His time and we will thrive. We are grafted into Him, the sacred Vine (see John 15).

Too often we think about what is wrong with us rather than about the gifts we have; and every one of us has important gifts to use for the good of the body of Christ. As we use our personal gifts, we grow spiritually and experience ever-greater success.

Scientific research is now concurring with what the Bible has always said about the need to focus on our strengths. The field of positive psychology has been developing this focus throughout the past twenty years. It scientifically examines what makes people happy and successful in life. It helps people understand and define their strengths and talents. It helps them comprehend how they can contribute to the larger community more effectively. Positive psychology is yielding a precise language that helps us understand the factors that contribute to a productive, meaningful life.

Positive psychology's focus is on strength and wellness rather than weakness. There is a shifting away from pathology and victimhood and toward positive emotion, virtue, and strength. Seligman sees mental health as more than the absence of anxiety, depression, neurosis, obsessions, paranoia, and delusions. He feels it should be something akin to a "vibrant and muscular fitness of the human mind and spirit."[14]

In his book *Authentic Happiness*, Seligman denotes three components of happiness: 1) pleasure, 2) deep engagement/involvement with family, work, romance, and hobbies, and 3) meaning. Meaning is found by using personal strengths to serve some larger end, including the altruistic giving of self.[15]

When you delve into the Word, you learn how to live a truly meaningful life. Through the wisdom the Word imparts to you, you become empowered to make a new start with confidence and joy. When you rely on Jesus, He helps you fulfill your mission.

In Jesus, you can find the faith, love, and hope to live beyond merely surviving; you can actually thrive. You can identify your strengths. You can carry out the distinct assignment God has planned for you.

This book is divided into four sections. The first section explores strengths as demonstrated by Bible characters. You might want to incorporate aspects of some of those strengths into your everyday life. You will also have an opportunity to think about how to best maximize your personal strengths.

The second section emphasizes the importance of building a support system. In 2002, Seligman and his colleague Deiner surveyed students at the University of Illinois and found that the most salient characteristics shared by the 10 percent of students with the highest level of happiness and the fewest signs of depression were their strong ties to friends and family and commitment to spending time with them. "Word needs to spread," Diener concluded. "It is important to work on social skills, close interpersonal ties, and social support in order to be happy."[16] As important as fellowship with others is, however, in the final analysis it is God whom we must fully and completely trust and depend on to meet our needs.

The third section of this book addresses the subject of finding your calling. Once you know your strengths and have your support system in place, you must answer the question, "What of value am I going to do with the rest of my life?" As the title of this chapter indicates, God has something special for you to do—something only you are tailor-made to accomplish. This will incorporate your strengths and your passion. Joseph Campbell, who wrote about mythology and comparative religion, said, "If you follow your bliss, you put yourself on a kind of track, which has been there all the while, waiting for you, and the life that you ought to be living is the one you are living."[17]

The final section of this book deals with the sole source of true empowerment—our triune Creator and Sustainer. It will clarify the self-control the Holy Spirit gives. It will embrace the hope of Jesus Christ, and it will explore the love our heavenly Father has for each of us, and for you in particular.

I don't know what difficulty you are facing today. Wherever you are, whatever the enemy is doing to thwart your progress, you can reach higher ground. As you study the Word and mature in your Christian faith, you can learn to become more comfortable in your own skin.

When my father passed away after being married to Mom for forty-eight years, she had a big adjustment to make. After they had both retired, they co-pastored a small country church in Indiana. They taught Sunday school together. They visited the sick, usually making an outing of it and stopping for lunch. They delighted in one another.

After my father's kidney failure became serious, he went on dialysis. They had to leave the little church they loved and concentrate on keeping Dad as well as he could be. When Dad felt well, they took drives, went to see movies, shopped around in malls, and took walks beside the river.

When Dad died in 2006, Mother provided a catered meal after the funeral. She said she wanted Dad's funeral to be a celebration of his life. We appreciated what a large turnout there was at Dad's visiting hours and funeral. He had made a lot of friends over the years.

Somehow we made it through the funeral. But after that we realized Mom's world had been totally turned upside down. Among other things, Dad was an electrician and could fix almost anything that needed upkeep in the house. He took out the trash and did the bills. Most importantly, he was Mom's best friend with whom she could share anything. They were still in love. And now he was gone.

Mom had a choice to make. She chose life. She battled through grief and moved to a condo in Kentucky where family and friends were near. Gradually she revived her usual zest for life and began to become more and more active in her church. Today you could pretty much say she is in church every time the doors open. In her late sixties, she loves to do all kinds of jobs at church. She loves teaching vacation Bible school and playing with the children. She is a gifted Bible study leader. Church is where she feels most at home.

In addition, Mom meets a lot of different friends and relatives for lunch. She enjoys their company and she is a joy to those with whom she spends time. Mom also continues the greeting card ministry she has been doing for years. If there is a birthday or someone is sick, he or she is sure to get a card from her.

Mom and I have grown closer and closer. We enjoy reminiscing about fun times with Dad and also some of the wonderful things he did for others. The point is that Mom did not lie down and die just because Dad did. She may have wanted to, but she stood strong. She reconfigured her life so that it would be meaningful and packed with interaction with others. Her main goal is to be a blessing wherever she goes. Mom is an example of the truth that no matter what your situation or circumstance, God has something special in mind for you.

Just as my mother is an original, God has made you unique. You have an important assignment to fulfill that God created with your specific aptitudes and attitudes in mind. When you combine a better understanding of yourself with an ever-growing understanding of God through His word and your prayers, you invite Him in. You open the door to knowing He is with you, guiding and loving you. You can accept His healing and grow beyond your challenges. The day may come when those challenges have hardly any impact on your life anymore. Be open to that possibility. You can be fully alive and flourishing. You can feel that you have encountered your real self and the rest of your life lies ahead as a great adventure.

CHAPTER 2

FAITH: BELIEVING EVERY PROMISE FOR YOUR LIFE

> Does the God who lavishly provides you with his own presence, his Holy Spirit, working things in your life you could never do for yourselves, does he do these things because of your strenuous moral striving or because you trust him to do them in you? Don't these things happen among you just as they happened with Abraham? He believed God, and that act of belief was turned into a life that was right with God.... So those now who live by faith are blessed along with Abraham, who lived by faith—this is no new doctrine! And that means that anyone who tries to live by his own effort, independently of God, is doomed to failure.
> (Gal. 3:5–6, 9 MESSAGE)

DO YOU REALIZE that every promise God has made to you in His Word is foolproof? He will never renege on even one pledge. Do you understand that He will bring to fulfillment everything you ask that is in line with His will if you take Him at His word? In *Sparkling Gems from the Greek,* Rick Renner instructs, "If you're planning to take a long, adventurous exciting faith journey, you better dive into the Word of God."[1]

When we know the Word, we know God's heart. We must, therefore, value an intimate communion with Him above all else. Out of that vibrant relationship, we get to know His will and can express desires that honor Him. It is imperative to place our faith solely in God to meet those desires and trust Him to lead us to the right desires. It is folly to try to live independently of God.

In Galatians, Paul wrote that God lavishes us with the Holy Spirit's presence. This is truly the greatest gift anyone could ever receive. If we have the Holy Spirit alive and active in us, our lives will move to a level of functioning that far outweighs the value of mere riches or human glory.

We can do nothing to earn this great blessing. All we must do is believe in our Lord Jesus Christ's absolute power and sovereignty. In other words, it is not a matter of willpower on our part but a realization of God's power.

We must rest in God's arms; we must live by faith. When guilt and shame snare our consciousness, we must run into His open arms. In our own might, we can never right the wrongs we have created. We are all sinners. The Bible's most important message is amazingly simple: Christ died for our sins. He paid the ultimate price so we could come freely before God as though we had never sinned.

That freedom comes through the power of believing. We must make a conscious act of the will to surrender the past completely to God, and then be done with it. Throw it away. He covers the stench of our sin not because of any works we do, but because of who He is. If we are fully repentant, we must only believe. "Faith is the substance of things hoped for, the evidence of things not seen" (Heb. 11:1 NKJV).

With that faith, you can return to a right relationship with God and our Christian family. All you have to do is trust God completely and your life will be restored. Blessings will emanate through your life. God will even give you back anything the devil has stolen from you. Hold on firmly to the promise in Joel 2:25 in which God says, "I will repay you for the years the locusts have eaten."

To continue your growth with the Almighty, you must feed regularly on God's Word. Learn to apply basic truths to your everyday life. In this way, you will live an orderly, pleasing life, and be whole and happy. After all, faith is the opposite of fear.

What role has faith played in your life? Are you thriving with a strong, unflappable trust in God?

Did you know the Bible tells us 365 times to "fear not"? That is one "fear not" for every day of the year. When we fear, we are demonstrating lack of belief in what God can do for us. We need to break free and trust God completely. By believing every promise the Bible gives us, we can enjoy a dynamic life filled with purpose.

Abraham had just such a life. He always chose to "trust and obey" whenever and wherever God led him. Studying Abraham's life through the eyes of positive psychology is affirming. Abraham awesomely depicted the character strength of faith. He trusted God so completely that he did not bother to worry about much of anything.

Abraham's story begins in Genesis 11 and ends at chapter 25. In those fourteen chapters, Abraham stepped forward as a wonderful example of what can happen when a person chooses to have absolute faith in God regardless of the situation.

Genesis 12 reports Abraham's first major act of faith. God instructed him to leave the familiar friends and surroundings of his own country and depart for an undisclosed land.

Try to put yourself in his position. Surely it was extremely frightening and daring to leave behind everything with which he was acquainted.

How do you think you would respond if God asked such a sacrifice of you? There exists deep within you that same intensity of faith that God found in Abraham. That faith is there because, through Christ Jesus, we Christians became the spiritual descendants of Abraham. I am sure Abraham felt great trepidation in leaving all he knew. Yes, he struck out for an unknown location, but what a grand adventure God took him on. He waits to do the same for you.

Because Abraham faithfully obeyed, God promised, "I will cause you to become the father of great nations; I will bless you and make your name famous, and you will be a blessing to many others. I will bless those who bless you and curse those who curse you; and the entire world will be blessed because of you" (Gen. 12:2–3).

APTITUDES FOR GROWTH; ATTITUDES FOR SUCCESS

Throughout the unfolding of this story of beautiful intimacy between God and Abraham, God promised that Abraham's descendants would obtain the promised land of Canaan. He promised they would flourish there, and He compared Abraham's descendants to the countless stars in the big night sky.

Abraham's name had originally been Abram, but God changed it because Abraham means "father of nations." God made a covenant with Abraham that their relationship would continue from generation to generation and never end.

Abraham never doubted God's promises. He paused frequently to build altars to worship the Lord. Can you conceive of adopting this type of trusting attitude with God when you are facing enormous challenges? Do you see how faith grows a person's character? Can you sense how this trusting attitude brought success into Abraham's life? You can legitimately claim such an attitude for yourself as a spiritual descendant of Father Abraham.

In an excerpted article from his book *Become a Better You*, Joel Osteen says, "If you will have the right attitude, you will give birth to more in the future than you've lost in the past. Quit looking back. This is a new day. It may seem like your dreams have died, but God can resurrect your dead dreams and give you brand-new ones. He is a supernatural God, and when we believe, all things are possible."[2]

Perhaps you can relate to your difficult past more easily than to Abraham's immediate faith and obedience. If so, what Osteen is saying becomes vitally important for your life. Letting go of the past and its mistakes is letting go of fear and trusting that with God in charge, your future will be a good one. If you can grasp that kind of faith, you can expect complete restoration. In order to reach that plane, however, you will have to trust God implicitly.

It could have been difficult for Abraham to believe he would have any descendants. He and his wife, Sarah, were very old, and she had been barren for many, many years. However, Abraham stood firm and believed God's Word. As promised, in their old age, the couple conceived and bore Isaac. Isaac's name meant "laughter" because Sarah laughed when the Lord predicted Isaac's birth. Eventually, God transferred the contract he had made with Abraham to Isaac and to all the posterity to come.

It is evident in reading Abraham's life story that he was not afraid to talk things over with God and make requests of Him. In Genesis 18, Abraham was so confident in his relationship with the Creator that he talked God into letting him try to find some godly folks in Sodom. God was angry because of the putrid sin abounding in the town and wanted to destroy everyone in it. Abraham bargained God down from finding fifty good men in Sodom to just ten. God promised to save Sodom if Abraham could find just ten good men in the adulterous city.

Because of Abraham's intercession on behalf of Sodom, his relative Lot and Lot's daughters were able to evacuate the area before God, in His disgust, destroyed it. Would you have the kind of faith and confidence Abraham had to bargain with God? Could you intercede and beseech the Lord to give wicked people just a little more time to turn their eyes and hearts over to Jesus? Is that not why God is waiting to return—so that as many people as possible can be saved from destruction?

We find Abraham's most amazing demonstration of absolute trust in and obedience to God in Genesis 22. God asked Abraham to do the unthinkable—to sacrifice the apple of his eye, his long-awaited, precious son, Isaac.

Surely Abraham's heart was breaking at the thought of slaying the much-cherished son through whom he was to propagate his descendants. Again, Abraham refused to question God. Nor did he argue.

Abraham could have questioned: "God, You can't be serious! You told me my descendants would be as dust, that I would not even be able to count their number. How can I ever have these promised descendants if You take my treasure, my heart, my one and only son?"

Nevertheless, Abraham did not question God at the moment of the most devastating possibility in his life. No. Stalwartly, doggedly, Abraham walked up a hill with Isaac and prepared to offer Isaac as his ultimate sacrifice. What kind of a depth of belief in

God did Abraham have to be able to do as God instructed? Does it make you rethink your answers and priorities when God makes a difficult request of you?

Abraham lifted his hand to slay Isaac. At the last moment he was instructed, "Lay down the knife; don't hurt the lad in any way for I know that God is first in your life—you have not withheld even your beloved son from me" (Gen. 22:12).

Abraham demonstrated his faith by allowing nothing and no one to reign supreme over his love other than God Himself. We can only marvel at the depth of a love like that.

Contemplate the fact that although God saved Abraham from sacrificing Isaac, the day would come when God would require such a heart-wrenching agony of Himself. God loved us so much that He offered his beloved, only Son, Jesus, on a cross to save our souls.

Jesus came from Abraham's lineage, and through His shed blood we have become Abraham's spiritual descendants. Do you have the level of trust and obedience Abraham had?

Jesus lovingly gave you the ultimate gift of eternal life through the cross. He bore the punishment for every moral and spiritual wrong you have committed or will commit. He paid the price so He could declare you "not guilty." He loved you that much.

Let go of the condemning thought that you never will be good enough. It would be true if you were standing before God on your own, but you are not on your own. You are good enough because the blood Jesus lovingly shed for you covers you. Jesus paid the price for your brand new life in Him. Now you are free to walk uprightly in society.

While we know Jesus is God and that His thoughts are higher than ours, we can compare our lives to that of a human being: Abraham. Does Abraham's obedience intimidate you when you think about exercising your own faith? Lest we get too discouraged, let's look at some of his foibles.

Because his wife, Sarah, was so beautiful, he would at times try to pass her off as his sister. This greatly aggravated both the Pharaoh of Egypt and the ruler, Abimelech. They both tried to sleep with Sarah, not realizing she was Abraham's wife. God intervened so that both men returned Sarah safely to her husband. Doesn't it seem strange that Abraham had such faith in big issues but feared these men? How typically human he was.

A sadder infraction occurred when Sarah and Abraham grew impatient because they had not produced an heir. After all, they were growing extremely old, and still no sign of a child was forthcoming. So Sarah got a bright idea.

Have you ever had a bright idea? Have you ever figured out the "perfect" shortcut to make sure God's promises come to pass, only to realize that waiting on the Lord is a crucial part of His plan for your life?

Sarah's bright idea was this: since she had not conceived, she would give Abraham her handmaiden, Hagar. Through this channel, an heir could come forth. Abraham was as gullible to his wife's suggestion as Adam had been when Eve offered him the apple in the Garden of Eden. So Abraham took Hagar to bed, and she conceived Ishmael.

This was not a plan built on great insight or even common sense. Inevitably, Sarah grew exceedingly jealous and eventually insisted that Abraham banish Hagar and Ishmael from their home.

The subsequent treatment Hagar and her son received was cruel and unjust. Have you ever found yourself in the ironic circumstance of blaming others for messing up the plan, when you yourself launched everything in the wrong direction?

Take heart! God never stopped loving Abraham and Sarah. His commitment to them never wavered. His promises never faltered. It was so because God's promises did not depend on Abraham and Sarah's obedience but on God's grace and faithfulness. All they had to do was accept the promises by faith. What was good for Sarah and Abraham is still good for us today.

God took Abraham on an extended journey and a fascinating adventure. A similar adventure is available to us today. Are you ready for an adventure with God?

If so, you must believe that every promise for your life can come true. What are these promises? The only way to discover them all is to read His divinely inspired Word, the Bible. Contained within the covers of God's Book are the answers to any questions you might have.

By all means, read the Bible. Start memorizing Scripture. Fill your mind with Words of life. Why not start by studying the Bible five minutes each day, and then incrementally add more to your devotional time? Keep a list nearby of people who need your prayers. Start small and stay consistent, but keep pushing yourself.

God has many promises in His Word for you. He has a good plan and purpose for your life, but you need to cooperate with Him. Once you lay hold of these promises, be careful not to let passion push you to move too quickly. Wait patiently for God's timing. Otherwise, you will birth Ishmaels that may not have been in God's best plan for your life.

Still, a poor performance cannot strike you out of God's plan. Just keep pursuing in His will. Can you even imagine the wonders God has stored up for you if you will heed Him as Abraham did?

Stand fast. Have faith. There is still time for God's design for your life to come true if you only will yield everything you have to Him. Getting and keeping a clear vision for yourself is pivotal to your success. Most of all, like Abraham, you must believe.

Mark 9:20–24 depicts a desperate father pleading for Jesus to remove a terrible demon from his son. The child was writhing and foaming at the mouth. When Jesus asked how long the child had been suffering, the father replied, "Since he was very small, and the demon often makes him fall into the fire or into water to kill him. Oh, have mercy on us and do something if you can."

"If I can?" Jesus asked. "Anything is possible if you have faith." The father instantly replied, "I do have faith; oh, help me to have more."

No matter how desperate a situation you are in, regardless of the challenges you face, there is always the possibility of a miracle from God. Never give up. When your faith is wavering, be like the father in the Mark 9 story. Ask Jesus for help to believe. Then your faith, a living force within you, will continue to grow.

Positive psychologists are beginning to take notice of the positive effects spirituality can have on a person's life. Through scientific study they are beginning to see a connection between religious belief and well-being. In the growing empirical body of literature, psychologists are observing how religion, or spirituality, aids mental health functioning, addiction problems, marital success, effective parenting, stress management, and coping with the death of a loved one.[3]

Positive psychologists look at faith under a basic concept called *transcendence*. People who have strengths in this area are able to forge connections to the larger universe and can find meaning in life. Under the umbrella of transcendence are awe, gratitude, playfulness, and spirituality.[4]

These positive psychologists view spirituality as having coherent beliefs about the universe's higher purpose and meaning. It includes knowing where you fit within the larger scheme. It is having beliefs about the meaning of life that shape conduct and provide comfort.[5]

In the U.S. spirituality resonates primarily through the Judeo-Christian religion. Ninety-five percent of Americans believe there is a God. Eighty-six percent believe God can be reached through prayer. Eighty-six percent identify religion as important or very important to them.[6]

Research helps define religion as a search for the sacred. Searching indicates that spirituality is a process involving the discovery of the sacred. This discovery must be followed by efforts to hold on to the sacred once it has been found. The sacred has to do with all that is holy, the concept of God the Divine, and transcendence. Sacred things are set apart from the ordinary and are worthy of respect and veneration.[7]

Believers consider a variety of things as sacred. As such, these things take on great power by virtue of their association with the divine. Think of the importance believers give to the time and space associated with the Lord's Day and churches. Big transitions such as birth and death have a sacred significance. Material items such as the bread and the wine or a crucifix have special meaning to believers. Sacred music and literature help people to experience their beliefs more fully.[8]

Leaders and fellow believers can augment the spiritual journey. Community is highly valued. The sacred has to do with social attributes such as treating others with compassion.[9] William Bennett in *The Book of Virtues* contends, "A shared faith binds people together in ways that cannot be duplicated by other means."[10]

The National Opinion Research Center has surveyed more than forty thousand Americans over three decades. The data indicate that people active in faith communities more often report being "very happy."[11]

This happiness occurs because these peoples' faith helps them understand the purpose of their existence. Meaning is derived from believing in Someone greater than self. That Someone, God, can give worth to the self of the believer in a way nothing and no one else can. Holding a view of the sacred affects the way people conduct themselves in their marital, parental, and working lives.[12]

Research defines spiritual strivings as goals concerned with ultimate purpose, ethics, and a commitment to God. Spiritual strivings are more highly related with measures of well-being than any other type of striving.[13] This means that even though our primary purpose in worship is to honor God, such worship also pays off in terms of greater psychological and physical health.

Researchers have also investigated the individual's relationship with the sacred by looking at methods of prayer. Some people prefer to pray ritualistically, such as reading from a prayer book. Other prayers are petitions—the believer asks for material things. Often, prayer is a conversation. The believer, for instance, might ask God for forgiveness.[14]

Meditative prayer seems to be the most effective. A person meditates by choosing to just bask in God's presence. You deepen your relationship with your Lord and Creator by spending time with Him. This helps you feel closer to God and is the most beneficial of all the types of prayer to your health.[15]

Having this type of relationship with God is especially helpful in difficult circumstances. Many believers are able to maintain their faith in a just and loving God in the midst of trauma and loss. They see a larger spiritual purpose behind the negative event.

This is called *reframing* and can help turn a crisis into a spiritually meaningful experience and an opportunity for growth.[16]

I have a friend, Sharon Anne, who suffers with bi-polar illness. Instead of focusing on her own problems, she is always concerned with helping others in need and bringing more believers into the Kingdom.

Every morning she puts on praise music and lies down with her face to the floor and prays. She dedicates everything she has—herself, her resources, her abilities and her money—to God for the day. She entrusts everything that is vital to her life into God's capable hands and then watches in awe as He works throughout her day in unexpected and satisfying ways. She delights in seeing how God can use her as His instrument to meet the large and small needs she encounters during her day.

No matter how much she suffers nor how many problems appear, she simply turns them over to the Lord. "Thy Will be done" is her motto for living. Because of her faithfulness she is an inspiration to many, including me.

Spirituality has much to teach social scientists. Much of psychology in the U.S. has been control focused. Making the unconscious conscious, increasing behavioral and cognitive control, and empowerment of the disempowered are all hallmarks of an American psychological movement to help people develop greater control over their lives. The trouble is, some aspects of our lives are completely out of our control.[17]

The language of our religion includes letting go, forbearance, suffering, faith, mystery, finitude, sacrifice, grace, and transformation. Limitations are a part of the human condition. A spirituality that helps us come to terms with what is out of our control may conversely help improve a psychology attempting to enhance our power and control.[18] Positive psychologists are open to learning more about religion and spirituality through scientific validation.

Seeking the sacred is a life-long pursuit. It begins in childhood. Young ones often have an amazing grasp on the Infinite. These are the words of a nine-year-old Jewish boy: "I'd like to find God! But He wouldn't just be there, waiting for some spaceship to land! He's not a person, you know! He's a spirit. He's like the fog and the mist. Maybe He's like something—something we've never seen here. So how can we know? You can't imagine Him, because He's so different—you've never seen anything like Him.... I should remember that God is God, and we're us. I guess I'm trying to get from me, from us, to Him with my ideas when I'm looking up at the sky!"[19]

Out of the mouths of babes! Artists and writers seem to retain that child-like connection to the Divinity. These are the sentiments of Emily Dickinson in a poem entitled, *I Never Saw a Moor*:

> I never saw a moor,
> I never saw the sea;
> Yet I know how the heather looks,
> And what a wave must be.
>
> I never spoke with God,
> Nor visited in heaven;
> Yet certain am I of the spot
> As if the chart were given.[20]

Having faith in God is what makes life worth living. Believe that God wants to provide for you. He wants you to depend on Him in trust to meet all your needs. He is our wonderful Father, but in the human sphere, we see a metaphor for His love in the way a mother holds her infant.

Kenneth Pargament and Annette Mahoney said it well: "Spirituality is a process that speaks to the greatest of our potentials. The capacity to envision, seek, connect, hold on to, and transform the sacred may be what makes us uniquely human."[21]

CHAPTER 3

OPTIMISM: YES, WE CAN!

> Be strong and courageous, for you will lead my people to possess all the land I swore to give their ancestors. Be strong and very courageous. Obey all the laws Moses gave you. Do not turn away from them, and you will be successful in everything you do. Study this Book of the Law continually. Meditate on it day and night so you may be sure to obey all that is written it. Only then will you succeed. I command you—be strong and courageous! Do not be afraid or discouraged. For the Lord your God is with you wherever you go.
>
> (Josh. 1:6–9)

LIFE IS FULL of decisions. You can choose to look on the brighter side of life or to see only the gloomy side. You can keep a positive attitude in the midst of adversity or choose to despair. You can face your daily life with either hope or hopelessness. You can choose to stick with a decision or ditch it.

One crucial difference between a good decision and a bad decision is how you talk to yourself about it. A good decision occurs when you own your choice and have the courage to support that choice rather than continually doubting yourself and rehashing every move you make.

Joshua set a sterling example of resolute decision-making. Whenever God gave Joshua a command, no matter how unusual or difficult, he performed the task with optimism. The Lord appointed Joshua to usher the Israelites into the Promised Land and he did so with great pizzazz.

Joshua based his optimism on his relationship with an all-powerful, loving, and creative God. His confidence rested solely in the Lord and what He could do through His people.

Just like the Israelites in the Old Testament, you have the choice to turn your life completely over to God's will. When you give yourself to the Lord and cast your cares on Him, you can rest in the certainty that He will take care of you and help you use your full potential.

Joshua's mentor, Moses, trusted God completely. He was, however, timid and easily overwhelmed. Yet God saw Moses' humility and honored it. Because he trusted God, Moses was the perfect leader to get the Israelites out of Egypt. Still, it was Joshua whom God equipped with optimistic faith to lead them into the Promised Land.

When Joshua and Caleb looked over the Promised Land for the first time, they were positive that with God's help the Israelites could defeat the native tribes and inhabit the land successfully. Unfortunately, they were only two of twelve spies who completed a forty-day exploration of the Promised Land.

The other ten spies told the people the situation was hopeless. Oh, it was true, they explained, that the land was "flowing with milk and honey." They had brought back luscious fruit as evidence of the Promised Land's abundance. However, the resident tribes were fierce, entrenched, and intimidating. They reported seeing Anakim giants so tall that the spies felt like grasshoppers before them. In their complete pessimism and fear, the ten spies rejected God's plan and sovereignty.

Caleb, however, reassured the people as they stood before Moses, "Let us go up at once and possess it, for we are well able to conquer it" (Num. 13:30).

Caleb sided with Joshua, embracing the minority position. He agreed that Canaan was well fortified but he believed his God was mightier than any enemy. Yes, he saw the obstacles as clearly as the other spies. Despite the intimidation factor, he believed God's Word.

The Israelites chose to disregard Caleb and Joshua and accept the majority view. They refused to march into the land God had promised them. Caleb knew this was wrong and stood up for what was right. He was more interested in God's approval than the people's.

The situation may have appeared desperate, but Caleb knew that by turning his will and his life over to the Lord he would achieve victory. Caleb had the optimism to grab on to the hope of all God had promised. He was reading the situation accurately and determining that his God was more powerful than any other force in existence.

Perhaps there are portions of your life that seem hopeless. Just as it was for Caleb, so it is for you today. If you turn your will and life over to Jesus, your victory is incontrovertible. When trouble comes, this is the time to trust God the most.

Decide today that you will never give up until you have completed the race God has ordained you to run. This decision will help you to grow in strength and resilience. Then when frustrations or failures bombard you, you will be able to quickly bounce back and achieve your victory.

When your heart is heavy with fear and disappointment after a setback, dispute the negative ruminations your mind projects. After a mistake, chalk it up to being human. Write down your automatic negative thoughts and then disagree with them. Trump your negative thinking by choosing to be more optimistic about your situation. Most importantly, fight back using God's Word as a tool.

You could quote, for example, Hebrews 10:35, 38–39: "Do not throw away your confidence; it will be richly rewarded.... My righteous one will live by faith. And if he shrinks back, my soul will have no pleasure in him. But we are not of those who shrink back and are destroyed, but of those who believed and are saved."

Affirm inside yourself that you choose to focus on the positive. Stir up the joy of the Lord. Relax, trusting that God's plan for your life is unfolding as it should because you have surrendered to Him completely. This is optimism.

Optimism is like an underground river running deep below the surface in the caverns of your innermost being. It is a choice that can become a way of life. When you choose optimism, your inner river runs strong, pure, and clear.

Choosing optimism is choosing calmness, balance, and increased physical health. It works as a buffer against depression. When you build the muscle of optimism, you can improve the quality of your life. It can help you grab hold of the joyful life that is your birthright as a Christian. It can assist you in finding within yourself the belief that with God's help, you can improve your life.

Optimism can encourage you to make positive changes in your life. It can inspire you to set some goals. It can prompt you to move forward on the cherished dreams you hold deep within your heart of hearts. With patience, creativity, and God's blessing, you can follow your bliss and achieve your mission.

God has desires for your life too. He wants you to feel respected and admired, as well as sought after and loved. Through His acceptance, embrace your personal power. If you are to live a fulfilling and authentic existence, you must take up the challenges God sends your way.

This was the choice both Joshua and Caleb made—and because of their faith, they were rewarded by being the only two of their generation to successfully enter the Promised Land. God blessed both men.

God exclaimed, "But my servant Caleb is a different kind of man—he has obeyed me fully. I will bring him into the land he entered as a spy, and his descendants shall have their fair share in it" (Num. 14:24).

God strongly supported Joshua, too. When Moses was old and ready to die, God instructed him to hand the mantle of leadership over to Joshua. Moses was 120 years old when he presented Joshua to the people as their new commander. He reassured the Israelites that the Lord would deliver the Canaanites to them.

"Then Moses called for Joshua and said to him, as all Israel watched, 'Be strong! Be courageous! For you shall lead these people into the land promised by the Lord to their ancestors; see to it that they conquer it. Don't be afraid, for the Lord will go before you and will be with you; he will not fail nor forsake you'" (Deut. 31:7–8).

The people of Israel were under a lot of what we today term *stress*. The old fight or flight syndrome was surely in full fury. In studying stress, researchers assert the importance of positive beliefs, such as optimism, in adapting to a negative situation.

Many patients with life-threatening illnesses say they learned they were stronger than they would have believed prior to their illness. Many began to see advantages in their situations of which they previously had been unaware, and they report they were able to appreciate and accentuate the positive aspects of their lives in a creative manner.[1] This is the wisdom gleaned from meeting tough life challenges head on.

In *A Psychology of Human Strengths*, Lisa Aspinwall and Ursula Staudinger say, "That people deliberately accentuate the positive in life to better deal with the negatives is surely a human strength. That people can draw on these strengths without ignoring or diminishing the negative realities of their situations is also important."[2] This balanced viewpoint has been referred to as *flexible optimism*. This is not a rose-colored world, and reality must be acknowledged if you are to modulate a better way for yourself.

You put optimism into effect when you pursue a goal that is meaningful to you. You also have to have an expectancy that eventually you will be able to achieve that goal you set. To succeed, then, you need the positive attitude and aptitude of optimism in order to persist until you achieve that goal. In "Three Human Strengths," Charles Carver and Michael Scheier conclude, "Often enough, from the expectance-value approach this translates directing into building people's confidence about successful outcomes to the point where effort is self-sustaining. Put simply, the attempt is to turn pessimists into optimists."[3]

Dr. Richard Davidson from the University of Wisconsin-Madison, has concurred with much recent research that the adult brain is changeable or "plastic" as opposed to being completely set in adolescence. "What this means is that although an individual may be born with a predisposition toward gloominess or anxiety, the emotional floor plan can be altered, the brain's furniture moved to a more felicitous arrangement; with a little training, you can coax a fretful mind toward a happier outlook," he said.[4]

Aristotle's concept of *eudaimonic well-being* encapsulates a way of striving toward excellence based on one's unique talents and potential. Davidson commented, "The positive emotion accompanying thoughts that are directed toward meaningful goals is one of the most enduring components of well-being."[5]

Another way to increase happiness and optimism is to deliberately design your life around the activities that bring you the most joy. Small changes can make a difference in your level of joy. Taking that afternoon walk around the lake can help a lot. Thinking about what you like and don't like, however, can also lead you to questioning some of your long-held assumptions.[6] If in your assessment you discover you are really hassled by your job and seldom enjoy it, you have some soul-searching and decision-making ahead.

Avoiding "if only" fantasies can rid your mind of a lot of negative thinking. When you counter reality with wishful thinking about things that have happened that you could not control, you become vulnerable to depression. Research shows that most of us are surprisingly bad at picking out what will make us happy.[7] If that "if only" had come to pass, the results might have been disastrous. You can be assured that if Christ is the Lord of your life, He will make your life a grander adventure than anything your limited mind could imagine.

Spending quality time with God is a great way to grow your optimism. Research has discovered, also, that spending quality time with a good friend can boost your level of positive emotion. The nature of the relationship is the crucial element in friendships. More joy arises from hanging out longer periods of time with a close chum.[8]

Some of us, deep down, feel it is wrong to be happy and upbeat when so many people are suffering. The truth is, happy people are in more of a position to help the needy than a die-hard pessimist would be.[9] Keeping yourself in a mirthful mood can contribute to peace on earth.

In *Lighten Up: Survival Skills for People under Pressure*, C.W. Medcalf and Roma Feliable say, "Humor is a way of seeing, salving and solving the serious issues of our lives.... Now it may be that what we need to do most is to learn to laugh a little more, to take ourselves—even our pain—a little less seriously."[10]

Red Skelton, the famous comedian, once said, "I live by this credo: Have a little laugh at life and look around you for happiness instead of sadness. Laughter has always brought me out of unhappy situations."[11]

In truth, optimism is a very serious business. Most of the developed world is "experiencing an unprecedented epidemic of depression—particularly among young people," said Martin Seligman in *Learned Optimism*. "Severe depression is ten times more prevalent today than it was fifty years ago. It assaults women twice as often as men, and it now strikes a full decade earlier in life on average than it did a generation ago."[12]

Learned helplessness is synonymous with depression. It is a state of believing that you are trapped, that you have no choices, and that there is no way to avoid failure. It is reacting to the challenges of your life by giving up and quitting. It makes a person feel that whatever he or she would do does not matter. This is a pessimistic explanatory style.

An optimistic explanatory style stops helplessness. The way you explain events to yourself determines how helpless you become. How are you explaining everyday setbacks or momentous defeats to yourself? What you think and tell yourself will determine whether you grow more helpless or instead choose to believe you can change your lot and so become energized to do so.[13]

You can be encouraging to yourself when facing difficulties. This can make all the difference in the world in the outcome of your challenge. It can mean the difference between success and failure.

You can learn to increase your level of optimism and control over your life by thinking realistically and refusing to view adversity as a catastrophe.

"When bad events strike, you don't have to look at them in their most permanent, pervasive, and personal light, with the crippling results that pessimistic explanatory style entails," Seligman said.[14] This means realizing the adversity is not permanent but rather temporary. One bad grade at school does not have to mean you will fail to graduate.

You can avoid a pervasive sense of helplessness by working to contain a difficulty to the particular life area in which you are struggling. Do not allow the situation to be pervasively disabling across the dimensions of your home, work, leisure, and social lives. When a loved one dies, for instance, getting back to work after appropriate grieving can help you feel more in control of your life.

It is also crucial to learn not to take things personally. Most of the time when people mistreat you, it is coming from something inside of them that they have not figured out how to master on the emotional level. Realizing this can save you many hours of anger, hostility, and rumination.

The main thing is to dispute your negative distortions. When you find yourself responding to a situation with helplessness and depression, argue with yourself. Keep up the pep talk until you feel better. Then think about what you can do to improve the situation.

By taking these steps, your health and general well-being will increase. "Findings show that learned helplessness doesn't just affect behavior; it also reaches down to the cellular level and makes the immune system more passive," Seligman said.[15]

These findings are interesting in light of researcher Daniel Gilbert's comparison of the psychological immune system with the physical immune system. That is, the mind defends against unhappiness much the way the body defends against illness. As the physical body strikes a balance between recognizing and destroying foreign invaders like viruses while respecting the body's own cells, likewise the psychological immune system must not defend you too well ("I'm perfect and everyone is against me") and must not fail to defend you well enough ("I am a loser and I ought to be dead"). Stick to the facts and realize that rather than being defenseless or defensive, you need to be tenderly defended by your own self-talk.[16]

William James, the father of American psychology, wrote *The Varieties of Religious Experience.* It was a bold tribute to the view that religion "gives some serenity, moral poise, and happiness, and prevents certain forms of disease as well as science does, or even better."[17]

This thinking is right in line with that of Joshua and Caleb. Both were optimists and were able to flourish amid great challenge. It was Joshua's job to secure his people in the land God had given to them. Surely there must have been a great weight of responsibility on his shoulders. Nevertheless, he was an optimist and a believer.

The Israelites fought many battles to win their beloved Promised Land. The most famous was the Battle of Jericho. You can find it in children's Bible stories and in Sunday school lessons for all ages.

God told Joshua, "Jericho and its king and all its mighty warriors are already defeated, for I have given them to you!" Of course, Joshua had complete faith in what the Lord told him. The entire army walked around the city of Jericho once a day for six days, followed by seven priests walking ahead of the Ark, each carrying a trumpet. On the seventh day, they all walked around the city seven times with trumpets blowing. With one loud blast, all the people shouted and the walls of the city fell down. Then the Israelites army moved in from all directions (see Josh. 5:2).

Gibeon was the spot for another memorable battle. At Joshua's request, God let the sun and moon stand still so the Israeli army could complete the destruction of their enemies.

Joshua 11 tells us, "So Joshua took the entire land just as the Lord had instructed Moses; and he gave to the people of Israel as their inheritance, dividing the land among the tribes. So the land finally rested from its war" (Josh. 11:23).

Right before his death at 110 years old, Joshua admonished the people to "revere Jehovah and serve Him in sincerity and truth" (Josh. 24:14). Yes, Joshua was faithful. He was a thriver as well. Perhaps as you face your challenges, whether family issues, job

APTITUDES FOR GROWTH; ATTITUDES FOR SUCCESS

stress, or chronic illness, you can reflect on how Joshua and Caleb conducted themselves in difficult times. With optimism in your heart, you can say along with Joshua and Caleb, "Yes, we can!"

Optimism believes in the best. It is having the hope that good things will happen. It is letting go of yesterday after learning whatever lesson yesterday offered, and moving forward into a world of brand-new possibilities.

My adopted grandfather, James Lester, just turned eighty-five years old. His wife passed away a couple of years ago. He nursed her through her illness with great tenderness.

Soon after her death, he had several nasty falls. One day while trying to retrieve his garbage can from the street, he fell backward and landed on the pavement, knocking him unconscious. Fortunately, a neighbor driving by saw him on the ground and did not run over him. James was hospitalized for this and various other serious illnesses over the next year.

James made the decision to enter an assisted living center. Many of the people there were very sick and not as high functioning as he was. But because James has always been content in whatever state he has found himself, he was able to adapt to his new environment in an optimistic and cheerful manner.

He looked at all the pluses of his situation. Meals were provided three times a day. There were parties and outings and all variety of groups to attend. People often came in and entertained, such as a children's Christmas choir and an Elvis impersonator.

James thrived on all the interaction and activity. He made lots of friends at the assisted living center and also continues to go out to eat with his many friends who stop in to visit.

He purchased some additional workout equipment for the center in what is now referred to as "Jim's Gym." He exercises daily, grows tomatoes on the back patio, and arranges the fresh flowers for the tables every week. It is usually a three-hour job.

James's upbeat nature never falters. He always seems content and positive, never complaining about anything but taking full advantage of every bit of fun he can squeeze out of life. He believes his life is a gift from the good Lord and James thanks Him every morning for the chance to live one more day.

He inherited his positive outlook from his mother. A devout Christian, her desire when she died was to float on a cloud and play a harp. Sometimes when James is out fishing, he almost thinks he can hear her playing her harp floating on a nearby cloud.

James enjoys showering love on all his friends and looks forward to the day when we will all be in heaven together. James Lester is truly a wonderful friend and a great optimist.

Dietrich Bonhoeffer, a German Lutheran pastor and theologian who participated in the German Resistance movement against Nazism, once said, "The essence of optimism is that it ... enables a man to hold his head high, to claim the future for himself and not abandon it to his enemy."[18]

Life is not an ordeal to be survived; it is an adventure of choices to be lived. I hope you choose optimism and joy.

CHAPTER 4

FORGIVENESS: LET GO AND BE FREE

> Then if my people will humble themselves and pray, and search for me, and turn from their wicked ways, I will hear them from heaven and forgive their sins and heal their land. I will listen, wide awake, to every prayer made in this place. For I have chosen this temple and sanctified it to be my home forever; my eyes and my heart shall always be here.
>
> (2 Chron. 7:14–16)

THIS VERSE CONTAINS one of God's most wonderful promises. He made it specifically to Israel, but it can be fulfilled in our lives today. Because Jesus went to the cross for us, God listens to our prayers. He will forgive our sins if we confess them. It is simply part of God's nature to forgive sins. This truth can give us great comfort as we deal with failure, and it can help us extend mercy to those whom we need to forgive.

Forgiving and receiving forgiveness unfold together as a process that takes time and commitment. Stress seems to infuse our fast-paced lives. We often find it difficult to slow down and attend to our spiritual and emotional needs. We rush around irritable and impatient, and seldom take the time to get to the heart of our problems.

Many of us are carrying around heavy burdens. Toxic emotions such as anger, disgust, and guilt block our effectiveness and level of fulfillment. Sometimes we direct these destructive emotions toward others, and sometimes we direct them toward ourselves. Fortunately, God has provided a healthy way to meet our hurts and needs through the power of forgiveness. He can show us how to let go and be free.

The first step toward getting right with God involves our taking an honest personal inventory. This step inevitably leads to the recognition of sin in our lives.

First John 1:8–10 insists, "If we say that we have no sin, we are only fooling ourselves and refusing to accept the truth. But if we confess our sins to Him, He can be depended on to forgive us and to cleanse us from every wrong." This cleansing from sin is possible through the blood Jesus shed for each of us.

We have needed God's forgiveness since Adam and Eve's fall in the Garden of Eden. When Adam and Eve failed, God set His plan of redemption into play by sending the second Adam, his perfect Son, Jesus Christ, to die for our transgressions.

The Holy Spirit repeatedly warns us to stay away from sin. Like Adam and Eve, however, we sometimes stray from God's will. Thankfully, through Jesus, God has provided a way to reconnect. First John 2:1–2 tells us, "But if you sin, there is someone to plead for you before the Father. His name is Jesus Christ, the One who is all that is good and who pleases God completely. He is the One who took God's wrath against our sins upon Himself and brought us into fellowship with God; and He is the forgiveness for our sins, and not only ours but all the world's."

Think of Jesus hanging on the cross. His concern was not for Himself but for others. He directed His compassion toward those who were torturing Him. He hung there in humiliation, more totally alone than we could ever understand; and in His darkest hour He prayed, "Father, forgive them, for they do not know what they do" (Luke 23:34 NKJV).

Jesus Christ is the great resource and advocate for all of us. He received the full force of God's anger against sin so we do not have to experience God's wrath for our past, present, and future sins. When we believe Christ suffered for our sins, we can come to the Father freely. We can approach Him with complete trust that He will accept us unconditionally. What a miracle! The God of the universe is willing to bind our wounds and care for us just as we really are.

Colossians 3:13 instructs, "Bearing with one another and forgiving one another, if anyone has a complaint against another; even as Christ forgave you, so you also must do" (NKJV). Since we accept the great gift of God's forgiveness toward our sin, we need to give that same sort of forgiveness to those who have hurt us.

My friend Betty showed incredible fortitude in bearing with her mother-in-law and caring for her as she lived her last years with dementia. She knew Sarah, her mother-in-law, had always said she wanted to die in her own home. So Betty hired a retired couple to check in on Sarah three or four times a day and give her needed medication.

Whenever she could, Betty brought Sarah back to her home to visit. It was about a three-hour trip each way. Sarah had a habit of rifling through Betty's things. One day she came out wearing Betty's rings and watch and asked Betty if she liked her new jewelry.

Betty could laugh off some of this behavior, but sometimes Sarah was pretty exasperating. She told Betty that Betty's family was not as good as hers. She said Betty's family consisted of lowlifes. Betty tactfully never pointed out that none of Sarah's other family was trying to help her at all.

Betty would come out in the morning in a modest gown and robe and Sarah accused Betty of "trying to show her legs off." Sarah would become indignant with Betty any time she was on the phone, wanting Betty's full attention at all times. This once genteel lady who was in church every time the doors opened threatened to "kick Betty's ass" several times.

Throughout the three-year ordeal, Betty never raised her voice to Sarah. Nor did she ever mistreat her. Betty continued to try to fix Sarah her favorite foods and play old Gospel music to calm her racing mind. Betty went through a lot for Sarah. But if you ask her she would say Sarah was ill and therefore needed understanding, not judgment. This is just one example from the life of a woman who excels at forgiving others and loving them fully, flaws and all.

Forgiveness is the act of excusing an offense and granting a pardon. It is letting go of resentment. If we hold on to resentment, it can drive us to fits of despair and anger. It can cause us to play scenes over and over again in our minds until we nearly break apart with pain and hurt. Relief seems hopelessly far away. Being unable to forgive keeps our emotions in an uproar. Unforgiveness blocks our minds from attaining serenity and peace. Is anything really worth that price?

The truth is that the past is gone and God wants us to look forward rather than back. In Isaiah 43:18–19 God says, "Do not remember the former things, nor consider the things of old. Behold, I will do a new thing, now it shall spring forth; shall you not know it? I will even make a road in the wilderness and rivers in the desert" (NKJV).

Paul expressed a similar sentiment in Romans 12:2: "Be not conformed to this world: but be ye transformed by the renewing of your mind, that ye may prove what is that good, and acceptable, and perfect, will of God" (KJV).

What if we dumped our baggage and left it in some wasteland never to be found again? What if we developed an overarching attitude of forgiveness? What if we allowed our burdens to lift, leaving us free to love others and ourselves fully? We could work to eliminate guilt, resentment, embarrassment, sadness, and hurt, and to fill our minds with satisfaction and joy instead.

The most effective way to do this is to speak God's Word. If we say aloud what He says in the Bible, we find ourselves on a path to wonderful health. Look up the topic of forgiveness in your Bible concordance. Write the verses that touch you on index cards so you can say and review them repeatedly.

In his book *Authentic Happiness,* Martin Seligman speaks of rewriting your past.[1] The concept of rewriting history means you can remember the good parts of the past and reframe the not-so-good parts. Fully enjoy the good memories from the past and then reframe the painful parts by thinking about them without pain or regret.

Sometimes it helps to simply accept what happened. It also helps to decide to forgive regardless of your feelings. The perspective of time helps us see formerly hurtful situations with more compassion. What a lift to be able to look back with eyes of love and forgiveness!

This process takes place in stages. As we practice forgiveness over time, we will eventually feel the negative emotions slipping away. If the memories come flooding back occasionally, we must make a conscious effort to practice forgiveness again. Each time we choose forgiveness over judgment, we achieve a private victory. Each time we choose compassion over a critical spirit, we take a step forward. No effort we make, no matter how small, is ever wasted. Do not ever give in to the mistaken belief that your efforts to become a more forgiving person are in vain. God notices every time you release a hurt from your past. He rejoices as He sees you let resentments go.

The longer we practice forgiveness the more our brains get into a healthy balance and a state of equilibrium. If we keep practicing we will reach a peaceful internal place in which we can charitably forgive the foolish mistakes of the past.

At each point in your journey toward total forgiveness of others and yourself, take your emotional temperature to see how you are progressing. Do you wish you could make the other person pay or that something bad would happen to him or her? Do you avoid the person or have trouble treating him or her warmly? Do you want to see the person miserable or hurt? Do you avoid the person or even sever the relationship?[2] Can you let go and move further along the continuum toward freedom and forgiveness?

If anyone in the Old Testament had a reason to feel vengeful, it was Joseph. Yet he never wallowed in self-pity. Joseph's story is found in Genesis, which records mankind's birth and early history. Joseph is considered one of the four great patriarchs of the Old Testament. Abraham, Isaac, and Jacob, his father, preceded him.

Jacob favored Joseph over all his brothers and so gave him a beautiful coat of many colors to show his love. As a young man, Joseph had a vision and a dream for his life. His boasting about this did not set well with his brothers.

His brothers sold him into slavery. An Egyptian military leader, Potiphar, purchased Joseph as a slave and put him to work. Soon Joseph was running all of Potiphar's business affairs. When Potiphar's wife failed to seduce Joseph, she falsely accused him of assaulting her. He was then hauled off to jail.

Joseph had such leadership ability that he was soon helping run the jail. He also showed a propensity to be able to interpret dreams. After several years of imprisonment, one of the king's court remembered how Joseph had accurately deciphered dreams and so Joseph was called before the Pharaoh.

People in the ancient Near East attached great significance to dreams and their interpretation. Both the Egyptians and the Babylonians compiled books of sample dreams with a key to their interpretation. Joseph consulted God to interpret dreams, but his interpretations lined up with that of the Egyptian dream literature.[3]

Eventually the Pharaoh called for Joseph to interpret his dreams. Pharaoh had dreamed that seven fat cows were consumed by seven skinny ones. Then he dreamed that seven beautiful ears of corn were followed by seven tattered and torn ears. Joseph explained the dreams: There would be seven years of plenty followed by seven years of drought. If the country stored the excess, everyone would survive the famine.

In time, Pharaoh made Joseph his second-in-command. He put him in charge of keeping resources available for Egypt and the surrounding lands to prepare for times of famine and drought.

In Genesis 42:21–22 we learn that Joseph's brothers went to Egypt because they were running out of food. Eventually they realized that the highly positioned administrator they were asking for help was actually Joseph—the brother they had abused and sold into slavery so many years before. Speaking among themselves, they murmured, "This has all happened because of what we did to Joseph long ago. We saw his terror and anguish and heard his pleadings, but we wouldn't listen."

Have you ever been in a position like that of Joseph's brothers? Isn't it terrible to realize the horrible sins you have committed for which you have no good excuse or defense? Instead of punishing his brothers, however, Joseph freely forgave them. Perhaps he even chuckled to himself as he saw how God had brought them all full circle. He would not have been able to help anyone had he not been mistreated at strategic points in his life.

In Genesis 45:4–7 he called the brothers to come closer, and said, "I am Joseph, your brother whom you sold into Egypt. But don't be angry with yourself that you did this to me, for God did it! He sent me here ahead of you to preserve our lives. These two years of famine will grow to seven, during which there will be neither plowing nor harvest. God has sent me here to keep you and your families alive so that you will become a great nation."

The writers of the *Archeological Study Bible* suggest, "Study the life of Joseph, from his years of slavery to his meteoric rise to power in a strange land to his revelation to his unsuspecting brothers. This book [Genesis] explains how and why the Israelites came to live in Egypt, setting the stage for what would happen to this special people in Exodus and beyond."[4]

In his magnanimity, Joseph foreshadowed the life and actions of Christ, who makes all things work together for good for those who love the Lord and are called according to his purpose (see Rom. 8:28). When we forgive, marvelous things happen. When we forgive, we become more positive and generous. When we forgive, we give people a second chance. When we forgive, our guiding principle becomes not revenge, but mercy.

In her ministry to countless people, Joyce Meyer shares the experience of years of sexual abuse she endured from her father.[5] Looking back, after much suffering and many years of reflection, she fully believes God's word in Joel 2:25: "I will restore to you the years that the swarming locust has eaten" (NKJV).

Moreover, she believes she is more successful, has better character, and can help more people because of all she went through.

Instead of resisting what happened, Meyer accepts what happened. She even believes God can use her suffering ultimately to do more good than if she had never been so deeply wounded.[6]

Meyer devoted her May 2008 issue of *Enjoying Everyday Life* to the topic of forgiveness. She explained that even if we had no other reason to forgive, we must do it because God said so. He expects His children to obey His dictates. Without forgiveness, our relationship to Him is blocked. She asks, "What is so unforgivable that I would let it hinder my personal relationship with God?"[7]

She points out that forgiveness is a choice. Despite extreme physical, emotional, and sexual abuse, Meyer has chosen to forgive. Look at all the success she has and all the help she has been able to give others because she has chosen to forgive!

Meyer emphasizes that this is a process. Even after a person decides to act right and forgive, it will take time for his or her feelings to catch up with that decision. We must not lose faith just because at times our feelings disagree with the decision we have made in faith to forgive. Studying the Word can help us discern how to handle our emotions properly. After forgiving, we can stand firm in the fact that we have done our part and now God will do His part.[8]

It is not easy, but it is the right thing to do. Forgiveness gives you a peace and a freedom that nothing else can. Jesus said, "I say to you who are listening now to Me: [in order to heed, make it a practice to] love your enemies, treat well (do good to, act nobly toward) those who detest you and pursue you with hatred, invoke blessing upon and pray for the happiness of those who curse you, implore God's blessing (favor) upon those who abuse you [who revile, reproach, disparage, and high-handedly misuse you] (Luke 6:27–28 AMP).

What we are really doing in this process of forgiving is asking God to bless the person with His presence. The truth is that 99 percent of the time people have no idea of the hurt they have inflicted upon us. When we bless someone, we speak well of him or her. We can say, with Jesus, "Father, forgive them, for they know not what they do" (see Luke 23:34).

Love covers a multitude of sins. This means that in love you can reach the point where you make excuses for your enemies. You can cover the one who hurt you by saying that the person did not understand what he or she was doing.

When you obey the Word of the Lord, Luke 6:35 says, "your recompense (your reward) will be great (rich, strong, intense, and abundant), and you will be sons of the Most High." Meyer says, "We will get double for our trouble if we will do things His way."[9] Wow! I'd like that kind of reward. Wouldn't you?

In *Conflict-free Living*, Meyer devotes a chapter to how to "Make Forgiveness a Lifestyle." She opens with, "I lived far too long behind walls I had built to protect myself from emotional pain because I was determined not to give anyone a chance to hurt me a second time…. I was no longer being abused, but I held the abuse in my heart. It continued to cause pain in my life because I refused to trust God to vindicate me."[10]

Can you relate to what Meyer is sharing? Life's hurts sometimes can cause us to harden our hearts as a protection from more pain. But the answer lies not in shielding our hearts through unforgiveness but rather in giving our hearts fully and completely to God's care. He will never fail to take care of us when we trust in Him.

The truth is when we refuse to forgive others, we open a door for the Devil to torment us. The Devil is always trying to stir up hatred and bitterness. He loves to see us feel disappointed with the circumstances of our lives, because that can develop into a disappointment with God Himself. Forgiveness and trust in God safely close the doorway to our hearts so the Devil cannot build a stronghold of anger and strife there.

Peter asked Jesus how many times he should forgive someone. He wondered if seven times would be sufficient. Jesus answered, "I tell you, not up to seven times, but seventy times seven" (see Matt. 18:21–22). Being longsuffering develops character. Having character gives us a strong foundation on which to build successful lives.

Meyer concludes by encouraging us to "make forgiveness a lifestyle by choosing to trust Him with the things you don't understand."[11]

We will not have all the answers until we meet Jesus face to face. While in this world we see through a glass darkly. Even though we don't understand now, we will then. And if we are obedient to God's Word, we will build up a storehouse of treasures in heaven by following the examples of Joseph and Jesus.

Forgiveness is such an important component of your walk with Jesus. When you forgive others by trusting in Him, Jesus takes you to higher and deeper levels of relationship with Him. So be gentle and forbearing when people lack insight or discretion.

Positive psychology has demonstrated that revenge has corrosive effects. Retaliation leads to escalating cycles of vengeance and is implicated in much of the violence that plagues our world.[12] Being accommodating when someone is behaving badly means refusing to respond negatively. There is a lot of strength in that.

What is this character strength we call "forgiveness"? It is "a freely chosen motivational transformation in which the desire to seek revenge and to avoid contact with the transgressor is lessened, a process sometimes described as an altruistic gift," say Frank Fincham and Todd Kashdan in *Positive Psychology in Practice*.[13]

Don't confuse forgiveness with similar constructs. It is not the act of living in a state of denial refusing to acknowledge your injury. Also, it is not the act of condoning the other person's actions. The offense happened. The hurt was real. Forgiveness is not the act of giving a pardon as a judge would. It is not synonymous with forgetting, nor does it necessarily involve reconciliation.

Forgiveness is a decision, and a wise one at that. There is now some MRI evidence to show that forgiveness activates a specific region of the brain. It is so specific as to be distinct from brain activation when feeling empathy.[14]

Decreased hostility enhances physical health. Forgiveness fights heart disease and lessens hormonal and physiological responses to stress. But to be effective, forgiveness must come out of a heart of love rather than from an insincere gesture made out of a sense of obligation.[15]

The link between forgiveness and mental health shows that people who have been "helped to forgive someone" are more successful in overcoming addictions, guilt, and discouragement. Any improvement in relationships with others helps boost mental health. Refusing to forgive however, by being preoccupied with blame or ruminating on the injustice, is bad for you mentally and physically.[16]

A caveat to bear in mind, however: The amount of time a person spends thinking about forgiveness is critical to his or her success in forgiving. Thinking about the hurt without pondering the virtues of forgiving the cause of that hurt is counterproductive.[17]

Research has demonstrated that training childhood sexual abuse victims in how to forgive properly increases hope and self-esteem while decreasing anxiety and depression. The changes were maintained over a yearlong period.[18]

Interventions that can help with forgiveness include writing about past traumatic experiences. Enhancing relationship abilities like basic communication skills has been shown to be helpful as well.[19]

Some of these techniques have been implemented successfully with reformed criminals, say Fincham and Kashdan: "By allowing for forgiveness, restorative justice programs empower the victim and allow the perpetrator to be affirmed both by the victim and the community as a person of worth and to regain—or for many gain for the first time—their respect and be reintegrated—or integrated—into society."[20]

We are all sinners in search of redemption. Healing occurs in a context where we are prepared to let love penetrate our hearts to give and receive forgiveness out of a place of warmth, affection, and tenderness.

Do you want everything God can do for you? Do you wish to reach your full potential? The only way to achieve these outcomes is through obedience. If you will humble yourself and pray, both to forgive and be forgiven, your level of personal fulfillment will deepen. God asks you to turn from your evil ways. Those evil ways include nursing grudges. Think of the pleasure you will give God if you make your search to know Him better worth anything, even if it means forgiving a horrendous offense.

Copy Jesus' example by practicing forgiveness until it becomes a basic trait of your character. Think of all the possibilities that can manifest in your life by releasing old hurts. Think of the adventure that awaits you.

CHAPTER 5

COURAGE: I COME TO YOU IN THE NAME OF THE LORD

> David shouted in reply, "You come to me with a sword and a spear, but I come to you in the name of the Lord of the armies of heaven and of Israel—the very God whom you have defied. Today the Lord will conquer you, and I will kill you and cut off your head; and then I will give the dead bodies of your men to the birds and wild animals, and the whole world will know that there is a God in Israel! And Israel will learn that the Lord does not depend on weapons to fulfill his plans—he works without regard to human means! He will give you to us.
> (1 Sam. 17:45–47)

LIKE THE COWARDLY lion in *The Wizard of Oz*, we all want to possess courage. With threats of terrorism, natural disasters, and random crime, there seems to be plenty to frighten us. But we also have fears about ourselves. We wonder if we have the strength to be the best people we can be—the people God created us to be. We fear we will fail to complete the mission God has planned for us.

However, we find an answer to our deepest fears and anxieties through belief in Jesus Christ. When we turn our lives over to Him, we receive all His blessings and protection. Psalm 31:24 challenges: "Be strong and let your heart take courage, all you who wait for and hope for and expect the Lord!" (AMP).

Often, we think of courage as a facing of fears through the brute force of willpower. Nothing could be farther from the truth. Ultimately, courage is not something we muster out of our own power. Trusting in the Lord opens a gateway through which courage can flow. It requires holding fast to hope and waiting patiently with faith for God to act. To be truly courageous we must believe in and expect that the omnipotent God will do what is best. We must believe he will act in His time, which is always the right time. And we must stand our ground until He does.

Think of the courage young David displayed as he faced the giant Goliath with the hope, faith, and love of Israel. He boldly stepped forward to recover the dignity of his people, the Israelites. He shouted to Goliath, "You come at me with a sword and a spear, but I come to you in the name of the Lord of the armies of heaven and Israel" (1 Sam. 17:45).

William Bennett, in *The Book of Virtues,* quotes Aristotle from his *Nicomachean Ethics*: "We become brave by doing brave acts ... by being habituated to despise things that are terrible and to stand our ground against them we become brave, and it is when we have become so that we shall be most able to stand our ground against them."[1]

David's days as a protective shepherd—fighting off bears and lions—stood him in good stead to face Goliath. As we examine David's fascinating life, we see him as a shepherd, a musician, a warrior, and a king. Also, we see the best and worst characteristics of humanity in him. Throughout his life, David had an incredible bond with God. He was called a man after God's own heart. We would be wise to emulate the kind of intimate relationship David had with God. Nothing is more important for each of us than vital union with our Savior. David's story shows us what that union looks like.

In some important ways, David prefigured Jesus Christ. In fact, the two shared a common genealogy. Both were descendants of Judah, one of the sons of Jacob. Through our study of David, we can gain insights into the meaning of Christ's life. David's life was far from perfect, but his life foreshadowed details of Christ's life.

COURAGE: I COME TO YOU IN THE NAME OF THE LORD

As David's saga illustrates, the Bible is full of important stories and information that, if applied, can transform our lives. I hope this book always points you back to the Bible. The Bible should be the centerpiece of all we do and say. It is the only Living Word.

In this study, we will delve into 1 and 2 Samuel, as well as portions of 1 and 2 Chronicles. We will also look at some of the Psalms. David wrote many of these songs and poems to sing praise to God as he played his harp.

We encounter David for the first time in 1 Samuel 16. God spoke to Samuel the prophet, telling him Saul was no longer fit to be king of Israel. He then sent Samuel to Jesse of Bethlehem, telling him that one of Jesse's sons was to be king.

Samuel studied each of Jesse's sons, but none of them seemed to be the right one. When Samuel asked Jesse if he had any more sons, Jesse explained that his youngest, David, was off tending the sheep. Samuel insisted that Jesse summon David at once.

The way Samuel found David tells me that no matter where I am or what I am doing, when God needs me to fulfill my purpose, He will find me. I will be right where I am supposed to be, learning exactly what I need to learn to fulfill my destiny.

In David's case, shepherding taught him a great deal. Psalm 78:70–72 tells us, "He chose David his servant and took him from the sheep pens; from tending the sheep he brought him to be the shepherd of his people Jacob, of Israel his inheritance. And David shepherded them with integrity of heart; with skillful hands he led them" (NIV).

God had been preparing David all his life. He has also been preparing you. The challenges you deal with are much like the bear and lion David slew while tending his flock—preparation. David's adventures led him from the grazing field to the battlefield. His first job in the palace was playing the harp for King Saul, but eventually David became the king over all Israel. Be open to the adventure that awaits you for the rest of your life.

As Beth Moore put it in *A Heart Like His*, "Never assume to follow Him means to throw away who He has made you to be. Few things seem less spiritual than keeping a bunch of smelly sheep, yet God used David's skills for eternal purposes."[2]

Think about your experiences, your strengths, and your talents. Realize you have the same potential David had. God made you for a unique and important purpose. How might the aptitude of courage help you grow into the Christian you want to be? How might a courageous attitude lead you to the same overwhelming success David experienced?

First Samuel 16:13 says, "So Samuel took the horn of oil and anointed him in the presence of his brothers, and from that day on the Spirit of the Lord came upon David in power" (NIV). You can have that same power if you will only invite the Holy Spirit into every area of your life.

Samuel finished his duty faithfully as the last of Israel's judges. The Israelites wanted a king to call their own, as the other nations had. At their insistence, Saul became the first king of Israel. He reigned for forty-two years.

Saul was self-centered, selfish, and insecure. As a leader, he was afraid of people, and so he became a people pleaser. This was a big mistake, because we must always rank pleasing God, not others, as life's highest priority.

David knew this truth even as a young man. If he feared God, he would not have to fear man. He was taking his older brothers some supplies when he heard Goliath, the nine-foot-tall warrior, taunting the Israelites as he had done morning and night for forty days. David was incensed. "Who is this uncircumcised Philistine that he should defy the armies of the living God?" he asked (1 Sam. 17:26 NIV). He volunteered to fight the menacing giant.

Saul gave David the king's armor. It did not fit. It was uncomfortable. David rejected the armor, and chose instead to be comfortable in his own skin as he battled Goliath. Are you comfortable in your skin as you go out to fight your battles? Are you so intimate with God that you know He sees you as the victor before the fight even begins? Do you approach every circumstance with the confidence that befits a member of God's army? Do you have the faith that

COURAGE: I COME TO YOU IN THE NAME OF THE LORD

God is active and alive—that He loves you and wants to bless you through every obstacle you encounter?

David trusted his God completely. He met Goliath with five smooth stones and a shepherd's slingshot. No giant will ever be as big as God is. No weapons will be too small to defeat the enemy if those weapons come from God. Even stones and a slingshot will do. David knew this and because of his faith, he was victorious.

David was extremely brave. The "Values in Action Classification of Character Strengths Inventory" describes bravery as an aspect of courage. Bravery means refusing to shrink from a challenge or difficulty. It is acting upon one's convictions even if they are unpopular.[3] David was brave in facing Goliath because he trusted his God to be with him.

There was perhaps only one facet of David's life that might have made him prouder than defeating Goliath. That was his lifelong devoted friendship and covenant with Jonathan.[4] Look at what happened right after Goliath's defeat. After King Saul had finished his conversation with David, David met Jonathan, the king's son, and there was an immediate bond of love between them. Jonathan swore to be David's blood brother, "and he sealed the pact by giving him his robe, sword, bow, and belt" (1 Sam.18:4).

Somehow, Jonathan knew David was destined to be Israel's next king. Although he was the heir apparent for the job, Jonathan believed the crown should rest on David's head. He did all he could to protect David, even at grave risk of danger to himself. Many years later, after Jonathan had died, David remembered Jonathan's son, Mephibosheth, who was crippled early in life. When David found him, he brought him into the palace to eat daily at the king's table (see 2 Sam. 9:7). David never forgot the unconditional love Jonathan had shown him. In doing so, David exhibited another characteristic "Values in Action Classification of Character Strengths" lists as a subset of courageousness—David acted authentically. He genuinely and without pretense wanted to show his willingness to take responsibility for Mephibosheth out of the deep feelings for Jonathan he cherished.[5] Perhaps the deep grieving David experienced when Jonathan died was somehow softened by his giving Mephibosheth such a comfortable life.

King Saul had no such sentiments toward David. After Goliath's defeat, David became commander of Israel's troops. As the victorious Israeli army returned home from a battle with the Philistines, everyone was singing and dancing with tambourines and cymbals. They exulted: "Saul has slain his thousands, and David his ten thousands!" (1 Sam. 18:7).

This celebration greatly angered Saul, and he kept a jealous watch on David from that time on.[6] Ironically, the only thing that soothed Saul's tormented spirit was David's harp playing. One day as David was playing music for Saul, Saul hurled a spear at David, but David quickly moved out of its path. This whole scenario was soon repeated, but David jumped out of the way again. Saul banned David from his presence and demoted him, but David continued to succeed in everything he did. The scriptures report that God left Saul and went with David. This divine act frightened Saul, as did David's popularity with the people. According to 1 Samuel 18:16, "All Israel and Judah loved [David] for he was as one of them."

David always proceeded with great zest. The "Values in Action Classification of Character Strengths" describes *zest* as approaching life with excitement and energy, living life as an adventure, and feeling alive and activated.[7] Unfortunately, Saul wasn't feeling very zestful.

It was becoming obvious that Saul wanted David dead. He used any and all tactics to snare David. Saul's daughter, Michal, was in love with David. So Saul sent her to be married to David even though the young man had no dowry. Saul set the price for the bride at "a hundred Philistine foreskins" (1 Sam. 18:25). Saul's plan was for David to die in battle. Michal double-crossed her father and helped David escape when Saul pursued him.[8] Jonathan did the same.[9]

Saul is a study in failed leadership. The culture of a company, or in this case, a kingdom, is determined by the way a leader communicates attitudes and standards. People are strongly influenced by the leader's behavior. To direct successfully, the leader must be willing to tolerate and even encourage open confrontation and debate as well as constructive criticism.[10] Saul made dysfunctional choices. The damage was permanent.

In describing how a business can be a center of excellence, Dieter Frey, Eva Jonas, and Tobias Greitemeyer say, "To achieve top performance as a global player in the international market, all employees must have a high achievement ethos, must constantly learn and improve processes, and must show responsibility and courage."[11] Sounds a lot like David, doesn't it?

Saul became even more determined to finish off David. So David learned a lot about life on the run. He also learned to run into his heavenly Father's arms. David penned Psalm 142 while hiding in a cave. Verses 5–7 record David's prayer: "You are my refuge, My portion in the land of the living. Attend to my cry, For I am brought very low; Deliver me from my persecutors, For they are stronger than I. Bring my soul out of prison, That I may praise Your name; The righteous shall surround me, For You shall deal bountifully with me" (NKJV). David found his strength and courage through his trust in the Lord.[12]

At one point in Saul's pursuit of him, David crept forward from his hiding place in a cave and cut off a piece of Saul's robe as Saul relieved himself. When Saul was away from the cave, David yelled to him, showing him the piece of robe. David was trying in every way to show Saul that he still respected him as king, regardless of how abysmally Saul had treated him. Unfortunately, this did not deter the tyrant.

King Saul took Michal away and gave her to another man. I guess back then women didn't have much say in such matters! Anyway, David and his band of men ran into a surly man named Nabal. Nabal was very rude to David and his men, but Nabal's wife, Abigail, was very wise. She took gifts to David and thereby kept the peace. David was so impressed that he later married her.[13] Unfortunately, this started the destructive practice of his taking more than one wife, which was an evil God had warned him against.[14]

APTITUDES FOR GROWTH; ATTITUDES FOR SUCCESS

Saul rampaged to find David again. This time, while Saul and his men slept, David bravely crept into the camp with a friend and stole Saul's spear and water jug. David showed the articles the next day to show Saul he meant Saul no harm. Again, Saul apologized and headed home.

But David knew the apology wouldn't last. *One of these days*, David thought, *Saul will destroy me*. In his exhaustion, he began to attack anyone who might talk to Saul about him. So he slaughtered the innocent people of Gath.[15] God had not told David to do this, and He did not condone the shedding of innocent blood. This is a lesson to us to lean solely on the Lord to guide our actions and keep claiming His promises.[16]

Meanwhile, Saul had resorted to consulting mediums about his future. The mediums summoned Samuel from the dead. Annoyed for being bothered, Samuel informed Saul that the kingdom would be taken out of his hands and given to David.[17]

Just as Samuel had said, the Philistines defeated Saul and his three sons. Saul took his own spear and fell upon it.[18] When David and his men returned to Israel and found out what had happened, they mourned, wept, and tore their clothes.[19] In his grief, David remembered Saul and Jonathan with great love, exclaiming, "Saul and Jonathan— in life they were loved and gracious, and in death they were not parted. They were swifter than eagles, they were stronger than lions" (2 Sam. 1:23 NIV).

David added, "I grieve for you, Jonathan my brother; you were very dear to me. Your love for me was wonderful, more wonderful than that of women" (2 Sam. 1:26 NIV).

David officially became king. He danced through the streets in jubilation when he brought the ark of God to Jerusalem (see 2 Sam. 6:14–15). Folly occurred, however, when he took many wives and concubines. This may have been acceptable in those times, but it was not acceptable in God's sight.

At this time, the prophet Nathan emerged as David's advisor. God told Nathan in a dream that David's house would endure forever before God (see 2 Sam. 7:16). And David ruled justly over all the people (see 2 Sam. 8:15).

Eventually, however, David began to shirk his duty. He stayed at home when he should have been leading his men on the battlefield.[20] One night he saw beautiful Bathsheba bathing on her roof, and summoned her to his quarters. They began an affair. Bathsheba became pregnant with David's child.[21]

In an attempt to cover his sin, David ordered Bathsheba's husband, Uriah, home from the battlefield. Uriah, ever loyal to his troops, refused to sleep with his wife. His heart was with his men in battle. And so David compounded his sin by having Uriah placed at the front of the battle lines so he would be killed.[22]

Using evocative language and intense storytelling, the prophet Nathan set the stage to convict David of his terrible crimes against God and Uriah. Nathan appealed to the king's imagination to lead David to the ultimate, horrible truth of what he had done.

Rather than coming right out and stating the fact that David slept with Uriah's wife, Bathsheba, and then had Uriah killed to cover up the pregnancy, which resulted from this adultery, Nathan skillfully approached the king with a moving allegory.

Nathan told about a rich sheep-owner and a poor man who had but one sheep. Nathan described the bereft man in detail: "And the very poor, owning nothing but a little lamb he had managed to buy. It was his children's pet and he fed it from his own plate and let it drink from his own cup; he cuddled it in his arms like a baby daughter" (2 Sam. 12:3).

When Nathan explained that the rich man took the poor man's lamb and roasted it and served it up to guests, he succeeded in raising David's great ire. Such a man, declared David, should be put to death. Now the boom was lowered. Can't you see Nathan point straight at the king as he declared, "*You* are that rich man"? It is as if Nathan was holding up a mirror to David. The image was ugly.

Nathan gave David a good dressing down. He laid out all the marvelous things God had done for David and all the great opportunities He had given to David. Through Nathan, God asked, "Why, then, have you despised God's laws and done this horrible deed?" What could David say? Indeed, what can you or I say when the prophet's mirror is held up to us?

Next, God delineated David's punishment. Staggering repercussions resulted from his brutal actions. His household was rebellious, and David's wives went to bed with other men. Perhaps, worst of all, his child died (see 2 Sam. 12:14).

The writer of 2 Samuel reports that David went without food and lay all night praying for the child's survival. Once the baby died, however, David accepted God's will, got up, and went about his business (see 2 Sam. 22–23).

He returned to his proper role as leader of the army by attacking Rabbah. To his credit, he made a fantastic comeback. Yes, he had made some very poor choices, but he went back to doing the things he should have been doing all along. And then, at last, with Nathan's blessing, Bathsheba bore David a son. His name was Solomon, and he became the wisest man who ever lived.

And so we see ourselves in David's story. Haven't we all, over the vantage point of many years of maturity, looked back with a sick heart on some of the things we have done? Perhaps the Holy Spirit brings those things to our remembrance. We, like David, must repent. We must accept divine chastisement. We must wear our sackcloth and ashes.

But then we must arise. God forgave David; he will forgive us too. In His great mercy, He sent His perfect Son to take the full punishment we deserved. After a personal failure, we must recover and again begin to do that special, distinct work God has for us to do.

This story inspires us to look at David's life and have the strength to try again. Something that might drive a person out of his mind can be buffered and avoided by banking on human strengths such as faith and courage.[23] With Christ's help, we can have the courage to do what we never could do alone.

Even years after God has forgiven us for a sin, we still may be dealing with the natural consequences accompanying that sin. David's household was replete with siblings, half-siblings, and the offspring of his concubines. All of David's sexual relationships must have been confusing to his offspring.

Amnon, David's eldest, plotted and schemed until he was able to get Tamar, his virginal half-sister, alone. Then he raped her.[24] This wicked act not only destroyed Tamar's life, it also led her brother, Absalom, on a path of wild vengeance. Absalom waited two years for David to punish Amnon. King David did not do so. So Absalom had his half-brother killed.[25] He hid out for three years and then waited two more years in Jerusalem for David to receive him. He never received satisfaction. Hence he spent the next four years plotting vengeance against his father.

When Absalom won David's highly respected adviser, Ahithophel, to his side, David responded by running.[26] Where was his trust in the God who had made him king? Where was the courage he had shown when he killed Goliath?

Finally, David's army battled the rebellious men who had sided with Absalom. David could not help but tell his men to be careful concerning Absalom (see 2 Sam. 18:5). Nevertheless, Absalom was killed, and David wept bitterly. He wished *he* could have died rather than his precious son. His grief was crippling.[27]

The pain and suffering David experienced throughout his life began to catch up with him. He became old and weak. There was just one last act to complete. Nathan, the prophet, told Bathsheba that Haggith's son Adonijhah was trying to seize the kingdom. Bathsheba told David, reminding him that it was her son, Solomon, who had been promised the throne. David decreed that Solomon would be the next king to sit upon the throne.[28] And so he was.

First Chronicles 29:26–28 tells us, "David was king of the land of Israel for forty years; seven of them during his reign in Hebron and thirty-three in Jerusalem. He died at an old age, wealthy and honored; and his son Solomon reigned in his place."

David's ability to protect Israel led to his divine appointment as the king over God's chosen people. Being a man after God's own heart, David dreamed of building a magnificent temple to honor his Lord. He commissioned Solomon, his son, to do the work, saying, "Every part of this blueprint was given to me in writing from the hand of the Lord.... Be strong and courageous and get to work.

Don't be frightened by the size of the task for the Lord, my God, is with you. He will not forsake you" (1 Chron. 28:19–20).

The same mandate applies to each of us. You never know what important work He will accomplish in your life if you ask Him to tell you what to do. He will answer you. When you feel His directing and prompting, take courage and move toward achieving your God-given dream with passion and diligence. Be secure in the fact that the outcome rests in His hands and that all the glory belongs to Him.

Just as Solomon faced the monumental task of building the temple David envisioned to give glory to God, the tasks ahead of you may seem overwhelming. Take comfort; God will be beside you every step of the way. Just keep taking small steps toward your ultimate goals. Head in the right direction, and then just put one foot in front of the other. Bravery is attainable when it is broken into doable parts.

Throughout his life, David exemplified the spiritual practice of emptying himself of his fears and realizing the battle was not his but the Lord's. Are you, like David, building an active history with the Lord? David believed with all his heart that God was with him, and so had the courage to believe his daunting mission would succeed.

God has a mission for each of us—a special destiny designed just for us individually. You can step out in faith and bravely ask God what that mission is. Wait with expectancy until He provides the answers.

Throughout history, great leaders have emerged with God-given visions that changed the world. Martin Luther King, Jr. worked nonviolently to create opportunities and equality for African Americans. FDR put the people of America back to work and pulled the country out of the Great Depression.

When God gives someone a vision, He also gives that person the passion, focus, and unwavering motivation to achieve that vision. He gives the tools necessary for the seeker to reach his or her vision and fulfill his or her mission. Courage is a crucial tool for success. There is a close relationship between courage and hope.

COURAGE: I COME TO YOU IN THE NAME OF THE LORD

Three basic elements help us enlarge our understanding of bravery: valor, diligence, and integrity. We display valor when we face challenge, pain, or difficulty without shrinking.[29] Think of Jesus' quiet strength as He prayed in the Garden of Gethsemane, where He sweat great drops of blood. Asking the Father to remove the cup from Him (His impending crucifixion), He prayed, "Not My will, but Thine be done." Courage is often affiliated with asserting one's own will, but we see in the Gethsemane experience that true courage is relinquishing our will to the heavenly Father.

No matter how difficult the circumstance, Christ never lost His dignity. Much of being courageous consists of taking a stoic and even cheerful stance needed to face serious ordeals and persistent suffering without loss of dignity. When we adopt Christ's mind, we develop the ever-growing ability to deal with difficulties with patience. When we seek to find and do His will, the Lord will cover and protect our dignity.

One of the biggest difficulties many believers face is that of accepting responsibility for past failures. As we learned from studying David's life, there is no escaping the consequences of our actions. It is a valiant act to face past wrongs squarely and change our ways. It may spare our loved ones and us years of additional pain. It is never too late to take responsibility and make a new start. The only truly fatal mistake is that of giving up.

Diligence is the ability to refuse to give up, to finish what we start, and to wait with expectancy on the Lord's power. When we possess this ability, we do what we say we will do and deliver what we had promised or even more. We must take special care not to be perfectionists.

Overcome the self-defeating thoughts and behavior of perfectionism with the character strength of courage. The first thing to remember is that there is a huge difference between setting high personal standards versus perfectionist ideals. This means making modest goals. Learn how to talk to yourself about keeping things reasonable. Don't be overly critical of your abilities or how you look. Having a nice appearance is different from obsessing in front of the mirror. Realize that competing and comparing are futile and destructive endeavors. Find out what you are best at and then make a realistic goal based on that attribute.[30] Strive to remain flexible, realistic, and industrious.[31]

Matthew 25:14–30 teaches about the virtue of industriousness. This illustration focuses on a master who left his residence and entrusted his money with three servants. Two of the servants took cautious risks and invested their money. They made profits on the money under their care. Unfortunately, the perfectionist, fearful servant buried his treasure in a hole because he was paralyzed by fear of failure or disappointing his master. Can you relate?

When the master returned, he gave greater responsibilities to the servants who had made profits, whereas he did not entrust the fearful servant with further responsibility. Just as the master expected his servants to prosper the resources he gave them, so God believes we should use the gifts He has bestowed on us. All that is required is that we make a reasonable attempt to do something useful with our abilities so they will bear fruit. It does, however, involve taking some degree of risk.

An anonymous Chicago teacher wrote some eloquent thoughts about how being a person of integrity entails certain risks:

> To laugh is to risk appearing the fool.
> To weep is to risk appearing sentimental.
> To reach for another is to risk involvement.
> To expose your feelings is to risk exposing your true self.
> To place your ideas, your dreams before a crowd, is to risk their loss.
> To love is to risk not being loved in return.
> To live is to risk dying.
> To believe is to risk despair.
> To try is to risk failure.
> But risks must be taken
> Because the greatest hazard in life is to risk nothing.

This teacher speaks with a great deal of integrity. Integrity involves not only honestly speaking the truth but also living life in an authentic and genuine manner. It means letting down our pretense and being "real."[32] These attributes do not magically appear because we wish to possess them. Courage, like any virtue, is similar to a muscle. You can possess more of any virtue through practice. With practice and dedication, courage can take root and flourish.

My husband, David, is a big fan of University of Kentucky basketball. He receives their publication, *The Cat's Pause*. He excitedly showed me the August 2009 issue. "I have the perfect story for your book that exemplifies courage," he exclaimed. The article talks about the life of Orlando Antigua. Antigua was made an assistant basketball coach at UK in April 2009.

From humble beginnings, Antigua overcame many challenges to become the success he is today. He cites his grandmother's prayers as pivotal to his achievements over the years.

Antigua was born into poverty in the Dominican Republic. His mom left his two brothers and him there while she made her way to the Bronx to give her family a better life. As soon as there was enough money, the boys joined her.

He is well positioned to help his players overcome obstacles because he himself overcame so many. Some of those included living on streets where drugs and violence were rampant. He avoided this life by finding a group of friends who played stickball, baseball, and basketball.

In addition to being homeless for a time, he was shot as an innocent bystander on the mean streets of the Bronx. The bullet hit near his left eye. He could have died. Fortunately, it lodged in his left ear and was safely extracted later.

Some good things were happening to him at that time too. In the eighth grade, Antigua shot up to 6'5". He was awarded a scholarship to Raymond's High School for Boys. After becoming senior class president and receiving the courage award from the U.S. Basketball Association, Antigua wrangled a scholarship to the University of Pittsburgh. While there he scored nine hundred points and four hundred rebounds. He stayed on at the university another semester to complete the degree as he had promised his mother he would.

With his degree behind him, Orlando went to play with the Harlem Globetrotters. He was the first Hispanic to do so. He stayed with them for seven years, traveling all over the world. The story explains, "He performed on the David Letterman show, matched basketball skills with Magic Johnson, and shook the hand of Nelson Mandela, the Noble Prize winner who was imprisoned for twenty-eight years for opposing South Africa's apartheid policy."[33]

Now Antigua is pursuing another challenging opportunity as the new assistant coach at the University of Kentucky. His mandate is to help others reach their dreams. Antigua put it this way: "God is the only one who can save your life. Basketball allowed me to live life. It has allowed us to better our circumstances, see the world, and make a living off something I absolutely love. Basketball has allowed me to live my life and my dream." [34]

Orlando Antigua is a perfect illustration of a person who succeeded by internalizing vital character strengths like courage. Character traits are like fruit; to be of quality they must ripen gradually.

So how do we ensure that we grow to flourish and bear good fruit—what we have been placed on Planet Earth to accomplish? The only no-fail manner in which to assure that we produce the fruit we are supposed to is to stay grafted to our source for all good things, including life itself. We must realize who we are in relation to Jesus and His Father. In John 15:5 Jesus promised, "I am the Vine, You are the branches. Whoever lives in me and I in him shall produce a large crop of fruit."

If we study the Word and pray regularly, we will acquire Christ's mind. Staying connected to the Vine means our joy will overflow and Jesus will call us His friends (John 15:6–14). Being Jesus' friend will give us a great deal of security. It will help us believe in things not yet seen. It will help us to be positive in a negative situation. It will allow us to believe that God will ultimately work out every suffering and trial for our good.

Courage is being willing to change and take moderate risks. It is about not fearing to move ahead with the plans the Lord has revealed to you. Passion and motivation are necessary if you are to reach your full potential. As you work hard on the projects that you care about and are interested in, your ability in those areas will increase.[35]

As the cowardly lion was required to reach inward to find the best that was within him, you can find the courage to become an unwavering believer. Glorifying and honoring the great and mighty living God is critical to our success. In Leviticus 22:31–33, God admonished, "You must not treat Me as common and ordinary. Revere Me and hallow Me, for I, the Lord, made you holy to Myself and rescued you from Egypt to be My own people. I am Jehovah."

The only way you can effectively be a courageous person is to have a heart for the Lord. He wants you to love Him and honor Him with all your heart, mind, and soul. When we do all we can, and then cast our cares on the Lord, we can be assured He will not forsake us. Have the courage within yourself to live out your purpose to the full and achieve all God designed for your destiny when He was yet forming you in the seclusion of your mother's womb.

CHAPTER 6

PERSEVERANCE: NEVER GIVE UP

> Take the old prophets as your mentors. They put up with anything, went through everything, and never once quit, all the time honoring God. What a gift life is to those who stay the course!
> (James 5:10 MESSAGE).

ARE YOU COMPLETING your most important goals? It takes perseverance to do so. Perseverance is an aptitude that can be either natural or acquired. By "acquired," I mean it can be learned. Simply put, perseverance is the aptitude of refusing to give up. Or, said another way, it is having the willingness to try again after losing or quitting. James 5:10 instructs us to use the old prophets as our examples. In this chapter, you will have the opportunity to examine the life of Nehemiah, a successful leader who persevered to the end.

An attitude is a manner of carrying oneself. Would you like to carry yourself with the persevering leadership style Nehemiah exhibited? What an adventure he had in completing his mission! The same can be true for you.

Leading and persevering are strengths you can build like muscles if you ask Jesus to help you do so. Whatever challenges you are facing, with Christ's help, you can reach higher ground. In this way, you can help others and glorify God with your service. It is amazing what can happen if you stay the course and take the risk of being responsible for the completion of your God-given mission.

Simply put, perseverance is the art of finishing what you start. It means taking on challenging projects and finishing them with, as Martin Seligman phrases it, "good cheer and minimal complaints."[1] The persevering person should remain flexible and realistic rather than perfectionistic—do what you say you will do or more, but never less.

Martin Seligman also says in *Learned Optimism* that success is more than having the aptitude and motivation to complete a project. He comments, "Success requires persistence, the ability to not give up in the face of failure."[2] He concludes that this persistence can occur when a person explains things to himself or herself in an optimistic style. He defines three characteristics necessary for ongoing success: aptitude, motivation, and optimism.[3]

John Maxwell speaks and writes about success to the corporate business world as well as to Christian community. "Leadership truly develops from the inside out. If you can become the leader you ought to be on the inside, you will be able to become the leader you want to be on the outside. People will want to follow you. And when this happens, you'll be able to tackle anything in this world," he says.[4]

What could be more exciting than trying to make the world a better place? Can you capitalize on your strengths to effect change both within and beyond yourself? Like perseverance, leadership is an aptitude you can grow into. It is an attitude that says with God's help, I can, you can, and we can.

One of the most astute decisions you can make as a leader is to help your employees discover their unused signature strengths. Let's say you supervise a group of lawyers. All of them possess prudence and high verbal intelligence, but each has distinct strengths that if used on a side project could really energize the productivity of each individual.[5] This is an instance when the results of the VIA Signature Strengths Survey can empower a leader and his or her organization.

PERSEVERANCE: NEVER GIVE UP

A certain African tribe was a puzzle to anthropologists. For hundreds of years this tribe enjoyed a 100 percent success rate with its rain dance. Other tribes did similar rain dances but did not always experience success. Their rituals, their costumes, and their methods of praying were all the same. Finally, someone discovered the truth behind this mystery. While all the tribes at times danced continually for days and even weeks, the tribe with total success refused to stop dancing until the rains came. That's perseverance!

Boredom, stagnation, and anxiety can lead to giving up. But if a person is working in one of his or her strength areas and can get into flow, those negative attributes can abate. Flow occurs when both the challenge and the skills to meet the challenge are at above-average levels. When a person experiences flow, he or she is encouraged to persevere. In fact, there is relationship between persistence and the quality of the worker's experience. Time spent in flow can improve self-esteem. Mastering the challenges of living can act as a buffer against negative outcomes.[6]

Perseverance is an essential quality for those of us who hope to lead others to Christ or to be effective in the body of Christ. The book of Nehemiah gives us an example of a man on a mission who possessed the vision and ability to set goals so he ultimately could succeed. Nehemiah had a specific and formidable task—to rebuild the broken-down wall around Jerusalem.

When Nehemiah first heard about the wall's devastation, he sat and wept.[7] He cared. First and foremost, leaders must care.

After drying his tears, Nehemiah took action. He did not start by writing his "to do" list. He did not make a grand announcement about the terrible state of the wall around Jerusalem. He did not immediately jump into action. No, he got on his knees and prayed.[8]

He began by putting first things first. His first act was to seek out God's direction. Repeatedly, throughout his story, Nehemiah slipped away in solitude. He beseeched God to show him His will. Because of Nehemiah's devotion to God, the workers under his leadership completed the wall of Jerusalem in an incredible fifty-two days.[9]

Nehemiah was wise enough to think clearly and pursue goals that would lead to ultimate fulfillment for his people rather than chasing goals that would give only the illusion of fulfillment. Wisdom is displayed when a person pursues positively framed goals that are good for the collective in a prudent, patient, and persevering manner.[10] Nehemiah moved forward in just such a manner.

The book of Nehemiah was written as an autobiography. Nehemiah discovered that the wall of Jerusalem was in a state of total disrepair. He wept and fasted for several days. He cried out to God and reminded God of the words He had spoken to Moses: "If you sin, I will scatter you among the nations; but if you return to me and obey laws, even though you are exiled to the farthest corners of the universe, I will bring you back to Jerusalem. For Jerusalem is the place in which I have chosen to live" (Neh. 1:8–9).

After confessing the Israelites' sins, Nehemiah reminded the Lord of His promises.[11] This is a great prescription for us today. When we go to God and repent, and then remind Him of His own words and promises, He can move miraculously in our circumstances.

At the time God convicted Nehemiah to lead the rebuilding of Jerusalem's wall, Nehemiah was serving as the cupbearer to King Artaxerxes of Persia. As a cupbearer, he was very close to the king. His job was to test the king's food and drink to determine whether it was safe. Nehemiah prayed that God would give the king a kind heart for the task he desired to accomplish. Then he waited—for four months.[12]

One of the things I would most like to emulate about Nehemiah is his habit of praying seriously for long periods before he undertook any action. This encourages me to talk to God about everything. I don't have to use fancy language; I just need to communicate in intimacy with my Maker. Then He certainly will be willing to guide my steps. It is so vital to check with God before beginning a project to make sure it is His and not just something we of ourselves take on.

One day as he was serving the king his wine, the king noticed Nehemiah was troubled, and asked why. This was Nehemiah's opportunity to share what had been on his heart. He fearfully asked the king to send him home to rebuild Jerusalem. The king's immediate response was simply, "How long will you be gone?"[13]

God moved the king's heart to grant Nehemiah's request.

Nehemiah 2 features him in Jerusalem. As a wise builder, Nehemiah proceeded cautiously. This habit was perhaps the secret to much of his success. When he arrived in Jerusalem, he realized the time was not right to tell anyone he was going to rebuild Jerusalem's wall. Instead, he waited until nightfall to inspect the state of the wall. As he toured the wall by horseback, he saw the rubble was too high to access many areas.

This moonlit excursion allowed Nehemiah to assess the situation accurately. He then had a good idea of his project's scope. He knew it was going to be challenging and rigorous.

At the right time, Nehemiah approached the city officials. He explained, "You know full well the tragedy of our city; it lies in ruins and its gates are burned. Let us rebuild the wall of Jerusalem and rid ourselves of this disgrace" (Neh. 2:17).

After Nehemiah had thoroughly diagnosed the problem, he took an active role in solving it. He did not sit back and tell city officials what they should do—he joined in. He suggested they rebuild the wall together. If you and I wish to make this world a better place, we too must do more than tell others what to do. We need to join in the labor and encourage our associates—we must be willing to get our hands dirty.

Nehemiah was successful in creating a team ready to work together. The officials agreed to begin the work at once. Rebuilding the entire wall of Jerusalem was a daunting task. Nehemiah prudently divided the work and assigned different parts of the wall to different groups. This greatly helped make the overwhelming nature of the task less frightening and more feasible. That's what leaders do: they inspire those they supervise by breaking up jobs into small, doable steps.

Even so, the challenges were not over for Nehemiah. Enemies rose up to oppose the successful rebuilding of the wall. Sanballat and Tobiah ridiculed him.[14] Isn't it encouraging that Nehemiah endured their sarcasm and persisted in the task set before him? Sometimes when people treat us poorly we want to throw up our hands and give up. We can learn from Nehemiah's example. He chose simply to keep his focus on God rather than on the ridicule. Christ made this same choice while He agonizingly hung on the cross to take the punishment for our sins.

Nehemiah's story shows us the importance of choosing to concentrate and focus on the right thing. Despite great odds and enemies, Nehemiah and his people completed the wall. With God's help, the group achieved in two months a job that had been left undone for a hundred years.

Nehemiah is a great role model. He was willing to lead by example. He sacrificed his own rights for the good of the people. If we can forget ourselves and persevere, letting nothing turn us from our purpose, we can join Nehemiah in saying, "I am doing a great work!" Seek God for clear direction. You have a calling no less important than Nehemiah's.

The optimistic person perseveres. Such optimism helps when the work gets hard.[15] When we persevere, we inspire others. Martin Seligman tells a story about his home-schooled son, Darryl, that humorously drives this point home. Darryl, who had a rock collection, accompanied a mineralogist to collect specimens. After hours of collecting, Darryl was urged back to the car. "Darryl, sweaty and dirty and sitting on top of a huge pile of rocks at a construction site, shouted back, 'Mineralogists don't take breaks,'" Seligman writes.[16]

An admirer once exclaimed to Theodore Roosevelt, "Mr. Roosevelt, you are a great man." Roosevelt responded, "No, Teddy Roosevelt is simply a plain, ordinary man—highly motivated."[17]

Think of people who are good at putting puzzles together. While others give up after making a good effort, the skilled puzzle player knows he or she has all the pieces of the whole on the table. It is just a matter of finding out which piece fits where. Once the person can do that, the puzzle is complete. As Vic Johnson explains, "Putting a piece in the wrong place is not a cause for concern; it is simply another step toward putting all of the pieces in their proper place."[18]

PERSEVERANCE: NEVER GIVE UP

A study of salespeople revealed that those who tested optimistic kept improving over those who tested pessimistic. Why did this happen? It became evident that optimism mattered because it produced perseverance. It was hypothesized before the experiment that talent and motivation would be as important to success as perseverance. As time went on and things got tough, it was those salespeople who persevered who did the best.[19]

It is interesting to notice Nehemiah did not retire immediately after completing his big project. He became the people's governor.[20] He devised a plan for guarding the wall. He also created a system to register all who had returned to Jerusalem now that its borders were secure.

Then Nehemiah did what is often the hardest thing of all for a leader—he handed the authority to someone better qualified for the next steps in God's desires for Jerusalem: Ezra.[21]

Nehemiah knew Ezra possessed the skills to lead the Jewish people to revival. He was happy his organizational skills had created a safe boundary for Jerusalem. Now the people were ready to move on to higher levels and reach spiritual maturity.

In *Hand Me Another Brick*, Charles Swindoll says, "Tucked away in the old book of Nehemiah is the first recorded revival."[22] Ezra 8 says Ezra read to the people out of the scroll of Moses' laws. The people bowed with their faces to the ground and worshiped the Lord. As they came to understand what Ezra was reading, all the people sobbed.

Then Ezra and Nehemiah instructed the people not to cry. "Don't cry on such a day as this! For today is a sacred day before the Lord your God—it is time to celebrate with a hearty meal and to send presents to those in need, for the joy of the Lord is your strength. You must not be dejected and sad" (Neh. 8:9–10).

The people participated in a seven-day feast. On the eighth day, there was a solemn closing—the people came together again to fast and clothe themselves in sackcloth. They sprinkled dirt on themselves. Ezra recounted the relationship God and his people should have. Then the religious leaders formalized a pact to be accountable to God. The people agreed to be obedient.

Positive psychology at the group level rests on institutions that move people toward better citizenship. Some of the attributes that help a collective thrive are responsibility, nurturance, altruism, civility, moderation, tolerance, and work ethic.[23]

Systematically, groups of Israelites returned to live in Jerusalem. There were now healthy boundaries of protection. The people held an ecstatic ceremony to dedicate the city wall. It turned out to be the happiest event Israel had experienced in more than half a century! It is amazing how happy we, God's people, become after we repent of our sins and renew our obedience to our awesome Creator and Sustainer.

With everything looking good, Nehemiah returned to his job under King Artaxerxes. However, it wasn't long before Nehemiah again needed permission to return to Jerusalem. He had heard that a temple storeroom had been made into a beautiful guestroom for a man who was not only not a Jew but also an enemy to the Jews' cause. Nehemiah angrily threw out the man's belongings and restored the space to its original purpose. He insisted that the people give the Levite priests their fair wage. He also swiftly put an end to any work that was being conducted on the Sabbath. Further, he forcefully prohibited marriage to the heathen. Isn't it predictable that even after a great revival and a declaration of obedience to God that the people fell away into sin again? Aren't they just so typically human? Can't you relate to their failure?

Leadership duties do not end after a mountaintop experience. When a prudent leader faces the fact that sin has reemerged among the group, he does not throw up his hands in disgust. He, like Nehemiah, must once again step boldly forward to put things back into their proper order.

Nehemiah showed himself to be an effective leader. He kept his focus on achieving specific goals without losing sight of "the big picture." He could see the results of his "now" ahead of time.[24] He influenced and organized his people so they might have all God had prepared for them. We should do no less.

Nehemiah did not entertain a self-serving agenda. He had a servant's heart. He understood that a person becomes an adult when he or she realizes that life is not about what you get, but rather about what you give. When you are motivated by intrinsic rewards rather than self-centered ones, you can use your curiosity and persistence to accomplish much.[25]

God never sends His leaders into any situation with a faulty plan or a plan to fail. If we are following God's desires, we will succeed mightily. We must always be aware to move forth God's agenda and His objectives, no more and no less. There is no place for ego in servant leadership. Think about your leadership in your home, your workplace, or your church. Are you aware that one of the stamps of great leaders is they spend much of their time training their successors?

The supreme example of this was Jesus' lengthy training program for His disciples. Think of the great selflessness of the greatest Self ever to grace the earth! Jesus successfully faced the powerful and universal temptations with which every leader must grapple. He did not need recognition or applause. He did not lust for power or use it improperly. He never caved in to acts of self-gratification.

He knew who He was. He knew without a doubt who His Father was. He never failed to obey God's Word. He knew the Word intimately. He was free of pride and just as free of fear. He knew very well what Proverbs 29:25 says: "Fear of man is a dangerous trap, but to trust in God means safety."

Trusting in the Lord means never putting something else in His place as the object of our worship. It means never relying on sources other than Him for our security. Trusting in the Lord means staying in intimate communion with Him and resting in His unconditional love.

If the Devil had a formula for self-worth it would be as follows: your self-worth is equal to your performance plus the opinions of others.[26] We demonstrate our trust in the Lord by putting our self-worth securely and completely in His hands. He is our Abba. We must grasp the truth! It is God who created us. It is God who determines our destiny. It is God to whom we will someday return. Selah! Ponder that.

We are not here to fulfill our own purposes. God created us to fit into His purposes. I need to realize I am not here to fulfill my plans for my life. God created me to fulfill His plans for me. If I don't fall into line with God's will for my life, I miss the best He has for me. What a waste my God-given life will have been if it has not been God-directed. How sad it would be if we did not trust Him enough to carry out the work He has for us confidently.

My friend Lorna was told by her high school guidance counselor that she was not college material. Frustrated, she graduated after the first half of her senior year and went to work at a pizza place. Soon she was manager. Eventually she put her experiences on the high school newspaper staff to good use and applied for a job working at a magazine that deals with antique guns. She got the job and before you know it she was Director of Publications. She successfully managed the magazine for several years.

In addition to the magazine, the association for which she works holds year-round events in the display and use of antique guns. Eventually the CEO and the COO of the company left and guess who was put in charge of the whole office and all the activities on the grounds? You guessed it: my friend Lorna. She is a no-nonsense, dedicated leader who puts in countless hours to keep both the organization and the magazine afloat. She took the raw intelligence and leadership ability she had and made the most of it. Refusing to believe she could not make the grade, she persevered and rose to the top of her company.

The cornerstone of positive psychology is that of having a commitment and confidence that foster perseverance even in the face of great adversity. It means having a goal that matters, one to which you will commit fully. It also means having the confidence that you *will* eventually achieve your goal, no matter how difficult.[27] It is pursuing the goal, as Nehemiah did, with ferocious fearlessness.

The only fear we should have is a healthy fear of the Lord. Psalm 111:10 says the fear of the Lord is the beginning of wisdom. When we faithfully trust in God's complete love for us, we push fear and pride out of our lives and leave no room for anything but His love.

In John 13:12–17 we see God's unconditional love embodied in the acts of Jesus Christ. He was our perfect and outstanding example of a servant leader. Just before the Last Supper, He knelt to wash the disciples' feet.

Jesus asked, "Do you know what I have done to you? You call Me Teacher and Lord, and you say well, for so I am. If I then, your Lord and Teacher, have washed your feet, you also ought to wash one another's feet. For I have given you an example, that you should do as I have done to you. Most assuredly, I say to you, a servant is not greater than his master; nor is he who is sent greater than he who sent him. If you know these things, blessed are you if you do them" (John 13:12–17 NKJV).

How can you incorporate the act of "washing the feet" of those in your life? Do you really believe that the servant who gives is happier than the person who takes? How have you seen this play out in your life and others' lives?

Examine the events that led to Jesus' crucifixion. In His dying, He saved all believers. He persevered through every challenge presented to Him. He kept reaching out to the crowds while training a small band of disciples in love and intimacy.

As Nehemiah returned home to rebuild the wall, so people today return to rebuild their homes in war-torn territories. "The ability of people to struggle forward, to persevere against great odds even in the face of failure, represents a very important human strength," according to Carver and Scheier in *A Psychology of Human Strengths*.[28] Let us, as instructed, follow Jesus and take up our cross. He beckons, saying, "My yoke is easy and My burden is light" (Matt. 11:30 NKJV).

In *A Leader in the Making*, Joyce Meyer tells us that joining others in our endeavors helps us to endure much longer. We certainly saw that truth portrayed in Nehemiah's life. On this note, Meyer expounds, "God does not have to anoint anything He does not tell us to do."[29] This means we must be earnest in following Nehemiah's example of much prayer and preparation before action. We must wait patiently for God's still, small voice.

Learn to be a God-pleaser rather than a people-pleaser. As Hebrews 12:2 tells us, Jesus is "the author and finisher" (KJV). Let us be diligent in completing that which He has begun in us. If we allow Him, He certainly will bring our efforts to fruition ... and we will thrive.

CHAPTER 7

PATIENCE:
I WILL WAIT UPON THE LORD

> My brethren, count it all joy when ye fall into divers temptations; knowing this, that the trying of your faith worketh patience. But let patience have her perfect work, that ye may be perfect and entire, wanting nothing.
>
> (James 1:2–4 KJV)

WOULD YOU AGREE that when the different aspects of your life are going well, you wish things would stay that way? Does anybody really want trials? When you are in the midst of acute suffering, do you secretly or openly beat your chest and ask, "Why, God, why?"

While we are on this earth, we never may know fully why people around the world have to endure abject misery. However, we see through a glass darkly. Clarity will come when we get to heaven.

After we receive the gift of salvation, which includes spending eternity with God, God works in our lives to grow us into mature and complete Christians. Trials help with that process. They help us acquire patience.

Notice that in the above Scripture, James did not write, "Let trials have their perfect work." Not at all! He wrote, "Let patience have her perfect work."[1]

In his book *31 Days of Healing,* Mark Brazee says, "You see, tests and trials don't perfect you. It is what you do with them that matters. You are not perfected because a bunch of problems come along. You are perfected because you resolutely believe the Word of God in the midst of those problems and patiently endure. That's when patience has its perfect work."[2]

Patience may be defined as consistent endurance. No matter what happens to you, patience enables you to stay on an even keel. The key to victorious patient living comes by basing everything about your life on God's Word. Rather than looking to an internal thermometer and asking, "Who am I and how do I feel?" open the Word and let God tell you who you are and how to think.

Faithfulness through challenges accounts for the difference between success and failure. The way you choose to handle your problems determines whether you will live a victorious life or give up in defeat. Rather than shrinking away from a challenge, allow faith to thrive in the midst of your suffering. This is the precise moment to put all your trust in God. Standing firm, you can say, "I don't care what it looks like, seems like, sounds like, or feels like. I believe what the Word of God says!"[3]

Patience is both an aptitude (an ability you can acquire) as well as an attitude (a state of mind in regard to some matter). It is a strength. Displaying patience as a strength means you are firm in your will, character, and mind. You determine you will reach your goals and fulfill your purpose no matter what. By applying patience to each difficult life experience, you can help others and glorify God.

Of all the characters of the Bible, Job is certainly the most frequently linked to the virtue of patience. Job was a good man, careful to keep the Lord's commandments. Yet he suffered horribly. He never received a complete answer as to why he had to go through the living hell he did.

Those who read the book of Job understand that Satan perpetrated Job's fall into the pit of despair. Job 1 in *The Living Bible* translation opens by telling us: "There lived a man in the land of Uz, a man named Job—a good man who feared God and stayed away from evil" (v. 1). The book says further that "he had a large family of seven sons and three daughters and was immensely wealthy" (v. 2). He was scrupulous in prayer, never failing to thank God for his blessings and for giving his family protection. Overall, Job had a great life.

Enter the great besplatterer. According to verse 7 of the first chapter of Job's story, Satan, also called the Accuser, presented himself to God. God asked where Satan had come from. Satan replied he had been watching everything on the earth.

In verse 8, the Lord asked Satan, "Have you noticed my servant Job? He is the finest man in all the earth—a good man who fears God and will have nothing to do with evil."

"Why shouldn't he when you pay him so well?" Satan scoffed. "You have always protected him and his home and his property from all harm. You have prospered everything he does—look how rich he is! No wonder he 'worships' you! But just take away his wealth, and you'll see him curse you to your face!" (vv. 9–11).

The Lord decided He would prove Job's faithfulness by letting the Devil test him. He allowed Satan to do anything except lay a finger on Job.

Almost immediately tragedy struck Job's household. A flurry of servants entered Job's home with bad news. The first servant informed Job that raiders had killed his donkeys and oxen, as well as all the farmhands. Another servant interrupted to say there had been a fire, and all the sheep and herdsmen had burned up.

Another servant entered and reported that three bands of Chaldeans had driven off Job's camels and killed the herdsmen. A final servant brought the devastating news that a mighty wind had swept in from the desert and collapsed the roof of the house where all Job's children had been eating. All of Job's children were dead.

"Then Job stood up and tore his robe in grief and fell down upon the ground before God. 'I came naked from my mother's womb,' he said, 'and I shall have nothing when I die. The Lord gave me everything I had, and they were his to take away. Blessed be the name of the Lord.' In all of this, Job did not sin or revile God" (vv. 20–22).

Soon after, God and Satan had another discussion in which God declared His pride in Job and how he had handled the loss of his wealth and family. Satan retorted that Job would curse God if he lost his health. God told Satan to go right ahead and test Job again but spare his life.

"So Satan went out from the presence of the Lord and struck Job with a terrible case of boils from head to foot. Then Job took a broken piece of pottery to scrape himself and sat among the ashes.

"His wife said to him, 'Are you still trying to be godly when God has done all this to you? Curse him and die.'

"But he replied, 'You talk like some heathen woman. What? Shall we receive only pleasant things from the hand of God and never anything unpleasant?' So in all this Job said nothing wrong" (2:7–10).

About this time, three of Job's friends, Eliphaz the Temanite, Bildad the Shuhite, and Zophar the Naamathite, arrived. They had heard of the tragedy that had befallen Job.

Job 2:12–13 explores their response to his trauma: "Job was so changed that they could scarcely recognize him. Wailing loudly in despair, they tore their robes and threw dust into the air and put earth on their heads to demonstrate their sorrow. Then they sat upon the ground with him silently for seven days and nights, no one speaking a word; for they saw that his suffering was too great for words."

Unfortunately, after the initial shock wore off, Job's friends began to pick at him. They suggested he had committed some horrific sin that had brought this calamity upon him. From chapter 3 until halfway through the last chapter of Job, chapter 42, a philosophical discourse ensued between Job and his friends and between Job and his God. In a series of long poetic soliloquies, all the major players weigh in with their opinions on the meaning of life and suffering.

Chapter 3 gives voice to Job's wish to die. In verses 2–10, Job lamented, "Let the day of my birth be cursed, and the night when I was conceived. Let that day be forever forgotten. Let it be lost even to God, shrouded in eternal darkness. Yes, let the darkness claim it for its own, and may a black cloud overshadow it. May it be blotted off the calendar, never again to be counted among the days of the month of that year. Let the night be bleak and joyless. Let those who are experts at cursing curse it. Let the stars of the night disappear. Let it long for light but never see it, never see the morning light. Curse it for its failure to shut my mother's womb, for letting me be born to come to all this trouble."

Rather than giving Job the comfort he so desperately needed at this dark juncture, Eliphaz lectured Job. In chapter 4 he accused Job of being faint and broken, whereas in the past Job had counseled many an afflicted soul to trust in God when trouble struck. Eliphaz's "sermon" continued through all of chapter 5. He repeatedly asserted that God was punishing Job for some sin. His advice to Job to repent echoes throughout all the coming chapters.

None of Job's friends believed he was innocent. Can you imagine how frustrating this must have been for Job? Yet he held his own. He had, as they say, "the patience of Job."

Job's reply to Eliphaz lasts through chapters 6 and 7—"One should be kind to a fainting friend, but you have accused me without the slightest fear of God" (6:14).

In chapter 8, Bildad had his say. "If you were pure and good, God would hear your prayer and answer you and bless you with a happy home" (v. 6).

Beyond chastising Job, Bildad waxed philosophical, as did all the main characters in the rest of the story: "Read the history books and see—for we were born but yesterday and know so little; our days here on earth are as transient as shadows. But the wisdom of the past will teach you. The experience of others will speak to you, reminding you that those who forget God have no hope. They are like rushes without any mire to grow in; nor grass without water to keep it alive" (vv. 8–12).

Bildad insinuated that Job had forgotten God and therefore God was punishing him. Job's response in chapters 9 and 10 allowed him to express his frustration not only with Bildad but also with God. In Job 10:8, Job pled with the Lord, "You have made me; and yet you destroy me. Oh, please remember that I'm made of dust."

Next Zophar took his turn in chiding Job: "Before you turn to God and stretch out your hands to me, get rid of your sin and leave all iniquity behind you. Only then, without the spots of sin to defile you, can you walk steadily forward to God without fear. Only then can you forget your misery. It will all be in the past. And your life will be cloudless; any darkness will be as bright as morning" (11:13–17).

Imagine how Job felt when his friends spoke that way. Their words must have left such a bad taste in his mouth! Job's reply stretched from chapter 12 through chapter 14. He defended himself by saying, "This is my case: I know I am righteous ... O God, there are two things I beg you not to do to me; only then will I be able to face you. Don't abandon me. And don't terrify me with your awesome presence" (13:18, 20–21).

The argument drags on chapter by chapter. In chapter 30, we find Job still suffering terribly in addition to dealing with the barbs of his accusers. He cried, "My skin is black and peeling. My bones burn with fever. The voice of joy and gladness has turned to mourning" (30:30–31).

In chapter 32, the last character of the drama, Elihu entered and enjoyed listening to himself talk so much that he carried on through chapter 37. Basically, he set himself up as someone with an upright heart who spoke sincerely, and yet he accused Job of being prideful for making the same claim. Like Job's other friends, Elihu assumed that external circumstances served as a measuring stick for the quality of a person's faith. He concluded that if Job was suffering, he was getting what he deserved.

In this case, Elihu's assumptions were ridiculously off target. Job's trials were not a consequence of sinful living. In reality, they were a testimony of God's belief and trust in His beloved Job.

In Elihu's opinion, God was a kind of dictator who watches our actions, takes note of our deeds, and punishes us without need of further examination. This is not an accurate portrayal of our God. God did not accuse Job as his friends did. Satan was Job's accuser.

God is infinitely patient, slow to anger and quick to forgive. He looks at the heart. Anyone who sincerely submits to God through his son, Jesus Christ, will find Him merciful.

In chapters 38 through 41, the Lord appeared in a whirlwind and answered Job's entreaties. In eloquent and lyrical prose, God used a series of questions to show how little Job knew about creation and God's ways:

> Where were you when I laid the foundations of the earth? Tell me, if you know so much. Do you know how its dimensions were determined, and who did the surveying? What supports its foundations, and who laid its cornerstone as the morning stars sang together and all the angels shouted for joy?
>
> Who decreed the boundaries of the seas when they gushed from the depths? Who clothed them with clouds and thick darkness and barred them by limiting their shores, and said, "Thus far and no father shall you come, and here shall your proud waves stop!"?
>
> Have you ever once commanded the morning to appear and caused the dawn to rise in the east? Have you ever told the daylight to spread to the ends of the earth, to end the night's wickedness? Have you ever robed the dawn in red, and disturbed the haunts of wicked men, and stopped the arm raised to strike?
>
> Have you explored the springs from which the seas come, or walked in the sources of their depths? Has the location of the gates of Death been revealed to you? Do you realize the extent of the earth? Tell me about it if you know! Where does the light come from and how do you get there? Or tell me about the darkness. Where does it come from? Can you find its boundaries, or go to its source? But of course you know all this! For you were born before it was all created, and you are so very experienced!
>
> Have you visited the treasuries of the snow, or seen where hail is made and stored? For I have reserved it for the time when I will need it in war. Where is the path to the distribution point of light? Where is the home of the east wind? Who dug the valleys for the torrents of rain? Who laid out the path for the lightning, causing the rain to fall upon the haven deserts, so that the parched and

barren ground is satisfied with water and tender grass springs up? (vv. 4–27)

Job knew nothing of God's mysteries, so he could not comprehend God's character accurately. We also wonder why we suffer. We wonder why bad things happen to us, to our family, to all of humanity. We must realize God's ways are infinite while we are simple and finite creatures. The best we can do in our challenges and trials is to praise God and wait on His deliverance.

In chapter 40, the Lord asked Job, "Do you still want to argue with the Almighty? Or will you yield? Do you—God's critic—have the answers?" (v. 2).

Then Job replied to God, "I am nothing—how could I ever find the answers? I lay my hand upon my mouth in silence. I have said too much already" (vv. 4–5).

Job's answer to God overflowed with gratitude, explains *The Life Recovery Bible*: "Where Job had once only heard about God, here he actually saw him—the loving, merciful, all-powerful, majestic Creator. This man, who was known as 'blameless and upright' before his suffering, was now even greater because of that suffering. God is good. He gives us good gifts; He works good from all things; and His intentions for us are always good. Pain is a privilege when it leads us closer to God."[4]

After Job and God came to an agreement, God gave Job's so-called friends a good tongue-lashing. He was angry with them, telling them they had not been right in what they had said about Him. He instructed them to present a burnt offering of bulls and rams as an act of contrition. He said Job would pray for them. He further decreed He would accept Job's prayer on their behalf rather than destroy them for their failure to speak appropriately to Job.

These pseudo-philosophers learned a lesson—friends in trouble need comfort and understanding, not judgment. Sometimes people choose to analyze rather than empathize because it is so very scary to put ourselves in the sufferer's position. In the back of our minds, at least on the subconscious level, we realize the same fate could befall us.

It is heartwarming to note that Job did not say one judgmental thing about how terribly unfairly his friends had treated him. No, he was quick to forgive and grant them mercy.

At this crucial juncture, Job was the epitome of patience. Billy Graham described it in his book, *The Holy Spirit: Activating God's Power in Your Life:* "Patience is the transcendent radiance of a loving and tender heart which, in its dealings with those around it, looks kindly and graciously upon them. Patience graciously, compassionately and with understanding judges the faults of others without unjust criticism ... Patience is a part of true Christlikeness."[5]

Surely this patience that enveloped Job's whole being was one of the reasons God felt so tenderly toward him. When Job prayed for his friends, the Lord restored Job's wealth and happiness. In actuality, He gave Job a double recompense for all he had lost.

Then all of Job's kin and friends gathered to give him a big party because God had brought him through his trials. Then God blessed him with enormous numbers of sheep, camels, teams of oxen, and female donkeys. He also gave Job seven more sons and three more daughters.

Chapter 42 concludes with this happy ending: "And in the land there were no other girls as lovely as the daughters of Job; and their father put them into his will along with their brothers. [Hurray for girl power and women's rights!] Job lived another 140 years, long enough to see his grandchildren and even his great-grandchildren. At last he died an old, old man, after living a long, good life" (vv. 15–17).

I love the dramatic manner in which Job is written. It reads with such lovely lyricism and poignancy. The soliloquies hold the reader's interest in a creative, fresh, and effective manner.

The most interesting aspect of the book of Job to me is that Job displays all kinds of negative emotions to God and yet he is greatly known for his patience. Isn't it fascinating that God did not expect Job to suffer in silence and play the martyr? No, God respected Job's frank response to what he perceived to be a very unfair situation.

We live out our years in a world where injustice and unfairness seem to predominate. Through no fault of his own, Job lost his possessions, family, and health. He never got a clear answer as to why. In his struggles, though, he came to know God in a more mature and profound way. As you and I face unfairness in our lives, we can still make it an opportunity to learn more about how to trust in our perfect, loving, and all-knowing God.

God is so far above our deepest thoughts. Many times we are unable to fathom His mysterious ways. Surely Job could not have helped but wonder why he had to suffer so much. It would have been easy for Job to wholeheartedly reject God for the seeming injustice of it all. But Job still believed that God was good, and despite lapses of despair and anger, Job trusted that in the end God would deal with him justly. He trusted God unconditionally.

The Life Recovery Bible says, "When life is going smoothly, trust is easy. The test of trust always comes when life stops making sense. Job gave us a very real example of how trust needs to work in our lives. Everything that Job enjoyed had been stripped away for no reason that he could understand. In spite of this, however, Job never gave up on God. He never placed hope in his experience, his wisdom, his friends, or his wealth. His trust was in God, even though he couldn't understand everything he went through. God alone is sufficient to help us with the ambiguities in life. We can trust in Him."[6]

God is in control of the universe. If we surrender to His plan for us, He will take charge of our lives and reward us both here on earth and in eternity. The future blessings that await us are greater than anything we can imagine.

Yes, being patient now will give us wonderful blessings throughout eternity. Yet God does not expect us to show a stiff upper lip and passively accept pain without complaining and seeking solace. In our character study of Job, we discover that it is all right to cry, doubt, fear, question, need, and wrestle with the very essence of our existence.

As our hearts cry against injustice and affliction, Job's saga reassures us that God wants us to be honest with Him. He wants us to communicate our true feelings to Him, even if that means expressing our anger. Being our Abba (Father), he wants us to run to Him when we are afraid. He can handle the strongest of emotions. They don't threaten or disappoint Him.

God longs for us to share our true selves with Him. He wants to participate with us even in the darkest times—especially then! He wants us to relate to Him as a whole person. This sets things into motion for Him to release the healing and hope He yearns to give into our lives. Our God is the supreme exemplar of what patience really is. We humans can only strive to approximate it.

Certainly Job's story helps us realize that the patience God calls us to exhibit is more complex than we might have superficially understood. Let's look at some other sources to flesh out our understanding of this intricate and deep-seated virtue we call patience.

Wikipedia.org defines *patience* as, "The state of endurance under difficult circumstances. This can mean persevering in the face of delay or provocation without becoming annoyed or upset; or exhibiting forbearance when under strain, especially when faced with longer-term difficulties. It is also used to refer to the character trait of being steadfast."[7]

Patience is often described as a core virtue in religious practices. Job's story is noted in research as a profound religious work. According to Wikipedia: "At its core, the theme is the co-existence of evil and God and the application of patience is highlighted as the antidote to the earthly struggles caused by that co-existence. The plot of the book is that Job endures near-apocalyptic calamities without losing his patience or reproaching Divine Providence."[8]

Wikipedia continues, "In the Christian religion, patience is one of the most valuable virtues of life. Increasing patience is viewed as the work of the Holy Spirit in the Christian who has accepted the gift of salvation ... patience is considered one of the seven virtues."[9]

The philosopher Friedrich Nietzsche said, "Being able to wait is so hard that the greatest poets did not disdain to make the inability to wait the theme of their poetry." Nietzsche cited Shakespeare's Othello and Sophocles' Ajax as literary examples of men so enflamed by their emotions that they refused to cool down and delay the instant gratification of acting out on their passions.[10]

These are feelings to which we can easily relate in our culture. Those of us who live in the United States can understand Jim Rohn's indictment that "Americans are incredibly impatient. Someone once said that the shortest period of time in America is the time between when the light turns green and when you hear the first horn honk." Rohn concluded that the twin killers of success are impatience and greed.[11]

A person is best able to be patient and giving when he or she is experiencing what positive psychology researchers Csikszentmihalyi and Nakamura call the concept of *flow*. A flow state is experienced when perceived challenges and skills are just above the actor's average levels. When the challenges or skills are below the average levels, apathy is experienced.[12]

Experiencing flow encourages a person to persist at and return to an activity because of the experiential rewards it promises. Each rewarding experience fosters the growth of skill over time. Children and adults who are able to habitually spend time in the flow zone would be predicted to have greater self-esteem than those who cannot. Mastering challenges in daily life may protect against negative outcomes.[13]

Evidence suggests a relationship exists between quality of experience and persistence in an activity. Professional athletes provide a good example of flow. In a game, the challenges are high but so is the athlete's skill. Those of us who are not super-gifted athletically would find the game highly challenging, but we would not have the high skill to master it as the pro does.[14]

But flow can happen with almost any activity. Think about your strengths. Can you remember times when you got so involved with what you were doing that time seemed to stop and fly by all at the same time? If you enjoy an experience and it is of quality for you, predictably you would have the patience to stick with that activity. You could enjoy working on the project for a longer time than someone for whom the activity does not suit his or her strengths very well.

I have to pause here a minute and insert another hurrah for girl power. Do you realize that women have larger prefrontal cortexes than men? It is true. This part of a woman's brain matures earlier than a man's. This is why women tend to have more patience than men.[15]

In a chapter in the text, *Flourishing: Positive Psychology and the Life Well-Lived*, positive psychologist Robert Emmons reported that patience "enables people to be attentively responsive to others, to be responsive to opportunities for goal attainment."[16]

Four primary meanings of patience are proposed: suffering with calmness and composure, forbearance and tolerance of others, willingness to wait without resentment, and constancy and consistency in effort. The authors view patience as a necessary condition for the accomplishment of anything worthwhile.[17]

So what conditions would tend to produce patience? "Engagement of effort requires both a goal that matters enough (value) and also sufficient confidence in its eventual attainment (expectancy)," say Carver and Scheier.[18]

We exhibit patience by refusing to give up. We have to be persistent if we are to overcome obstacles. To demonstrate that consistency we must have confidence that we eventually will succeed in our endeavors.

Can you think of some examples of patience? Carver and Scheier offer, "The struggling student may work for months toward the completion of a project that is very difficult. People return to rebuild their homes in war-torn territories. The ability of people to struggle forward, to persevere against great odds even in the face of failure, represents a very important human strength."[19]

Paul spoke to the Thessalonians about patience: "We are happy to tell other churches about your patience and complete faith in God, in spite of all the crushing troubles and hardships you are going through" (2 Thess. 1:4).

Christian writer Rick Renner elaborated in *Sparkling Gems from the Greek*, "The word *patience* is a favorite word in Paul's epistles. It is the compound Greek word, *hupomene,* and it paints the picture of one who is under a heavy load but refuses to bend, break, or

APTITUDES FOR GROWTH; ATTITUDES FOR SUCCESS

surrender because he is convinced that the territory, promise, or principle under assault rightfully belongs to him. The word denotes a refusal to give up and an attitude that is determined to receive what is promised or hoped for. The King James Version translates it *patience*, but a better rendering would be endurance."[20]

It is important to realize we have to be patient with our foibles and ourselves just as we are with others. St. Francis de Sales instructed, "Have patience with all things, but chiefly have patience with yourself.... Every day begin the task anew."

Life is messy and unpredictable. We might as well embrace it. People bumble through life the best they can. We must be merciful. And we desperately need to extend that mercy to ourselves. We must look upon ourselves with the compassion Jesus extends. What might happen if we treat ourselves in a tender, gentle manner, as a loving mother treats her newborn child? The more love and mercy we shower on ourselves, the more patience flows from our innermost being to our family, friends, and people in need.

We have looked at the attribute of patience to discern ways we can incorporate it into our everyday lives. In this hustle bustle world it is advantageous to slow down. We must be willing to wait for what we want. We must be willing to persevere until we successfully complete our life assignments.

My friend Eric developed muscular dystrophy at around twelve years of age. He had been a gifted baseball player when at some point he started noticing his legs were dragging as he tried to run the bases. A trip to the doctor told him he had only a few months to live. Fortunately, the doctors were mistaken. He has FSH muscular dystrophy, which means he will have a normal life span.

Eric's hands are not under his control but he can use his thumbs. He is a whiz on the computer with those thumbs. He acquired two master's degrees and landed a good job as a librarian when he finished school.

Two years ago Eric broke his kneecap from a fall in the shower and now cannot walk on his own. He gets physical therapy and rides a scooter, and he accepts all of this with great equanimity.

PATIENCE: I WILL WAIT UPON THE LORD

Eric enjoys his life. He likes to read and watch movies and have a good time.

Eric has another burden to bear, however. His wife, Anna, has mental illness. She struggles with depression and cries a lot. Sometimes she has to go to the hospital. Eric is tirelessly patient with his wife even on those days when she is quite distressed. It must not be easy for Eric but he believes it is his calling to help his wife. He believes she will get better. Eric certainly has the strength of patience.

You have distinct strengths. You also have a unique destiny to fulfill. God made us all with different gifts so we might effectively work together as a body. Moderate your pace so you can enjoy your interactions with your brothers and sisters in Christ. Take a little extra time to play with a child and talk to him or her about Jesus. Smile and say hello to the people you meet on the street. Visit the sick and infirm. Make sure you display the fortitude of Jesus to the non-Christians who are watching you.

Water and tend to the good seeds in your life. Have the patience to wait for the seeds to germinate and grow into a fruitful orchard. As you embark on the adventure called the rest of your life, take patience as your personal virtue that you may thrive and flourish.

CHAPTER 8

WISDOM: MINING FOR GOLD

> Have you ever come on anything quite like this extravagant generosity of God, this deep, deep wisdom? It's way over our heads. We'll never figure it out. Is there anyone around who can explain God? Anyone smart enough to tell him what to do? Anyone who has done him such a huge favor that God has to ask his advice? Everything comes from him; everything happens through him; everything ends up in him. Always glory! Always praise! Yes. Yes. Yes.
>
> (Rom. 11:33–36 MESSAGE)

IF YOUR LIFE is to be the greatest of adventures, surely wisdom will serve as a reliable roadmap to guide your path. It is easy to forget the awesomeness of the God, who wishes to travel with you throughout your life's journey. He is the alpha and the omega; He is glorious and praiseworthy; He is perfect. He knows all things—and He wants to share that wisdom with you. All you have to do is invite Him into your life.

Gaining divine wisdom is a fantastically freeing experience. In Hosea 6, God declared, "I desire mercy and not sacrifice, and the knowledge of God more than burnt offerings" (v. 6).

What does that statement mean to you? To me, it indicates there is a better way to go through life than to continually mess up and then apologize. God wants you to gain knowledge of His higher ways and follow them. Then you can proceed with wisdom. Your life will become exponentially easier and more fruitful.

God prefers to relate to us as a loving father more than as an angry judge. Often we hear an angry judge inside our heads and we think it is God. It is not. It is our own ego tearing us to shreds.

"If we could see how harshly we judge ourselves and how much we expect of ourselves, we would see that's not helping us accomplish what we want to," says Jenifer Westphal, quoted in *What Happy Women Know*. "It's actually letting go of judgment, coming to yourself, and saying, 'I'm an awesome person who is contributing much value to my family, to my spouse, and to my friends' that takes you to a happy place where you can start to get things done."[1]

Whatever challenges you are facing, you can get going in the right direction only by looking at yourself as primarily worthy rather than as unworthy. God doesn't want you to think poorly of yourself. He wants you to reach out to him in belief—to call those things that are not as though they were. He wants you to write a different story for your life, a story in which you do much good and have a great life. When you allow Him to be the author and finisher of that story, unimaginable dreams become a reality. God blesses you based upon your faith in Him, not on your neediness.

You can be as needy and messed up as it's humanly possible to be, but if you do not have the wisdom to turn it all over to God, you will not receive the blessing. When you believe in God, you can begin to realize who you are through His eyes. This is when you become capable of living out the special calling that He has for your life.

To discover that calling, be a seeker willing to swim into as yet unknown spiritual depths to find it. "The search for human strengths is a continuous journey with a long history," says Ute Kunzmann in *Positive Psychology in Practice*. "Since antiquity, one of the guideposts in this search has been the concept of wisdom. At the core of this concept is the ... integration of knowledge and character, mind and virtue ... wisdom identifies in the most universal sense the highest forms of expertise that humans can acquire. Studying wisdom helps reveal the strongest qualities of humans as they have evolved through the experience of succeeding generations."[2]

Wisdom is such a powerful strength. It is a fusion of enlightenment, goodwill, sober judgment, and the pursuit of excellence. It takes into account the broader view of the big picture. It values not only the interests of the self but takes into account others' interests as well.

"Wisdom is knowledge," Kunzmann continues, "about ways of developing ourselves not only without violating others' rights but also with co-producing resources for others to develop ... a central characteristic of a wise person is the ability to translate knowledge into action geared toward the development of self and others ... wise persons tend to be benevolent, compassionate, caring, and interested in helping others."[3]

How can we not thirst for this wonderful gift called wisdom? Don't we all want to possess a solid understanding of life, a sterling character, a sound mind, and a virtuous spirit? Could we possibly desire to go through life without learning to be a compassionate and caring person? Fortunately, we have an exemplar to turn to in this quest.

One man in the Bible fully exemplified wisdom. His name was Solomon. The book of Proverbs explores his insight in depth.1 Kings 3 tells the story of how God gave Solomon the opportunity to ask and receive anything he wished:

> Solomon replied, "You were wonderfully kind to my father David because he was honest and true and faithful to you, and obeyed your commands. And you have continued your kindness to him by giving him a son to succeed him. Oh, Lord my God, now you have made me the king instead of my father David, but I am as a little child who doesn't know his way around. And here I am among your own chosen people, a nation so great that there are almost too many people to count! Give me an understanding mind so that I can govern your people well and know the difference between what is right and what is wrong. For who by

himself is able to carry such a heavy responsibility?" The Lord was pleased with his reply and was glad that Solomon had asked for wisdom. So he replied, "Because you have asked for wisdom in governing my people and haven't asked for a long life, or riches for yourself, or the defeat of your enemies—yes, I'll give you what you asked for! I will give you a wiser mind than anyone else ever had or ever will have! And I will give you what you didn't ask for—riches and honor! And no one in all the world will be as rich and famous as you for the rest of your life! And I will give you a long life if you follow me and obey my laws as your father David."

(1 Kings 3:6–14)

Solomon received this wisdom because he carefully considered how God could best bless him and those he led. In *The Richest Man Who Ever Lived: King Solomon's Secrets to Success, Wealth, and Happiness*, Steven Scott points out, "Just as there are physical laws that govern the physical universe, Solomon reveals 'laws of living' that invisibly govern all aspects of life."[4] These "laws of living" collectively make up the concept of "wisdom."

Solomon was the wisest man in the world. He displayed his creativity in his writings and in the building of the temple and his kingdom. He was curious in many areas including mining. His mines represented a great portion of his wealth. He often used mining terms in his writings. In his asking God for wisdom, we see his love of learning. In his writings, we find an open-mindedness in which he was willing to look at situations from many angles.

He demonstrated his supreme mastery of perspective when two women came to him as a judge. Both claimed to be the mother of an infant whom they had brought before him. Solomon thought for a moment and offered to cut the baby in half. Of course, the real mother would not hear of this outrageous behavior, thus proving she was the rightful parent.

We expect to find the following four factors in wise people such as Solomon. First, the wise person comprehends the nature of human existence and tries to learn from his mistakes. Second, the wise person knows when to give and when to withhold advice.

He is a person to whom one would go for help with the problems that can arise in life. Sometimes it is not yet the season for God's plan to come to fruition so the wise person must be aware of God's timing as he counsels people.

Third, the wise person knows that life's priorities may change and there can be possible conflicts among different life domains. A child would need to be supported in an entirely different way than a senior adult. Their maturity levels and interests would be quite dissimilar. Also, at some junctures in life there will be clashes of duties with which a person must contend. Consider the working mom who is also trying to go back to college. The wise person must take all of this into account as he or she guides and mentors. Fourth, the wise person has an exceptional personality and social functioning. He or she is a good listener and a very humane person.[5]

Some significant factors that exemplify wisdom:

- Addressing important and difficult questions and strategies about the conduct and meaning of life.

- Including knowledge about the limits of knowledge and the uncertainties of the world.

- Representing a truly superior level of knowledge, judgment, and advice.

- Constituting knowledge with extraordinary scope, depth, measure, and balance.

- Involving a perfect synergy of mind and character, that is, an orchestration of knowledge and virtues

- Representing knowledge used for the good or well being of oneself and that of others.

Though difficult to achieve and to specify, wisdom is easily recognized when manifested.[6]

As we look at the wisdom Solomon shared in Proverbs, note that what he wrote always meets the criteria expressed above by experts who defined the concept of wisdom. There are several themes in the thirty-one chapters that make up the book of Proverbs. It is obvious from his writing that he held common sense in very high esteem. He emphasized the power of setting priorities that reflect God's will in our lives. He explored how vital it is to set boundaries and to have the ability to say no. He also firmly endorsed building and maintaining healthy relationships.

In Proverbs 1:2–3, we discover that King Solomon wrote Proverbs so the people of Israel would know how to live justly, fairly, and with understanding in every circumstance. He specifically mapped out how to live a good life, emphasizing that wisdom begins by revering and trusting in God. It brings with it the implicit understanding that we need God's guidance and care. We learn that living with wisdom gives us a level of protection the foolish person will not possess.

Proverbs 1:20 affirms, "Wisdom shouts in the streets for a hearing." It demands our attention. Those who heed it will be successful because wisdom comes from God. In Proverbs 3:21–26 we read:

> Have two goals: wisdom—that is, knowing and doing right—and common sense. Don't let them slip away, for they fill you with living energy and bring you honor and respect. They keep you safe from defeat and disaster and from stumbling off the trail. With them on guard you can sleep without fear; you need not be afraid of disaster or the plots of wicked men, for the Lord is with you; he protects you.

Fortunately, we can grow in wisdom—it is accessible to everyone. In Proverbs 4:8–10, Solomon advises, "If you exalt wisdom, she will exalt you. Hold her fast, and she will lead you to great honor; she will place a beautiful crown upon your head. My son, listen to me and do as I say, and you will have a long, good life."

As chapter 4 closes, we are told above all else to guard our affections. In chapter 5, Solomon "fleshes out" a warning against sexual sin. He points out that after an indiscretion only a bitter conscious remains, sharp as a double-edged sword; she leads you down to death and hell (Prov. 5:4–5).

Chapters 6 through 8 warn against foolish action: "haughtiness, lying, murdering, plotting evil, eagerness to do wrong, a false witness, and sowing discord among brothers" (vv. 16–19). In chapter 9 we learn that wisdom is its own reward: "I, Wisdom, will make the hours of your day more profitable and the years of your life more fruitful" (v. 11).

Chapters 10 through 24 cover many topics and thoughtful sayings about the practice of wisdom. Proverbs 10:14 advises, "A wise man holds his tongue. Only a fool blurts out everything he knows; that only leads to sorrow and trouble." Proverbs 11:2 says, "Proud men end in shame, but the meek become wise." Solomon spent quite a while talking about the foolishness of pride and conceit. Humility, he reiterated, is a virtue that is paramount to living successfully.

In Proverbs 12:11 we learn, "Hard work means prosperity; only a fool idles away the time." The topic of diligence is central throughout Solomon's writings. Steven Scott teaches, "Diligence is a learnable skill that combines: creative persistence, a smart-working effort rightly planned and rightly performed in a timely, efficient, and effective manner to attain a result that is pure and of the highest quality of excellence."[7] Diligence will give you ever-increasing success. It will put you in control of a situation, rather than letting the situation control you.

In Proverbs 13:17 we are told, "An unreliable messenger can cause a lot of trouble. Reliable communication permits progress." Communication skills were another of Solomon's major concerns. What we say and how we say it can have a life-changing impact on others.[8] Communication can either escalate anger or extinguish it. We can wound or heal through the power of words. Our mouths can either tear others down or build them up.

Proverbs 14:8 tells us, "The wise man looks ahead. The fool attempts to fool himself and won't face facts." Warnings about ignorance and irresponsibility pop up regularly in Solomon's writings. Ignoring the long-term consequences of our actions is dangerous.

Proverbs 15:2 says, "A wise teacher makes learning a joy; a rebellious teacher spouts foolishness." Solomon taught that effective communication brings material success, joy, fulfillment, and lasting friendships. In Proverbs 16:16 Solomon confided, "How much better is wisdom than gold and understanding than silver." Solomon wrote often of the foolishness of greed and avarice. He continued in the third verse of the next chapter: "Silver and gold are purified by fire, but God purifies hearts."

Proverbs 18:10 reiterates the paramount importance of revering God: "The Lord is a strong fortress. The godly run to him and are safe." Proverbs 19:2 continues, "It is dangerous and sinful to rush into the unknown." Proverbs 20:18 reads, "Don't go ahead with your plans without the advice of others; don't go to war until they agree." It is prudent to seek the counsel of mentors.

"He who shuts his ears to the cries of the poor will be ignored in his own time of need," reads 21:13. In addition to concern for the needy, God is also concerned that young ones receive help and support. In chapter 22, Solomon wrote, "Teach a child to choose the right path and when he is older, he will remain upon it" (v. 6). This thought continues in Proverbs 23:13, "Don't fail to correct your children; discipline won't hurt them."

Proverbs 24:13–14 says, "My son, honey whets the appetite and so does wisdom! When you enjoy becoming wise, there is hope for you! A bright future lies ahead!" There are many benefits to choosing a life of obedience and thoughtful action.

Chapters 25 through 28 teach about wisdom for leaders. Chapter 25 counsels, "Be patient and you will finally win, for a soft tongue can break hard bones" (v. 15). Patience is the sign of a wise man. A fool does not have sense. Proverbs 26:7 insists, "In the mouth of a fool a proverb becomes as useless as a paralyzed leg."

Chapter 27:21 conveys, "The purity of silver and gold can be tested in a crucible, but a man is tested by his reaction to men's praise." Proverbs 28:23 explains, "In the end, people appreciate frankness more than flattery." Choose truth over undeserved praise, even if that truth comes in the form of a criticism. Proverbs 29:1 says, "The man who is often reproved but refuses to accept criticism will suddenly be broken and never have another chance." Garnering wisdom is a serious business. Without wisdom, we will not succeed.

Scott presents the concept of apprenticeship to the God of the Universe. He instructs, "Begin to hold Him in the highest esteem, honor Him as God, and make Him the boss of your life."[9] The greatest honor we could give to God and to ourselves is immersion in an intimate, loving and trusting relationship with Him. Walk through your day with an awareness of His presence every step of the way. Pray to Him continually for guidance. He wants to hear your ideas and dreams. He also wants to experience your gratitude for the many gifts He dispenses daily.

So far we have limited our study on wisdom to the books of the Old Testament, principally to Proverbs. However, the never-ending story of God's love and wisdom continues in the New Testament. It contains the accounts of the birth, life, and death of God's only begotten Son, Jesus. Although mere humankind had miserably failed, Jesus fulfilled every letter of the law.

God sent Jesus to earth as a human being to help us understand God and His plan for our lives. Matthew 6:20 promises that when we ask Jesus into every aspect of our being, we are building up "treasures in heaven." Treasures in heaven cannot be stolen, destroyed, or tarnished by time.[10]

In Matthew 7:24–27, Jesus explained to His listeners how to live wisely: "All who listen to my instructions and follow them are wise, like a man who builds his house on solid rock. Though the rain comes in torrents and the floodwaters rise and the winds beat against that house, it won't collapse, for it is built on rock. But those who hear my instructions and ignore them are foolish, like a man who builds his house on sand. For when the rains and floods come, and the storm winds beat against his house, it will fall with a mighty crash."

It is astonishing to realize that we can actually develop the mind of Christ. Philippians 2:5 encourages, "Let this mind be in you which was also in Christ Jesus."

In 1 Corinthians 2:16, Paul asked, "For who has known or understood the mind (the counsels and purposes) of the Lord so as to guide and instruct Him and give Him knowledge? But we have the mind of Christ (the Messiah) and do hold the thoughts (feelings and purposes) of His heart" (AMP).

How encouraging!

James 1:5 enlightens us, "If any of you is deficient in wisdom, let him ask of the giving God [Who gives] to everyone liberally and ungrudgingly, without reproaching or faultfinding, and it will be given to him" (AMP).

John Wooden, named the greatest coach of the twentieth century by ESPN in 1999, displayed incredible wisdom in the manner in which he recruited players. Surprisingly, he was not a man preoccupied with winning. He never spoke to his team about winning. His focus, rather, was on potential and improvement.

While most recruiters scoured high school gyms in search of talent and athleticism, Coach Wooden's primary consideration was the student's transcript. To him, a student's discipline said a great deal about that player. Wooden wanted his players' first goal to be to graduate from college.

John Wooden's second criterion was the student's relationship with his family. Did the student treat his parents with respect and his siblings with kindness? The coach knew that these types of relational skills were a necessary part of teamwork and camaraderie.

The third criterion consisted of a composite evaluation by six coaches. He did not want to base his decisions on one game but rather on the player's consistency over time. So he had six experts watch the possible recruit at length.

The coach's final criteria in making player selections were based on the boys' quickness and natural ability. He knew talent was irreplaceable but refused to select a player without seriously deliberating on the player's priorities, relationships, and track record of solid and consistent performance.[11]

In the last book of the New Testament, Jesus, the greatest coach of all coaches, made a wonderful promise. He said, "Behold, I stand at the door and knock. If anyone hears My voice and opens the door, I will come in to him and dine with him, and he with Me" (Rev. 3:20 NKJV).

May we dine with Jesus always. It would be wise. It would be prudent—and it will be magnificent.

CHAPTER 9

PEACE: BEING A MARY IN A HEROD-RULED WORLD

> The angel answered, "The Holy Spirit will come upon you, the power of the Highest hover over you; therefore, the child you bring to birth will be called Holy, Son of God." ... Mary said, "Yes, I see it all now: I'm the Lord's maid, ready to serve. Let it be with me just as you say."
>
> (Luke 1:35, 37 MESSAGE)

IN OUR BUSY, overcommitted lives, we must pause to examine the health of our souls. Are we keeping ourselves in perfect peace, or are we dragging ourselves through an endless, stressful cycle of putting out fires?

Putting out those fires can inflate our pride, but pride can be dangerous. King Herod's life exemplifies just how dangerous a situation becomes when a huge ego feels threatened.

On the other hand, Mary, Jesus' mother, epitomizes peace. Her quiet manner infused every fiber of her being. She endured challenges humbly and obediently. When we consider how much Mary had to endure in her lifetime, we see her as a deeply inspiring heroine.

If positive psychology is characterized by the study of the truly good life, Mary's story provides a wonderful case study. In *What Happy Women Know* (2007), authors Dan Baker and Cathy

Greenburg note, "Happiness is far more than a mood or emotion; It is a way of being, a way of knowing what's right and good, and living true to that."[1] Certainly Mary had a most graceful and dignified way of living. She reached for God's will in every situation and placed her dependence and trust in Him. Hence, even in the darkest times, Mary's peaceful composure was the steady center of her personality.

This chapter is designed to help us tap into our essential peacefulness—a serenity Mary so beautifully exemplified. This is a peace that passes all understanding. It is the tranquility necessary to sustain you as you pick up and carry your cross. Your cross is borne as you live out your distinct calling despite the challenges you face. Like Mary, you are to complete the full purpose of your life on earth. To do that you will need the deep-seated equanimity that only faith in God can give.

It is interesting to note that the United Nations Educational, Scientific, and Cultural Organization (UNESCO) regards individual and group peace and human rights as essential human strengths.[2] This organization characterizes peace as a "dynamic, holistic and lifelong process through which mutual respect, understanding, caring, sharing, compassion, social responsibility, solidarity, acceptance, and tolerance of diversity among individuals and groups … are internalized.… This process begins with the development of inner peace … of individuals engaged in the search for truth, knowledge, and understanding."[3]

Mary's inner peace was so deep and reflexive that she could accept a visit from the angel Gabriel without missing a beat. Gabriel told Mary she was highly favored in God's eyes. He then proclaimed to her that she would bear God's Son, the Savior of the world.

Try to put yourself in Mary's situation. What would your first thoughts have been on receiving such news? Would you feel dumbfounded by the fact that God had decided to use you in such an astounding way? Would you marvel that, though you were a virgin, God would conceive a baby in your womb? Would you be terrified that your fiancé would never understand something so incomprehensible? What emotions might you have in such a situation? Would fear, doubt, disbelief, and lack of comprehension be just a few of your feelings?

Yet look at Mary's first utterance upon receiving such life altering news: "I am the Lord's servant, and I am willing to do whatever he wants. May everything you said come true" (Luke 1:38). Notice the feminine acquiescence. As quickly as Gabriel cast this reality on her, she moved into harmony with God's will. Her focus was not on her own well-being or the sacrifices she would have to make. Rather, she was pliant and willing to do whatever the Lord directed her to do. In fact, she was inspired to sing. What a lovely response—"For he, the mighty Holy One, has done great things to me" (Luke 4:9).

Mary displayed her inner beauty, strength, and abiding tranquility. Certainly, she must have wondered how her betrothed would accept all this. Fortunately, an angelic messenger brought Joseph up to speed. Joseph responded by making Mary his wife.

Another challenge arrived—tax time. An almost-due Mary rode atop a donkey all the way to Bethlehem. Once again, our heroine maintained her calm in the midst of discomfort. She and Joseph finally arrived in town only to discover there was no vacancy at the inn. They took shelter in a stable, where Jesus was born. Gently, they placed Him in a manger. Not exactly an ideal environment! Still, Mary maintained her serenity.

Soon shepherds entered the stable and disclosed an amazing story. Angels had appeared to them as they were tending their sheep. Accompanied by a multitude of angels, an angel of the Lord announced that the Messiah had entered the world.

Surely those shepherds were elated. However, the new mother "quietly treasured these things in her heart and often thought about them" (Luke 2:19).

Mary's countenance must have glowed. She had her beautiful, perfect child, Jesus. Twelve years later, though, she temporarily lost Him at a festival. After a frantic search, she found Him in the temple, where He was conversing wisely with the Jewish elders.

When Jesus was an adult, Mary told Him the wedding they were attending had run out of wine. In response, He turned water into wine. What joy she must have experienced at that festive celebration as He performed His first miracle.

But Mary also experienced sorrow at the end of Jesus' ministry. From the foot of His cross, she watched Him experience an agonizing death. She saw the blood running down His face from His crown of thorns. She heard His gasps for breath and His cries of anguish. She was there the moment God turned His face away from Jesus as Jesus took upon Himself the sins of the world. He hung there before His mother and endured His shame and degradation.

Mary did not scream. She did not shatter. Her heart was fully breaking within her and yet—even yet—she accepted God's will. She submitted herself to the nightmare—and she endured. Her thoughts were not focused on herself. There was no self-pity in her expression. She held strong to the belief that God had a larger plan and purpose in her son's suffering.

She chose to trust. She made a decision to abide in peace. In deference and faith, she turned everything in her soul over to her Lord. Amid the desperation of the moment, she maintained her composure. Is it any wonder that God chose her to be the most blessed among all women?

Paul's words in Philippians 4:6–7 reflect the way Mary conducted herself: "Be anxious for nothing, but in everything by prayer and supplication, with thanksgiving, let your requests be made known to God. And the peace of God, which surpasses all understanding, will guard your hearts and minds through Christ Jesus" (NKJV).

What does Mary's life teach you about the challenges you are currently facing in your life? What can you take away from her deep composure? Can you move beyond mere survival when faced with overwhelmingly difficult life issues? Can you empower yourself to meet them in such a way that you become a thriver as Mary was? There are many shades of the ability to thrive. Peter thrived boldly. Mary thrived with quiet dignity.

Susan, a retired schoolteacher, lost her son to suicide. How do you overcome something so devastating? It is very painful, but day after day Susan puts her son in God's hands. She plants marigolds at his grave and believes she will see him again someday. She lives out her heartache with the same quiet dignity Mary displayed while enduring Jesus' suffering on the cross.

Juxtapose such dignity and integrity with the actions of a man driven and obsessed by power—the infamous King Herod. There was nothing peaceful about him.

When the wise men arrived in Jerusalem in search of the infant Jesus, the King of the Jews, they asked Herod where they could find Him. Their inquiry deeply disturbed King Herod. He attempted to gather more information about this child's whereabouts because he considered the infant a direct threat to his throne. He was incensed when, after worshiping baby Jesus, the wise men took an alternate route home to avoid giving Herod any information.

Herod's paranoia continued to mount. He vowed to kill every male under two years old in the town and surrounding countryside to make sure he destroyed the King of the Jews. However, an angel foiled Herod's plan by appearing to Joseph, telling him to flee to Egypt with Mary and Jesus. They lived there safely until King Herod died.

Herod was controlled by greed. Power and possessions, his paramount values, gave him his inflated position and identity. He allowed things that had no eternal value to consume him. He built his house upon the sand instead of on the rock.

Herod did not blink when he ordered the slaughter of all those innocent male babies. He did not hesitate to destroy anyone he perceived to be a threat. Being extremely insecure and suspicious, he felt himself to be literally surrounded by such threats.

King Herod's paranoia became a self-fulfilling prophecy. His ugly jealousy created a life of ineffectiveness, failure, and evil. He was inflamed with imaginary fears that eventually swallowed him whole.

One Tin Soldier Rides Away is a song from the 1970s about a group of people who had a treasure that another group wanted. The group with the treasure suggested they dig up the treasure together and share it, but the other group was greedy and ruthlessly slaughtered the group that had the treasure on their property. After everyone from the group who had the treasure was dead and out of the way, the warring group dug up the treasure. The treasure was simply a rock—"peace on earth was all it said."

James 3:16 explains: "For wherever there is jealousy (envy) and contention (rivalry and selfish ambition) there will also be confusion (unrest, disharmony, rebellion) and all sorts of evil and vile practices" (AMP).

Misguided King Herod blatantly failed to acknowledge the truth that ultimately it is God and God alone who is in control. In his hubris, Herod refused to submit to God's will for his life. Peace does not come from forcing others to bow down before us, but rather from choosing to bow down humbly before the omnipotent Creator of the universe.

If we persist in refusing to trust God, we will be plagued with fear and anguish. We can live in victory only if we allow our lives to be clay in the Potter's hands. There is only one Potter. Having the audacity to "play god" in an attempt to control others always causes insecurity and hostility and leads inevitably to failure and destruction.

Throughout his manipulations and machinations, Herod refused to seek the one element he needed most of all—inner peace. It is not by winning contests or conquests that we find meaning in life. We can achieve peace through admitting our sins and our great need for God's involvement in every aspect of our lives. It is in crying out for help to our Father, our Abba, that healing and restoration occur.

Poor Herod—he never got it. He never understood the essential truth of life or came to any comprehension about what really leads to a meaningful and satisfying existence. He never took comfort in the Lord the way we can. Isaiah 54:10 declares: "For though the mountains should depart and the hills be shaken or removed, yet My love and kindness shall not depart from you, nor shall My covenant of peace and completeness removed, says the Lord, Who has compassion on you" (AMP).

For further reassurance, jump forward a few chapters to Isaiah 66:12–13: "For thus says the Lord: 'Behold, I will extend peace to her (Jerusalem) like a river, and the glory of the Gentiles like

PEACE: BEING A MARY IN A HEROD-RULED WORLD

a flowing stream. Then you (true worshipers and their offspring) shall feed; on her sides shall you be carried, and be dandled on her knees, as one whom his mother comforts, so I will comfort you; and you shall be comforted in Jerusalem" (NKJV).

It is no coincidence that the image of the mother is often synonymous with peace. These images of the comforting mother in the Old Testament foreshadow the great compassion and peacefulness of Jesus' mother.

How can we, like Mary, conduct our lives with dignity and equanimity? Philippians 4:8 give us clues: "Finally, brethren, whatsoever things are true, whatsoever things are honest, whatsoever things are just, whatsoever things are pure, whatsoever things are lovely, whatsoever things are of good report; If there be any virtue, and if there be any praise, think on these things" (KJV).

These are beautiful sentiments and would indeed be an ideal way to think and live. However, we cannot will ourselves to be good. On our own we are weak and ineffectual creatures. In our own power we will never be adequate. We have to look to and cling to Jesus to provide for all our needs and problems. In John 14:27 Jesus promises, "I am leaving you with a gift—peace of mind and heart! And the peace I give isn't fragile like the peace the world gives. So don't be troubled or afraid."

Jesus' peace, mirroring his mother's serene nature, fulfills and satisfies our deepest longings. When we trust in and rest in the arms of Christ, we will flourish and find lasting and impenetrable harmony with Him.

Take time out to examine your specific strengths and talents. Think about your strongest aptitudes. Are you willing to have an attitude that exhibits peace and stillness as you fulfill your unique calling? Are you grafted in an interdependent community of fellows to which you are able to give security and steadiness?

Leo the Great, who was pope from September 29, 440, to November 10, 461, once said, "Peace is the first thing the angels sang. Peace is the mark of the sons of God. Peace is the nurse of love. Peace is the mother of unity. Peace is the rest of blessed souls.

Peace is the dwelling place of eternity."[4] Choose peace as an aptitude for growth and an attitude for success.

Peace grows when people use self-control and wisdom in the way they conduct their lives. The great gift of peace arrives when such people have straightened out their priorities. When we truly think about what is important and what matters most, it has little to do with going around putting out fires all the time or rushing from one mindless activity to another. We can pause, slow down, and get in tune with the music of God's soul. When we do this, we, like Mary, will be able to endure even the toughest of challenges.

CHAPTER 10

ENTHUSIASM AND COMMITMENT: WITH ALL HIS HEART; WITH ALL YOUR HEART

> When Jesus arrived in the villages of Caesarea Philippi, he asked his disciples, "What are people saying about who the Son of Man is? ... And how about you? Who do you say I am?" Simon Peter said, "You're the Christ, the Messiah, the Son of the Living God." Jesus came back, "God bless you, Simon.... My Father in heaven, God himself, let you in on this secret of who I really am.... You are Peter, a rock. This is the rock on which I will put together my church, a church so expansive with energy that not even the gates of hell will be able to keep it out."
>
> (Matt. 16:13–18 MESSAGE)

SO YOU WANT your life to be a great adventure? Giving your life over to Christ will lead you on an adventure more wonderful that your wildest dreams! Throw away your excuses and your fears. Let go of hurts. Let Jesus heal your wounds and wipe away your tears, and then reach for all Christ has to give you. If you do this with enthusiasm and commitment, your life will take on a new energy. Deep inside you lies a passion only Christ can ignite.

Simon Peter had just such a passion. His heart's desire was to magnify Christ and lead others to the Savior. By examining his life, we will be able to see that from his initial brashness and impulsivity as a crusty fisherman, he was refined through his experiences with

Christ into a man of vitality and dedication. Peter means "rock." Throughout his time with Jesus, Peter the "rock" became more and more polished.

The chief character strengths Peter exhibited throughout his lifetime were commitment and enthusiasm. Perhaps we can take away a little something from Peter's life that would improve our own walk with God. You and I can study Peter to find out how to be a foundation on which Christ will build His church.

We can also learn from Peter's character strengths of enthusiasm and commitment that it is OK to fail and try again. Seeing the humanness of his many foibles, we can be encouraged that we, too, can be cultivated under God's healing touch.

If we, like Peter, try to walk on the water to Jesus, Jesus will extend a hand to help us. We must try and keep on trying to connect with God. It is always worthwhile to abandon our human perspective to embrace God's total omniscience. On our own, we creep along the ground. Upon discovering the indwelling of Christ, we soar.

How do we connect with God and learn to soar? It is through regular study of God's Word that is alive and active. Prayer can help. Gathering with other believers can help. Doing things for others is beneficial. However, if we are to truly soar, we must take up our cross with all the enthusiasm and commitment we can muster.

Ponder how completing your daily tasks contributes to a larger purpose. God-given goals can lead you on your way. "For goals to be effective, people must be committed to them," says Edwin Locke in the *Handbook of Positive Psychology*. "This is especially critical when goals are difficult and thus require considerable thinking and effort. Action is the ultimate proof of commitment. After all, people can say they are committed and not really mean it. Two types of causal factors are critical in commitment: the belief that the goal is important and the belief that one can achieve or make progress toward it. For a goal to be important, it must be tied to an important value."[1]

Surely sharing the saving grace of salvation is a worthy value. Will you commit yourself here and now to the goal of furthering

ENTHUSIASM AND COMMITMENT: WITH ALL HIS HEART; WITH ALL YOUR HEART

God's kingdom? The narrow road will not always be the easy one to walk, but by taking one step at a time on that walk you are taking action that can change your life and the lives of others for eternity. This goal is of utmost importance. With the Holy Spirit's help, you can make significant progress toward helping gather Christ's flock for the day of redemption.

We can check our hearts and see if we are experiencing the deep satisfaction of discovering and carrying out our individual roles in the grander scheme of things. Every one of us needs purpose in our lives. God will joyfully bestow that purpose on you if you will only but ask.

What are your specific strengths and talents? Are you using your aptitudes to the maximum degree for God's glory and the redemption of those who are still lost? What attitudes are you displaying? Are you exhibiting zest as you fulfill your unique calling? Living zestfully means "approaching life with excitement and energy; not doing things halfway or half-heartedly; living life as an adventure; feeling alive and activated."[2] You can make living zestfully contagious by sharing your commitment and enthusiasm with others in the body of Christ.

Are you grafted into an interdependent community of fellows where you are able to give and receive support for the journey? Jesus Himself enjoyed the fellowship of His twelve disciples. Hopefully when we are in our Garden of Gethsemane, our entire support system won't abandon us in favor of a nap as the disciples did. While Jesus fervently prayed right before His time of crucifixion for the bitter cup of the cross to be taken from Him, His closest friends napped. Don't you think looking back that those disciples wished they had shown more commitment and enthusiasm in praying for their Master?

I have a friend whose husband was in a head-on collision with a dump truck one icy morning a few years ago. Throughout her husband's months of rehabilitation and recovery, she was like a solid rock. She is editor-in-chief of a magazine. She did all her work on a laptop in the hospital waiting room for many long weeks. She slept every night in that waiting room on an air mattress.

One example of her tenacity was the night the nursing staff was shorthanded and her husband was running a terribly high fever. They put him on a bed of ice. My friend had to cool him down by placing wet washcloths on him the entire night.

What does Peter's life have to say to you about the challenges you currently face in your life? How can you learn from his example? Can you see how Peter was able to thrive despite the mistakes and failures in his life? Do you have the inner strength to do likewise?

Jesus called Peter a rock because of his unswerving devotion. I saw my friend act with such strong commitment and unfailing love in this time of crisis that I knew Jesus was shining through her.

Peter made many mistakes, but he always let Jesus shine through him. Fortunately, God does not demand perfection. Peter truly loved God with a zestful heart though he often let Jesus and himself down. So, too, we often let Him or ourselves down.

Ponder for a moment all of the occasions that Peter disappointed Jesus. Think about the time Jesus told Peter he would deny knowing Christ three times before the cock crowed. Peter swore vehemently that he would never forsake Jesus, but within hours he did deny Jesus three times.

Can you imagine how Peter felt at that moment the cock crowed? I certainly remember many occasions in my own life when I recognized what a horrible sinner I was. Don't you imagine Peter probably felt he had completely failed in his mission, that he had utterly ruined his relationship with the Lord? However, this is not where the story ends.

After His resurrection, Jesus appeared to the disciples on the shore. They had returned to fishing. At a wonderful morning meal Jesus had prepared, Jesus asked Peter three times: Do you love Me? Three times Peter emphatically answered he did. Three times Jesus told him to feed His little lambs.

So Peter's denial was not the end of his relationship with Jesus. I sometimes think Jesus asked Peter three times about his allegiance to replace the three times Peter had denied Him.

Notice how Jesus focused on Peter's strengths rather than his weaknesses or the mistakes he had made? Likewise, Seligman,

ENTHUSIASM AND COMMITMENT: WITH ALL HIS HEART; WITH ALL YOUR HEART

speaking about positive psychology, exclaimed, "I do not believe that you should devote overly much effort to correcting your weaknesses. Rather, I believe that the highest success in living and the deep emotional satisfaction comes from building and using your signature strengths."[3]

So Christ Himself told Peter he had an extremely important mission and it was to be so. Jesus instructed His apostles to go and make disciples of all the nations, baptizing them and teaching them to obey God's commandments. This is called the Great Commission. As it was for Peter, it is our commission too.

Jesus promised never to leave His disciples, and it is as though He is speaking to us too. We have the Holy Spirit who comforts, counsels, and directs us if only we will hearken an ear to His still, small voice.

Well, guess what Peter ended up spearheading? On the Day of Pentecost, the Holy Spirit descended on Peter and the other believers. Peter preached to the crowd of Jews assembled for the Feast of Pentecost. He explained what was happening by reading prophecy from the book of Joel: "In the last days, God said, I will pour out my Holy Spirit upon all mankind, and your sons and daughters shall prophesy, and your young men shall see visions, and your old men will dream dreams" (Acts 2:17).

Pretty good preaching for a burly, unschooled fisherman, wouldn't you say? That is what Christ's presence in a life can do—and it is as true for you and me as it was for Peter.

After Peter's sermon, the crowd called out, asking what they should do. According to Acts 2:38 Peter instructed them to turn from sin, return to God, and be baptized in the name of Jesus Christ for the forgiveness of their sins. Those who did this received the gift of the Holy Spirit. At that point about three thousand people were baptized.

Soon after, this, Peter performed miracles and preached persuasively to fulfill the Great Commission. The authorities began to watch Peter closely. It was confounding to them how two uneducated and non-professional men such as Peter and John had grown so confident and well spoken since being with Jesus.

The Council of High Priests was intimidated, and told Peter and John to be silent. However, these two bold apostles refused to stop talking about all that had happened to them since following Jesus. May you and I be so enthused and committed. May we never stop telling others all the wonderful things that have happened to us since we began to follow our Jesus. This is the path to increased spiritual growth and personal success.

Peter's enthusiasm and commitment were unstoppable. He and the other apostles healed many. The sick actually vied for a position on the road just so Peter's shadow would fall across them as he went by. He restored to health all the sick and demon-possessed he encountered. That is the power of the complete faith Peter had in Jesus. Could you or I demonstrate such enthusiasm and commitment?

In Acts 10, Peter was meditating on a flat rooftop. He had a vision in which the sky opened and a great sheet settled on the ground. In the sheet were all types of animals that God had forbidden the Jews to eat. God told Peter to kill and eat any of them. Headstrong Peter refused. He retorted that he had never done such a thing. God replied that, if He said something is kosher, then it truly was. This vision challenging Peter's view on what was clean or unclean repeated three times.

Peter was perplexed. God was changing the rules and it was scary to leave known territory. Can you relate? The uncertainty of trying to follow God's will is only possible if we relinquish our ideas of how we think things ought to go. Throughout this confusing time, God was preparing Peter for his next great endeavor: to bring the Good News to the Gentiles.

God showed Peter that he should never think of anyone as inferior. Do an inventory of your prejudices. Is there anyone in God's creation to whom you secretly think you are superior? Peter, the proud man of Jewish ancestry, had to rethink his basic paradigms. He had to think on his feet, for he was going to be the vessel through which God would bring together peoples who had been separated by huge barriers. In Acts 10:34 Peter exclaimed, "I see very clearly that the Jews are not God's only favorites."

ENTHUSIASM AND COMMITMENT: WITH ALL HIS HEART; WITH ALL YOUR HEART

After this, when Peter began ministering to the Gentiles, the Holy Spirit fell upon those who believed. The Jewish leaders, however, were unhappy with what Peter was doing. They began to plot against him. They often imprisoned him for his preaching. Would you have the devotion to speak the Word of Christ if it meant great suffering would result from doing so? We will never really know what we would do in such a situation, but it is worth pondering.

One night while Peter was in jail, an angel came to him, released him, and escorted him out of the prison, opening each locked door they encountered. Amy Grant wrote a song about this—*Angels watching over me, every step I take.*

Peter, the burly fisherman, went on to write two epistles. At the time, around A.D. 64, Christians were being martyred for believing in Jesus Christ. Peter's first letter was written to encourage suffering Jewish Christians. In this writing, Peter passed on the shepherd's crook to the elders of the new Christian movement by saying, "Shepherd the flock of God which is among you, serve as overseers, not by compulsion but willingly, not for dishonest gain but eagerly; nor as being lords over those entrusted to you, but being examples to the flock; and when the Chief Shepherd appears, you will receive the crown of glory that does not fade away" (1 Peter 5:2–4 NKJV).

Did you notice the parallel between Peter's admonition to the elders to shepherd the flock and Jesus' earlier injunction to Peter to "feed My sheep"? As Peter grew incrementally in ability and wisdom, he was able to stay focused on the Great Commission to "feed My sheep." He did this, as always, with characteristic fervor. May we learn from his example how the fruits of enthusiasm and commitment can change the world.

Second Peter was written around A.D. 66–67. By this time Peter's message had expanded from Jewish Christians to all believers everywhere. As he wrote, Peter was not expecting ever to see his readers again. His words were meant to embolden the believers to be faithful to God and to warn them to watch out against false teachings. This second epistle opens with Peter's advice on how to grow spiritually:

> Giving all diligence, add to your faith virtue, to virtue knowledge, to knowledge self-control, to self-control perseverance, to perseverance godliness, to godliness brotherly kindness, and to brotherly kindness love. For if these things are yours and abound, you will be neither barren nor unfruitful in the knowledge of our Lord Jesus Christ.
>
> (2 Peter 1:4–8 NKJV)

What about you? What is your heart telling you to do? How are you to bear fruit in your individual situation with your unique gifts and talents?

Think of the marvelous enthusiasm Billy Graham has shown over the course of his lifetime. He has made it his mission to present the Good News to as many people as possible. He lives out his mission joyfully, skillfully, and faithfully. Over the years, as Billy circled the globe to share the Good News, his wife, Ruth, stayed at home and raised their five children. Billy later commented that because he was called away so often, Ruth became both mother and father to their children. Yet she never complained or asked him to stay home. She was brimming over with commitment to her husband, and significantly, she was filled with dedication to the Lord.

Our strengths and talents shine brightly through the broken jar of clay that is our identity. Peter was just such an imperfect vessel. God can use us in our humanness to accomplish important things. We must, like Peter, let go of fear and hold onto faith. When we trust God in an enthusiastic and committed manner, God can do great things with our lives.

We should desire above all else to further Christ's kingdom. Living to accomplish God's purposes is the most exciting adrenaline rush you can experience. You can serve the Lord each day with great enthusiasm and commitment if you will just surrender your life over to Him. Surely it is the truth to say that Peter served the Lord with his whole heart. Will you follow Peter's example?

CHAPTER 11

GRATITUDE: MARY MAGDALENE WASHES FEET AND THE CLEANSED LEPER GIVES THANKS

Do you see this woman? I came to your home; you provided no water for my feet, but she rained tears on my feet and dried them with her hair. You gave me no greeting, but from the time I arrived she hasn't quit kissing my feet. You provided nothing for freshening up, but she has soothed my feet with perfume. Impressive, isn't it? She was forgiven many, many sins, and so she is very, very grateful.

(Luke 7:44–46 MESSAGE)

SOMETIMES WE BECOME so bogged down in our trials that we forget to express gratitude. However, it is those very trials that help us grow and mature. As we look back over our lives with the perspective that only time allows, we can see that in accepting our hardships, we became more loving, more patient, and kinder.

Have you ever heard the expression "a Kodak moment"? This is a memory we want to cherish forever. Sometimes we have a camera handy. Sometimes just experiencing the moment's beauty through the windows of our minds is the perfect response. We can hold those memories close to our heart always.

When we get to the end of our adventure on Planet Earth, we will see how each step of the way led us closer to our desired destination. We will see how Jesus was there with us at every step, and we will be grateful.

Whatever challenges you are facing today, remember this: a negative attitude is the only disability. We are enabled when we choose to think positively about our lives. When we spiral downward into negativity, we become disabled.

Emmit Miller, a TV news anchor in California, once said, "Gratitude has to do with feeling full, complete, adequate—we have everything we need and deserve, we approach the world with a sense of value."[1]

Luke 7 focuses on a prostitute strong enough to value herself. She knew her sins were many, but she also knew Christ could forgive her. What a tender, intimate moment in Jesus' life Luke revealed to us!

Notice Jesus' response to this raw, vulnerable expression of gratitude. He displayed overflowing compassion and tenderness to this deeply repentant woman. The Lord derives much pleasure from a sincere offering of gratitude.

In Leviticus, we learn that in ancient times the fat from the sacrificial animal was considered the choicest part of the offering. Symbolically this helps us remember that God deserves the very best from us. He wants us to commit our lives to Him completely, never counting the cost. We see that this woman discussed in Luke gave everything she had—body, mind, and soul—in overflowing appreciation for Jesus and His boundless mercy. Jesus responded to the pure gratitude of a wicked prostitute by completely forgiving and restoring her. Will He do any less for you and me if we sincerely repent?

Sometimes the way we live displeases and dishonors the Lord and disrupts our fellowship with Him. But when we make all-out heartfelt offerings of gratitude to Him, He reconciles with us and rescues us from ourselves. Our offering of thanksgiving, like the prostitute's, shows God we appreciate His blessings, healing, and aid in difficult times.

Gratitude has a way of giving us eyes to see all of life as a gift. It is a key element for sparking positive changes in individuals, families, and organizations.[2] Just as the prostitute Mary Magdelene's

GRATITUDE: MARY MAGDALENE WASHES FEET AND THE CLEANSED LEPER GIVES THANKS

act of adoration toward Jesus had a rippling effect throughout the community, so our gratitude affects those around us. Can't you just imagine that the disciples and town folk spent many a speculative conversation trying to understand this surprising mystery?

At the end of the story, Jesus told the (now former) prostitute that her faith had saved her. Then He told her to go and enter into peace. The Hebrew word for peace is *shalom*. It is a rich term that encompasses the concepts of vibrant physical health, robust emotional wellbeing, bounteous material prosperity, and ethereal spiritual wholeness.

An act of wholehearted praise—as this woman made by bathing Jesus' feet in her perfumed hair—can restore completeness and harmony to the penitent's life. The people that God blankets with love do not necessarily have wonderful past records. He can give people who have made deeply scarring mistakes, such as Mary, this former prostitute, a blessed and power-filled future.

Wouldn't you like to have been able to wash Jesus' feet with costly perfume? Do you know you can spend your day in such a way that it is a sweet aroma lifted to the Lord? How would you spend such a day?

How about if you had been at the Last Supper? What if you had been given the experience of having Jesus wash your feet? It has been said that demons feed on the dust on the feet. What dust remains on your feet from roads you have walked? Would you be willing to ask Jesus to wash all the dust off your feet and make you clean? What past events in your life need to be cleared of their dust? Keep your feet "dust-free" through prayer, forgiveness, confession of your sins, and praise.

It means a lot to the Lord when we, like the "wicked sinner" in the story above, choose to praise Him in a public forum. When we make our thanks visible to others we grow spiritually and can be an examples for others to follow. The seventh chapter of Leviticus confirms that God wants us to praise Him publicly.

David was never bashful about being demonstrative about his God. He wrote many "thank you" letters to Him in the Psalms. In Psalm 92:1–4, he said, "It is a good and delightful thing to give thanks to the Lord, to sing praises [with musical accompaniment] to Your name, O Most High. To show forth Your loving-kindness in the morning and Your faithfulness by night, with an instrument of ten strings and with the lute, with a solemn sound upon the lyre. For you, O Lord, have made me glad by Your works; at the deeds of Your hands I joyfully sing" (AMP).

The act of praise brings honor to God. It also helps us feel positive about ourselves and our lives. Endorphins are released when we show praise because it feels good to think about what is right with us and our world. It makes for a happy and satisfied life. Praising the Lord will always bring joy and contentedness. This is especially true when God has done something extraordinary in our lives. Particularly if we have been an outcast, perhaps for many years, we are overwhelmed with the wonder of redemption.

Let's take another look at Jesus' graciousness when thanksgiving is offered:

> And as He was going into one village, He was met by ten lepers, who stood at a distance. And they raised up their voices and called, "Jesus, Master, take pity and have mercy on us!" And when He saw them, He said to them, "Go [at once] and show yourselves to the priests." And as they went, they were cured and made clean. Then one of them, upon seeing that he was cured, turned back, recognizing and thanking and praising God with a loud voice; And he fell prostrate at Jesus' feet, thanking him [over and over]. And he was a Samaritan. Then Jesus asked, "Were not [all] ten cleansed? Where are the nine? Was there no one found to return and to recognize and give thanks and praise God except this alien?" And He said to him, "Get up and go on your way. Your faith (your trust and confidence that spring from Your belief in God) has restored you to health."
>
> (Luke 17:12–19 AMP)

Think of it—ten lepers were healed, but only one came back to thank Jesus. As we think of all God has done for us, let us always remember to go to Jesus and thank Him for His kindness and mercy.

GRATITUDE: MARY MAGDALENE WASHES FEET AND THE CLEANSED LEPER GIVES THANKS

Some startling similarities are apparent between the forgiven prostitute and the newly cleansed leper. Both were of a socially unacceptable caste. Both felt a deep need to show their appreciation to Jesus. They both fell prostrate at His feet, thanking Him repeatedly. Each of their expressions of thanks was wholehearted, deeply passionate, and public.

Jesus pulled up the former leper and sent him on his way, telling him his faith had restored his health. Similarly, He told the prostitute that her faith had led to the great peace she would experience the rest of her life.

Gratitude changes people! It creates a proactive energy that can move us to a higher, deeper level of living. Giving thanks is an art. It can be cultivated. It brings with it the ability to give and receive joy every day. It is living with an open heart.

My friend Anna has an attitude of gratitude. She suffers from bipolar disorder. She has a very difficult time getting her medications regulated and hence experiences a lot of discomfort and anxiety on a continual basis. Her thoughts frighten her sometimes and she struggles with tears and pain. She has a problem called *rumination* where she continues to think and obsess about things in her past that upset her greatly.

Anna is working hard in therapy to rid herself of self-defeating beliefs but it is excruciating work at times. Still, no matter how sick or unsteady she feels, Anna never forgets all the things for which she is grateful. In fact, every night she writes out three things that happened that day for which she is thankful.

It is important to Anna that she not dwell solely on her own problems. Sometimes even when her ears are so sensitive that it hurts to listen, she gets on the phone and calls her friends in hopes of offering support and a listening ear. She watches Christian programs on TV and feels that by contributing her money to worthy charities she in some way is partnering with the ministries in helping the suffering and downtrodden. Anna displays the strength of gratitude in the midst of her suffering.

The Lakota Indian's daily prayer gives us a great example: "Let us give thanks for this beautiful day. Let us give thanks for this life.

Let us give thanks for the water without which life would not be possible. Let us give thanks for grandmother earth who protects and nourishes us."

It is so easy to lose sight of for how much we have to be grateful. Notice the thankfulness the Native American prayer expresses for very simple and basic things—things necessary for life.

Think about something as basic as clean water. Much of the world lacks this most central element for health and survival. As we ponder how wealthy and materially blessed we are compared to most people in other parts of the world, we should feel moved to help. We need to be grateful for every resource we have while setting up systems to share our wealth with those less fortunate.

Is gratitude one of your strengths? Do you feel you have much for which to be thankful? If you wrote a gratitude list, how long would it be? Can you appreciate the situations and relationships that have made up your past? Can you express gratitude simply to give glory to God?

If you aren't as grateful as you think you should be, remember that we are promised in Romans that we can be transformed by the renewal of our minds. We have the ability to learn and change.

Perhaps all of us, to some degree, are saddled with at least a few ingrained negative responses we may have formed in early childhood. In the process of growing up, we experienced emotional wounding that was hurtful and hard to understand. It is only when we fully realize the depth and breadth of God's love for us that we can heal and grow beyond our hurts. We can change the way we think and so change our experiences. We have the possibility to create a robust and mature adulthood when we seek out and integrate attributes such as hope, joy, and, yes, gratitude.

We are here on earth "to grow our souls, to heal our wounds—or at least bless our woundedness—and become more loving, kind, fearless, and hopeful," Emmit Miller said.[3]

It is impossible to feel both the positive emotion of thankfulness and a negative emotion, such as anger or fear, at the same time. By focusing on all for which we are grateful, fear, anger, and bitterness

GRATITUDE: MARY MAGDALENE WASHES FEET AND THE CLEANSED LEPER GIVES THANKS

melt away. Learning to "let go of the struggle" is an amazing feat. It usually happens a little at a time.

As I spend time in the Word, I learn that God is love personified. He forgets every transgression I have made once I have repented. Through this process, I become lighter and lighter. What I mean is, I lighten up. Joy is mine because what Jesus has done for me buoys me.

Certainly, I am endlessly grateful for the salvation He gave me. I am also immensely grateful for the freedom from bondage He gives me while I am here on earth. My personal experience with suffering gradually transformed me from an unhappy person to a very grateful one. I'm so thankful that we can progress beyond our ignorance and become wise, disciplined people. This, too, is a process.

It happens when we immerse ourselves in the Word. It deepens when we ponder His ways. I have a long way to go, but I make it a habit to pause and think of God (Selah). I find that with practice and humility, I can increase the amount of time I am thinking of Him and His precepts. We are instructed in Philippians 4:8 to think on what is good and pure and edifying. Start where you are. If you are faithful to do what you can, God will miraculously do the rest.

Study the Word diligently to understand all that will bring gratitude. We are forgiven. We are restored. The One who made us loves us deeply and completely.

The following message was found as graffiti on a wall in Berkeley, California: "Gratitude makes us feel good. Mental sunshine will cause the flowers of peace, happiness, and prosperity to grow upon the face of the earth. Be a creator of mental sunshine."

The practice of gratitude is far reaching. When we are grateful, it rubs off on other people. When we feel free and joyful, we can help others frame their lives and experiences in a new and more positive way. You can plant flowers of peace, happiness, and prosperity in the hearts of others. This will help some and rescue many. If people see you have a robust life, they will believe they can also.

Gratitude serves as an important antidote to stress, which flourishes in our culture today. Positive feelings can actually release endorphins throughout the body. Thanksgiving can lead you down the road to greater health.

That road begins with a change of heart. Gratitude opens up your heart so you can receive all of the good God waits to give you. Our destination is never a place but rather a new way of looking at things and a new way of perceiving that can lead to greater health and well-being.

If we live deeply and authentically long enough, gratitude, like any practice, can become second nature. Meister Eckhart said, "If the only prayer you say in your whole life is 'thank you' that would suffice."[4]

So often our prayers are requests. We ask for help. We ask for favor. We ask for miracles. However, if you are unable to see the beauty and grace that is already all around you, how can you expect to be able to receive anything else? Do you spend time just thanking and praising God for all He is doing in your life? Developing the aptitude of being grateful is not only a result of meeting challenges successfully, it is a key to personal and spiritual growth.

Surely we can understand we are more eager to help people who show gratitude for what we have done for them. Don't you imagine that God feels the same way? Why would He bless you with more if you do not even appreciate all He has done for you? God must love an attitude of gratitude.

In *Attitudes of Successful Learners,* motivational speaker Chris Widener (2008) says choosing the right attitude will significantly determine new circumstances. It will change the world around you. Widener suggests four attitudes that successful learners possess:

"I can."
"This is a long-term approach."
"Learning is valuable."
"I will make a difference in the lives of those around me."[5]

Gratitude is graceful. It is a mysterious and powerful tool that can open your eyes to see that which you could not see before.

GRATITUDE: MARY MAGDALENE WASHES FEET AND THE CLEANSED LEPER GIVES THANKS

The Ojibway have a beautiful saying, "Sometimes I go about with pity for myself and all the while the Great Winds are carrying me across the sky."

"In the history of ideas, gratitude has had surprisingly few detractors," say Bono, Emmons, and McCullough in *Positive Psychology in Practice*. "Nearly every thinker has viewed gratitude as a sentiment with virtually no down side.... But the fact that people typically consider gratitude a virtue and not simply a pleasure also points to the fact that it does not always come naturally or easily. Gratitude must, and can, be cultivated. And by cultivating the virtue, it appears that people may get the pleasure of gratitude, and all of its other attendant benefits, thrown in for free."[6]

Oh, what an adventure the grateful life can be. It connects us with the vast, fierce vibrancy of the universe and its Maker. Let us say with David in Psalm 116:16–17, "O, Lord, You have freed me from my bonds, and I will serve You forever. I will worship You and offer You a sacrifice of thanksgiving."

CHAPTER 12

HAPPINESS: FOUND ON A ROAD AND UP A TREE

> We pray that you'll live well for the Master, making him proud of you as you work hard in his orchard. As you learn more and more how God works, you will learn how to do your work. We pray that you'll have the strength to stick it out over the long haul—not the grim strength of gritting your teeth but the glory-strength God gives. It is the strength that endures the unendurable and spills over into joy, thanking the Father who makes us strong enough to take part in everything bright and beautiful that he has for us.
>
> (Col. 1:10–12 MESSAGE)

AS WE LOOK at Bible characters, we see their lives were grand and exciting adventures. Yours can be grand and exciting too if you ask Jesus to take control of your life.

By studying the Word, you will be able to step out of fear and guilt and live in the happiness of communion with the Lord. No matter what type of situation in which you find yourself today, no matter how paralyzed, embittered, or scarred you are, Jesus can lift you out of your troubles and bring you into a new life of happiness and fulfillment. As positive psychologist Martin Seligman put it, "The good life is using your signature strengths every day to produce authentic happiness and abundant gratification."[1]

In his seminal work, *Authentic Happiness,* Seligman talked about positive psychology researcher Barbara Fredrickson's concept of broadening and building. The basic idea is that developing more positive emotion builds friendship, love, greater health, and more powerful achievement. He commented, "Barbara Fredrickson's theory and all these studies utterly convinced me that it was worth trying hard to put more positive emotion into my life.... Broadening and building—that is, growth and positive development—are essential characteristics of a win-win encounter."[2]

He continued, "Fredrickson claims that positive emotions have a grand purpose.... They broaden our abiding intellectual, physical, and social resources, building up reserves we can draw upon when a threat or opportunity presents itself. When we are in a positive mood, people like us better, and friendship, love, and coalitions are more likely to cement. In contrast to the constrictions of negative emotion, our mental set is expansive, tolerant, and creative. We are open to new ideas and new experiences."[3]

Creating happy experiences is a good task for Christians to aspire to and practice, because as Seligman said, "It turns out that adults and children who are put into a good mood select higher goals, perform better, and persist longer."[4] To live in a consistently productive state so you can successfully approach and meet challenging goals, you must let go of all the baggage of the past so you are free to run your race fully with nothing weighing you down or holding you back.

Your yesterdays do not dictate your tomorrows. Leave the hurts and sins of the past behind and make the rest of your life a glorious adventure with Jesus Christ. That's what Paul did.

If anyone had valid reasons to sink into the miry quicksand of guilt, it was Paul. After all, he had ruthlessly orchestrated the deaths of countless innocent Christians. In his religiosity and zeal, he had killed the Lord's own children. How in the world could he live with himself? There was only one way—he had to relinquish all control and live the remainder of his life in harmony with the wishes of his Savior, Jesus Christ. The same is true for you and me.

HAPPINESS: FOUND ON A ROAD AND UP A TREE

In the epiphany he experienced on the road to Damascus, Saul's estimate of himself was completely demolished. A self-righteous Jew of privileged background and impeccable credentials, he had been reduced to an awful monster. Can you imagine the shame and guilt that overcame him in that moment of realization?

In the same moment that Saul fully recognized the hopeless wretchedness of his life, he was given the greatest gift anyone could be given—a chance to know the living Christ personally. This gave him the courage to face himself for the horrible sinner he was and reach out to a perfect Savior.

Saul had the strength to face his own evilness, because in that flash of insight he very personally felt the love of a holy and perfect Christ. Regardless of how disastrous his choices had been, he had a fresh chance to live in a way that brought purpose, satisfaction, and happiness to his life and the lives of innumerable others. Saul received a new name, Paul, to commemorate the depth of meaning in this new beginning.

Paul was strong enough and humble enough to receive immediate and total forgiveness. This forgiveness is available to you right now if you only will believe in the risen Christ. Feel Christ's boundless love and receive it for yourself. Realize there are no second-class citizens. You are not second-class no matter what your heritage, no matter how vile your sins.

God chose Paul to take the Good News of Jesus Christ to the Gentiles. As a Jew, Saul had looked down at the Gentiles with great scorn. Now they would become the precious recipients of all he had discovered in Christ.

I imagine Paul's view of himself traversed through three lines of thought very quickly. He went from (1) an arrogant Pharisee, highly privileged in birth and ethical standing, to (2) a despicable murderer of God's people to (3) a grateful sinner saved by Jesus Christ's grace.

Though Paul was an undeserving sinner, God declared him "not guilty." In Romans 4:7–8, Paul reminisced on how centuries before, David had said, "Blessed and to be envied are those whose sins are forgiven and put out of sight. Yes, what joy there is for anyone whose sins are no longer counted against him by the Lord."

When we think of King David, a man after God's own heart, we can feel hope for our own lives. I am sure Paul could relate to David's laundry list of sins, including the murder of Bathsheba's husband.

Nevertheless, David looked to a higher source for his security. After coming face to face with his own sinfulness, he sang. "O, God in Zion, we wait before you in silent praise, and thus fulfill our vow. And because you answer prayer, all mankind will come to you with their requests. Though sins fill our hearts, you forgive them all. How greatly to be envied are those you have chosen to come and live with you within the holy tabernacle courts! What joy awaits us among all the good things there" (Ps. 65:1–4).

How could vile sinners such as David, Paul, you, and me find lasting happiness? Paul wrote in Romans 3:23–24, "Yes, all have sinned; all fall short of God's glorious ideal; yet God declares us not guilty of offending him if we trust in Jesus Christ, who in his kindness freely takes away your sins." When God takes away our sins, He does it absolutely and completely, removing them as far from us as the east is from the west (see Ps. 103:12).

The realization of this glorious truth brings with it ultimate joy. It is a transforming moment when we discern that eternal salvation comes through Christ's suffering on the cruel cross. We need only to believe and it will be so, despite the sinful mess we made of our lives. This is the happiness Paul refers to in Philippians 4:4–7:

> Always be full of joy in the Lord; I say it again, rejoice! Let everyone see that you are unselfish and considerate in all you do. Remember that the Lord is coming soon. Don't worry about anything; instead, pray about everything; tell God your needs, and don't forget to thank him for his answers. If you do this, you will experience God's peace, which is far more wonderful than the human mind could understand. His peace will keep your thoughts and your hearts quiet and at rest as you trust in Christ Jesus.

HAPPINESS: FOUND ON A ROAD AND UP A TREE

Paul also wrote in Colossians 2:4–7 about the joy found through new life with Christ:

> For though I am far away from you my heart is with you, happy because you are getting along so well, happy because of your strong faith in Christ. And now, just as you trusted Christ to save you, trust him, too, for each day's problems; live in vital union with him. Let your roots grow down deep into him and draw up nourishment from him. See that you go on growing in the Lord, and become strong and vigorous in the truth you were taught. Let your lives overflow with joy and thanksgiving for all he has done.

Paul was a thriver. He grew to be content in whatever circumstances he found himself. Instead of complaining, he looked for a way to make the most of each situation. He viewed even the most treacherous of situations as opportunities. We can learn how to conduct our own lives in the courageous and fulfilling manner Paul demonstrated. No matter what we have done and no matter what has been done to us, we, too, can have a joyful life with a happy ending. Don't miss all the bright and beautiful things in store for you when you are living in dynamic fusion with the Lord.

Paul was a perfect example of a strong and vigorous believer. His circumstances were often far from ideal, yet he always managed to keep the faith. He was often beaten, brutalized, and imprisoned. It is said that some of his writings occurred while he was in a prison with knee-high in sewage. Yet he kept the faith. He was happy because he had Jesus. He knew nothing and no one could ever take Jesus away.

Once while Paul and Silas were imprisoned, they were praying and singing hymns to the Lord around midnight when an earthquake occurred. The prison was shaken to its foundation. The cell doors flew open, and all of the prisoners' chains fell off. The guard awoke and assumed all the prisoners had escaped. So he drew his sword to kill himself. Paul yelled to the man not to kill himself. "We are all here," he assured the jailer.

The guard was so impressed and grateful that he fell before Paul and Silas and asked what he must do to be saved. They told him and his household the Good News—they could be saved by believing on the Lord Jesus. After washing the stripes on Paul and Silas's backs, the jailer and all his family were baptized. They all shared a meal together and rejoiced.

Happiness is perhaps most sweet when we get to impact another human being's life for eternity. Paul and Silas found joy by giving the jailer and his family the greatest possible gift: a life lived in communion with Jesus Christ. How loving and thoughtful Paul and Silas were, even in the midst of their own suffering.

It was the attitude these brave heroes took that made them so effective. Paul described our bodies as perishable containers holding "this light and power that now shine within us" as a precious treasure. This glorious power within is from God.

Paul was said to have buffeted his body because he cared not for his physical self but rather gloried in having Jesus in his heart. He said, "We are pressed on every side by troubles, but not crushed and broken. We are perplexed because we don't know why things happen as they do, but we don't give up and quit" (2 Cor. 4:8).

Paul was wise enough to lubricate the irritations in his life with God's love. He knew that it is through such a process that a clam creates a pearl within itself. Think about the things in your life that irritate you. How can you surround (lubricate) these things in love?

Have you ever thought you could transform every day into a pearl of a day? How? Make conscious contact with God through prayer. Pray for guidance in the morning and pray with gratitude at night. Give each of your days to God for his purposes. In this way you can make your life into a strand of pearls—many days lived well unto the Lord.

Paul demonstrated this way of thinking when he said, "Not that I was ever in need, for I have learned how to get along happily whether I have much or little. I know how to live on almost nothing or with everything. I have learned the secret of contentment in every situation, whether it be a full stomach or hunger, plenty or want; for I can do everything God asks me to with the help of Christ who gives me the strength and power" (Phil. 4:11–13).

HAPPINESS: FOUND ON A ROAD AND UP A TREE

A significant theme threads its way through the book of Philippians, and it is this: Blessedness does not come from outward circumstances but rather from inward strength. Joy comes from knowing Christ personally and from depending on His power on a daily basis.

True happiness, Paul taught us, comes from turning our wants, needs, and indeed our very lives over to God in complete obedience. In Romans 12:1–2 he exhorted, "I beseech you therefore, brethren, by the mercies of God, that you present your bodies a living sacrifice, holy, acceptable to God, which is your reasonable service. And do not be conformed to this world, but be transformed by the renewing of your mind, that you may prove what is that good and acceptable and perfect will of God" (NKJV).

Paul understood that we are good and acceptable only because we have Christ within. In Romans 7:18 he wrote, "I know I am rotten through and through so far as my old sinful nature is concerned. No matter which way I turn, I can't make myself do right. I want to but I can't."

Paul demonstrated great humility in his writings. Paul, former torturer and murderer of Christians, was the supreme example, showing that it is never too late while we are still here on earth to exchange hubris for humility.

Thank God for the crucifixion of Jesus Christ and all that it meant! Romans 6:6 states, "Your old evil desires were nailed to the cross with him; that part of you that loves to sin was crushed and fatally wounded, so that your sin-loving body is no longer under sin's control, no longer needs to be a slave to sin."

Galatians 5:24 agrees. It says, "Those who belong to Christ have nailed their natural evil desires to his cross and crucified them there."

What was God accomplishing with creation? How was He saving his creation through the life and death of his only begotten son? Acts 17:27 explains, "His purpose in all of this is that they should seek after God and perhaps feel their way toward him and find him—though he is not far from any of us."

The seeking after God is a lifetime endeavor. It will involve, as it did for Paul, considerable suffering. However, if we depend on the Holy Spirit to testify from within, we, like Paul, can finish the race with joy.

He put it this way:

> Therefore we also, since we are surrounded by so great a cloud of witnesses, let us lay aside every weight, and the sin which so easily ensnares us, and let us run with endurance the race that is set before us, looking unto Jesus, the author and finisher of our faith, who for the joy that was set before Him endured the cross, despising the shame, and has sat down at the right hand of the throne of God.
>
> (Heb. 12:1–2 NKJV)

Paul's deep and penetrating devotion to Jesus made him happy. Why do you think this is so? Research has shown why, said Seligman: "The data on the positive psychological effects of faith started to provide a countervailing force. Religious Americans are clearly less likely to abuse drugs, commit crimes, divorce, and kill themselves.... The increase in optimism which increasing religiousness brings is entirely accounted for by greater hope.... The relation of hope for the future and religious faith is probably the cornerstone of why faith so effectively fights despair and increases happiness."[5]

Living in this way elevates your mind, health, and general level of wellbeing. Break free from daily stressors and focus on the little things in life that bring you joy. An aptitude for happiness is as available for you as it was for Paul.

You can take small steps to a healthier and happier life. One of the best habits you can cultivate is the ability to focus on your strengths and pay scant attention to your weaknesses. There are also other easy ways to promote health and happiness.

Simplifying your life, for instance, can increase happiness. Feeling like you have enough time to pursue the things you want to pursue is a better indicator of a satisfied life than income. The term for this is *time affluence*. Do you take time to draw away from your work and refresh yourself? Jesus withdrew often to pray and receive power from His Father.

You might be interested to know that while it is positive to achieve a reasonable quality of life, beyond a basic level of financial security money does not bring happiness. Possessions will not bring lasting happiness.

Taking time to develop a hobby can make you happier. It increases your satisfaction and self-esteem. When you are creative, you become more flexible and open.

Have you ever become totally absorbed and focused while working on a hobby or participating in a sport? Positive psychologist Dr. Csikszentmihalyi refers to this heightened state of consciousness as *flow*. Finding activities you love that put you in a state of flow is relaxing and enjoyable.

If you want to be happy, don't continually seek out the very best decision in every area of your life. Make the best choice you can and then move on. Continually revisiting decisions creates anxiety. Good enough is good enough.

Widen your circle of friends. All kinds of positive relationships with others can contribute much to the level of happiness you experience.

Forgetting your own problems to help someone else is among the most effective strategies to becoming happy. Doing a good deed resonates within your heart much longer than if you had spent the time in a more frivolous manner. Practice altruism and watch your life satisfaction take a leap in the positive direction.

Bring happiness into your life through realizing that some people will not like you. Don't take everyone's judgment to heart. In doing so, you surrender your own ability to view yourself clearly.

Think more about your accomplishments than your defeats. Remind yourself of times when people you respect complimented you. It is amazing how much we needlessly torture ourselves about past mistakes rather than move on to greater levels of happiness.

An effective way to distract yourself from negative self-talk is to exercise. The activity will strengthen your mind and body. Exercise increases happiness and life satisfaction.

Happiness combines self-satisfaction, general contentment, and the ability to enjoy life. A happy person is cheerful and enthusiastic. Have dreams and be willing to take risks, if only on a modest scale. Derive pleasure and meaning from what you do. Stay in balance to keep feeling good.

Reflect on how happy Paul became after his encounter with Christ on the road to Damascus. He wanted to share the Good News with as many people as possible. We can see a similar change of heart toward others in Zacchaeus's life.

In the beginning, Zacchaeus, the tax collector, was very unhappy. He absconded with as much of other peoples' money as he could. But that lifestyle did not work well for him. It had not brought him happiness. So the little guy climbed the highest tree he could find in hope of glimpsing Jesus as He passed.

Various aspects of our life experiences can converge to make us, like Zacchaeus, unhappy people. Sometimes we have unrealistic expectations. Sometimes we want to get something we desire without putting in the necessary effort or obtaining the knowledge or skill needed to achieve the goal. Sometimes we feel so deflated that we completely give up on our goals and dreams, in the process becoming hopeless and helpless. We can correct this situation by modifying our expectations and setting reasonable goals.

One of the useful tools you can acquire to help you move toward victory is an understanding and application of emotional intelligence. It is important to understand what motivates you and what motivates others. Emotional intelligence arises through being observant of people and listening carefully to what they say. It also means being in touch with what you are thinking and feeling in the moment.

Success in modulating emotions and positively influencing situations brings buoyancy, inspiration, fervor, and zest. The experience of success attracts other people to you. Thus, you draw more people into your support system.

HAPPINESS: FOUND ON A ROAD AND UP A TREE

My friend Elizabeth is filled with just this kind of zest. She makes friends wherever she goes. She was on the bus once and heard a blind lady talking about how much it was going to take to pay workers to paint the interior of her home. Elizabeth offered to do it for free on the spot. She followed through, and in fact now cleans weekly for that blind woman and for a blind couple.

Elizabeth has done missionary work with Native American children and in Haiti and South Africa. When she goes on these trips she takes all the luggage she can, filled with things like clothes and shoes to leave for the people to whom she is ministering. She comes home pleased and empty handed.

Elizabeth participates in a Christian clown group through which she entertains children, senior citizens, people with disabilities, and those from low-income communities. She is a bike enthusiast and rides to many of the events on her bicycle. It is nothing for her to ride a hundred miles in a day. Her energy is infectious and she channels that energy through healthy exercise, and more importantly through helping anyone in need who happens across her path.

As you can imagine, Elizabeth has many friends. She has succeeded at being herself and she is a happy person because of it. It is infinitely easier to build strong and lasting friendships if you are satisfied and happy with your life as Elizabeth is with hers. Don't envy what others have. That is coveting, and there is a commandment against it. Be happy for the goodness you see in others' lives.

Let's look at the story of Zacchaeus to examine how an envious, bitter, and stingy person became a very happy man who reached out to others in love and joy. After an encounter with the living Christ, Zacchaeus learned how to be truly happy with himself. This biblical character is known for his short stature. Let's also remember his great transformation from a life of greed to a life of meaning through helping others:

> Then Jesus entered and passed through Jericho. Now behold, there was a man named Zacchaeus who was a chief tax collector, and he was rich. And he sought to see who Jesus was, but could not because of the crowd, for he was short in stature. So he ran ahead and climbed up into a sycamore tree to see Him, for he

was going to pass that way. And when Jesus came to the place, He looked up and saw him, and said to him, "Zacchaeus, make haste and come down, for today I must stay at your house." So he made haste and came down, and received Him joyfully. But when they saw it, they all complained, saying, "He has gone to be a guest with a man who is a sinner." Then Zacchaeus stood and said to the Lord, "Look, Lord, I give half of my goods to the poor; and if I have taken anything from anyone by false accusation, I restore fourfold." And Jesus said to him, "Today salvation has come to this house, because he also is a son of Abraham; for the Son of Man has come to seek and to save that which was lost."
(Luke 19:1–10 NKJV)

Zacchaeus had earned a reputation as a sinner and a swindler. But in the twinkling of an eye, he went from being unscrupulous and greedy to being happy, loving, and giving. The Living Word cries out through Zacchaeus's life, as it does through Paul's life, that no one is so despicable that he or she cannot be completely transformed through Jesus Christ's love and mercy. Along with Zacchaeus the thief and Saul (Paul) the murderer, join the ranks of errant human beings acutely aware of just how much we need a perfect Savior:

The Lord [earnestly] waits [expecting, looking, and longing] to be gracious to you; and therefore He lifts Himself up, that He may have mercy on you and show loving-kindness to you. For the Lord is a God of justice. Blessed (happy, fortunate, to be envied) are all those who [earnestly] wait for Him, who expect and look and long for Him [for His victory, His favor, His love, His peace, His joy, and His matchless, unbroken companionship]!
(Isa. 30:18 AMP).

How can we ever know the end of happiness once we grasp the reality of Jesus' unbroken companionship? If we are Christians, we will happily fellowship together forever and ever.

CHAPTER 13

USING YOUR STRENGTHS FOR GROWTH AND SUCCESS

> This Book of the Law shall not depart from your mouth, but you shall meditate in it day and night, that you may observe to do according to all that is written in it. For then you will make your way prosperous, and then you will have good success.
>
> (Josh. 1:8 NKJV)

GOD LOVES YOU unconditionally just the way you are. Using your signature strengths to grow as a person and achieve success will not make Him love you more. In your own power you can do nothing to earn His love. No matter how good you are at using your strengths or how many wonderful things you do, if you have not received salvation through faith in Jesus as the One who died for you and rose again, everything you do is futile. Growth and success are simply fruits derived from having a relationship with God and intimate knowledge of "this Book of the Law," the Bible.

These fruits result from a connection with Jesus. When you trust in Him, you are grafted into Him, the Living Vine. When you accept Him as your personal Savior, you will begin to see yourself growing in the areas that are your strongest. Opportunities will arise where you can use those strengths to achieve success.

What is success? You would probably get a different answer from each person you ask. I believe the best answer to the question is this: Success is the experience of living a Christ-directed life. Such a life is centered in Christ and empowered by the Holy Spirit. With the power this gives you, you will be compelled to share the Good News to a hurting and dying world. You will want others to find out about the glorious truth of God's love as well as all His promises to those who believe. You will need to spend time in prayer and in the Bible. Then you begin trusting God and obeying Him.

Living this kind of life automatically opens doors for you to experience ever-increasing personal and spiritual growth. Think about your top strengths. How could you use them in service to our Lord? A Christ-directed life can be full of love, joy, peace, patience, kindness, faithfulness, and goodness.[1] Pretend there are blank spaces here and add in your own unique specific character traits. If you will surrender them to Him and make the Living Word a priority in your life, I guarantee you God will use you and make your way prosperous.

You will want to use your strengths to the fullest for the kingdom. That requires faith, determination, and an unwillingness to give up no matter how rough the journey. Paul was brutally persecuted for his declaration that Jesus is Lord. Remember in the previous chapter I said Paul wrote some of his New Testament letters from a jail swimming in sewage? But Paul had that faith, determination, and unwillingness to give up; and so he persevered and ran the race to achieve his prize—eternity with Jesus Christ in a glorious heaven where there is no suffering, pain, or injustice.

But heaven will be much vaster that the sufferings we leave behind. When we all get to heaven, it will be a day of rejoicing. We can't even begin to imagine how wonderful our experience throughout eternity is going to be.

This all will happen and we can prepare ourselves by using our aptitudes and attitudes to live out our allotted time with purpose, making efforts that will count for something in the next life. Even though he was suffering terribly, Paul had the inner fortitude to encourage the church in Philippi. He wrote: "There has never been the slightest doubt in my mind that the God who started this great work in you would keep at it and bring it to a flourishing finish on the very day Christ Jesus appears" (Phil. 1:6 MESSAGE). This same message is true for you today.

Yes, Paul was an encourager, and he reached the highest level of development a Christian can possess—he worked to help people in the body of Christ become all they could be.

Another example of Paul's ability to be inspirational is found in Romans 12:2, "And do not be conformed to this world, but be transformed by the renewing of your mind, that you may prove what is that good and acceptable and perfect will of God" (NKJV).

If we are to grow and succeed, we must leave the past behind and allow ourselves to go through the process of having God transform us. This transforming occurs from glory to glory as we slowly develop into Christ's image. I won't kid you—effective change is difficult, slow, and gradual. But with God, all things are possible.

Perhaps you are letting the past get the better of you. Maybe your mind is entangled with guilt and shame. If you accept what Romans 12:2 teaches, you can drop all that baggage, turn your eyes to the future, and begin the transformation that leads to full maturity.

Did you know that some guilt is actually false guilt? And guess where it comes from? You are right! It travels from the Devil's lips to your ears. If you are bothered by a sin you have already sincerely confessed to God, you are being pulled into the mire of quicksand we call false guilt.

On the other hand, when the Holy Spirit convicts you, He will point out a specific sin in your life. As soon as you confess that you have sinned, the guilt can lift immediately. At that time you will be restored to full fellowship with your heavenly Father. Then all you need do is thank Him that His forgiveness is complete.[2]

Aptitudes for growth and attitudes for success become evident as we are being filled with the Holy Spirit. "To be filled with the Spirit is to be controlled by the Holy Spirit. When I am filled with the Spirit, Christ's Spirit will dwell in my body and live His resurrection life in and through me,"[3] said Bill Bright in *5 Steps to Christian Growth*.

So what must we do if we want our strengths to be anointed and available for God to use as He pleases? We must pray. Philippians 4:6–7 tells us we must pray about everything. John 14:14 instructs us to pray specifically. First Thessalonians 5:17 urges us to pray continually.[4]

Talk to Jesus. He is your friend. Be patient in waiting for Him to respond to your requests. He knows your goals, aptitudes, and character. Display a positive attitude of expectancy and God will come through in a way only the Great Creator can—with a flourish! He will make a way where there is no way.

Just offer up your gifts and dreams to Him and His blessings will overflow in your life and you will be able to accomplish the mission you were placed on earth to fulfill. Never forget that God loves you and that He has a wonderful plan for your life.[5] Knock yourself off the throne and place Christ there. Yielding to Christ will catapult you into harmony with God's plan. From there, the sky is the limit!

Choose Jesus, and you will succeed. To truly succeed and grow you need to know your purpose, grow to your maximum potential, and sow seeds that benefit others. Success is for everyone, and success is a journey.[6]

A "benefit of focusing on the journey of success instead of on arriving at a destination or achieving a goal is that you have the potential to become a success today. The moment that you make the shift to finding your purpose, growing to your potential, and helping others, successful is something you are right now, not something you vaguely hope one day to be," said [6]John Maxwell in *Your Roadmap for Success: You Can Get There from Here.*[7]

The story of Milton Humason should encourage you if you are starting with humble beginnings. He dropped out of school at age fourteen and then became a janitor at Mount Wilson Observatory in 1917. Because it seemed interesting to him, he volunteered to be a night assistant at the observatory. He was so talented that he was hired on as staff. He ended up becoming an indispensable help to Edwin Hubble in creating Hubble's law, and he also discovered a comet. Humason shows how we can thrive and succeed even with impoverished or seemingly limited circumstances.

USING YOUR STRENGTHS FOR GROWTH AND SUCCESS

A majority of people believe that having good health is a key to success. We have all heard the saying, "If you have your health, you have everything." Certainly we pray for good health for our families and ourselves but we must also take into account that many people learn how to thrive through very dire and difficult physical circumstances. We must pick up our cross and bear it with determination to finish the race, as Paul would say.

Think of people in war-torn countries who rebuild and go on to have great lives. These are the people who thrive, the people who flourish. Would you believe the prevalence of flourishing is barely 20 percent in the adult population?[8]

Corey Keyes created a thirteen-dimension system to help us evaluate where we stand in terms of our ability to flourish.[9] Your answers to the following questions should give you some clues about where you are and where you want to go.

First, let's look at your emotional well-being. Are you usually cheerful and peaceful? If not, how could you make improvements to be in good spirits more often? Are you satisfied with your life as you are currently living it? Or do you need to make a change in your life that allows you to use your signature strengths more fully?[10]

How about a glance at your psychological well-being? Do you have a positive attitude about yourself? If not, how could you shake things up by learning to appreciate your unique personality? Do you seek challenge and growth? If not, think reflectively about your potential.[11]

Examine your psychological well-being. Does your life have direction and meaning? If not, try writing a paragraph about what gives you purpose in life or what could, if in place, make you feel more purposeful. Can you create and manage your environment to suit your aptitudes and attitudes? If not, try fantasizing about what your world would look like if you had mastery over your environment.[12]

Ask yourself if you feel you live your life by your internal values and standards. If not, how can you build more autonomy into your life? Do you have warm, trusting relationships with others? If not, what can you do to reach out and have more positive relations with the people you encounter?[13]

Now let's explore your social well-being. Are you accepting of human differences? If not, think of how you might more effectively embrace those differences encountered in others. Do you believe society can grow positively? If not, ponder what self-actualization might look like in your life and then broaden that out and imagine what society-wide actualization might create.[14]

Continuing your quest for social well-being, detect whether or not you believe your daily activities are useful and valuable to society and others. If you think they are not, consider how you might expand your sense of social contribution. Are you interested in society? If not, how might you engage in society in a more meaningful way? Finally, do you have a sense of belonging to a community from which you get comfort and support? If not, can you think about how you might reach out to people with similar interests and values in a more extroverted way? Think about how you might more effectively integrate into the general society.[15]

World renowned author and speaker Zig Ziglar gave a comprehensive definition of what he terms "the success formula": "The right attitude, plus specific skills, plus the right philosophy and the right objectives, all built on a character base, enables you to have winning relationships with friends, family, associates, and members of the community at large."[16]

So to what is Ziglar referring when he talks about having the right attitude? It is the difference of personal choice as to whether you are a pessimist or an optimist. A pessimist will look for difficulty in the opportunity, while an optimist looks for opportunity in the difficulty.[17]

No doubt in your life so far you have encountered some sadness, disappointment, rejection, and maybe even trauma. Sometimes after being hurt, a person will slip into a pessimistic mindset. While we can understand the roots of thinking negatively, making a willful decision to be more optimistic will pay big dividends for your personal peace and health as well as your relationships with others.

USING YOUR STRENGTHS FOR GROWTH AND SUCCESS

"Two men looked out from prison bars—one saw mud, the other saw stars," Ziglar said in *Success for Dummies*.[18] If you look around, there are many things on which to focus your attention and concentration. Have you ever had the experience of having a great day but then one bad thing happens and you let it cloud everything in a negative cast? You can choose to focus on something good amidst the situation—be it a beautiful flower, a friend's smile, or a delicious meal. In fact, decide to savor every good thing that happens to you. Dwell upon it, roll it around in your mind, and then express thanks and gratitude for what is going well.

Decide to let go of the bad habit of cynicism. "A cynic is someone who would demand a bacteria count on the milk of human kindness," Ziglar said.[19] So how do we move out of the painful effects of cynicism to lead a happier life? Talk to yourself. Instead of talking negatively to yourself, slowly begin to add more and more positive talking. We all have lots and lots of thoughts going through our heads. We pick the ones on which to dwell. Whenever you can, dwell on the positive.

Repeat affirmations over and over in your mind to affirm yourself to change. For instance, you could say to yourself, "Today I will look for the good in every situation." To magnify the effect, say it aloud several times a day.

Personal growth requires seizing the now while planning for the future. It also requires commitment, goal setting, and responsibility.[20] When you take responsibility by setting goals and then following through with commitment, you win. Each small win will motivate you to move forward again. After enough experiences of succeeding, living a life of personal growth will become a habit.

That is not to say there will not be mistakes and failures along the way. The truth is they are inevitable. How you look at them can either make you or break you. If you use the mistake as a lesson and learn from it, then you will be ready to try again with a fresh spirit.

Some of the benchmarks of success Ziglar revealed in *Success for Dummies* are: Understanding that failure is just an event; seeing bright things in your future; filling yourself with faith, hope, and love; thinking of your responsibilities rather than your rights; standing up for what is morally right; being secure in who you are; gaining love and respect from enemies and friends alike; understanding that happiness comes from doing things for others; giving hope, love, and encouragement to those in need; forgiving those who have wronged you; being a servant friend; recognizing and using your talents; and serving God well.[21]

So why is it is so important to follow Ziglar's suggestions? Because those suggestions are founded in optimism and teach you to be strong in yourself. This leads to increased mental health. By the same token, adopting a "learned helplessness" or pessimistic type of attitude will lead to depression.[22] Carefully look over Ziglar's list again and try to apply each one to your life. It is worth the effort and will pay you dividends until the day you pass into eternity.

Did you know, according to George Vaillant in the *American Journal of Psychiatry*, that "in the absence of disease the brain works surprisingly well until age 80 and that neurologically optimal brain development requires almost a lifetime? Prospective studies reveal that individuals are less depressed and show greater emotional modulation at seventy that they did at thirty."[23] Another fact worth embracing is that people who were denied love as children recover and find it in mid-age adulthood.[24] All this news is exciting! You don't have to be pessimistic about getting older. Indeed, like a fine wine, your passing years can add depth and joy.

What do you expect for yourself and your future? Well, whatever it is, you are probably right! I am talking here about self-fulfilling prophecies. You have a choice. You can become what you fear or you can expect the best. "The winners in life, believing in the self-fulfilling prophecy, keep their momentum moving upward by expecting better jobs, more money, good health, better family relationships, financial security, warm friendships, and success," said Denis Waitley in his e-zine.[25]

Pessimism and cynicism lead to nothing but trouble. Optimism and reality are the keys to problem solving. Look at problems as opportunities. No matter how tense the situation,

USING YOUR STRENGTHS FOR GROWTH AND SUCCESS

stay relaxed and friendly. Calmness and courage are habits that can be learned by actually using them in real life. Instead of griping, praise. Have a big dream and get excited and enthusiastic about it.[26] You can succeed if you think you can. What you see is who you will be.

The more frequently and intensely you experience positive emotions will help mold your future. Dr. Barbara Fredrickson is a positive psychology researcher who is well known for her groundbreaking Broaden-and-Build Theory of positive emotions. In a recent interview, she shared some research nuggets from her lab. They include the fact that positive emotions broaden the scope of your vision. Just as negativity spirals down into misery, positivity sparks upward spirals that open people's minds, build their resources to cope with life, and promote health. Though positive emotions are often far milder than negative emotions, they are the key to rebounding from adversity. A ratio of positivity to negativity of 3 to 1 is the tipping point that predicts whether or not people flourish.[27]

The implications of Fredrickson's work and how Christians can apply it to their lives effectively lies in her statement, "Flourishing is distinct from mere happiness—it entails not only feeling good, but also doing good, adding value to those around you."[28]

Wanting to add value to others' lives is an exciting venture. It can make you want to get up in the morning. "Success is waking up in the morning, whoever you are, wherever you are, however old or young, and bounding out of bed because there's something out there that you love to do, that you believe in, that you're good at—something that's bigger than you are, and you can hardly wait to get at it again today," Maxwell said.[29]

The key to living a life worth getting up for every day is a life in which you discover and work toward your dream. What would you do with your life if you could do anything you wanted? Extract a viable way to significantly incorporate your dream into your life from your answer to that question.

Your dream is the ticket to your destiny. It is something worthy of sacrifice and commitment. It gives you a sense of direction.

APTITUDES FOR GROWTH; ATTITUDES FOR SUCCESS

Having a great vision for yourself increases your potential. To achieve your potential you will need to exert a lot of effort, a belief in yourself, and an ability to prioritize your life around your most important goals.

Work becomes a joy when done in service to your big dream. Working actively on your dream is the most likely predictor of your future. It is a roadmap to get you where you want to go.

Let go of the past. What are you doing now to further your dream? If it is something constructive, it indicates a successful future. Keep your dream the front and center of your focus. "Dreams don't die—they fade away. It takes, hunger, tenacity, and commitment to see a dream through until it becomes reality. Once you discover your dream, go after it," Maxwell said.[30]

A dream in its early stages while it is under construction can be fragile. Be tenacious about that which is most dear to your heart. Don't let anyone take that desire away from you. "Your ability to live your dream may be closer that you think," Maxwell said.[31] Persevere. Your breakthrough might be right around the next corner.

I keep underscoring the power of having a positive attitude. No matter how much aptitude you have, unless you approach your dream with the right attitude, you will not see results. Ultimately, your attitude determines whether you will succeed or fail in your endeavor to make your dream come true. "When our attitudes out distance our abilities, even the impossible becomes possible," Maxwell said.[32] There is great power in the way you think. Be decisive in training your mind to be positive.

Following through on your goals requires decisiveness and dedication. Growth is something that should be planned. It is a decision. Did you realize if a person would spend an hour a day on the same subject for five years, that person would be an expert on that subject?[33] At what do you want to be an expert? What's stopping you? Start now. Set some goals. Make an action plan.

"Your dream determines your goals. Your goals map out your actions. Your actions create results. And the results bring you success."[34]

USING YOUR STRENGTHS FOR GROWTH AND SUCCESS

Be dedicated to being a growing person. It will motivate you to keep learning and finding ever more ways to apply what you know. Turn every adversity into an opportunity. Keep moving forward, even when you hit a detour. The two major detours are fear and failure.[35]

Naturally, any time we undertake a dream that means everything to us, there will be fear. "Fear breads inaction; Inaction leads to lack of experience; Lack of experience fosters ignorance; and Ignorance breeds fear."[36] A vicious cycle is the result. So what are we to do? We must face the fear and move ahead anyway. Focus on the aspects of your situation over which you do have control. Place your faith in God. He will help you cope with any trepidation you may be feeling.

Trusting in God will help you when you fail. And you will. It is a part of the process. The trick is learning from your mistakes without letting them paralyze you. See your failures as growth opportunities. If you find out you are going down the wrong road, review your direction and take another route. "Your goal is to finish the race—to do the best you're capable of doing."[37]

It takes character to finish the race. And while each person may not be good looking or physically resilient, all people can aspire to have strong character.[38] Each of us should make it a practice to develop and use as many strengths of character as possible.[39]

So what exactly do signature strengths do to help us in our everyday lives? They have many benefits. These include: a sense of ownership—"this is the real me," a feeling of excitement, a rapid learning curve in the strength area, a continuous drive to learn new ways to use the strength, a sense of yearning to act in accordance with the strength, feeling like you can't be stopped from using the strength, being invigorated rather than exhausted when using the strength, the creation and pursuit of projects that revolve around the strength, and intrinsic motivation to use the strength.[40]

In the next section of this book, we will be exploring the vital importance of meaningful relationships with others. It is good to know that character strengths that orient us toward others make us happy.[41]

APTITUDES FOR GROWTH; ATTITUDES FOR SUCCESS

In *Your Road Map for Success*, John Maxwell encourages you to paint a picture of your dream to others so they can catch your vision. Give them a horizon to see the incredible possibilities ahead. Give them the sun for warmth and hope. Give them the mountains to represent challenges ahead. Give them birds to inspire them to soar like eagles. Give them flowers to remind them to enjoy the journey along the way. Give them a path to offer direction and security. Give them yourself to demonstrate your commitment to the dream. Finally, reach out to them to show them where they fit in and that you believe in them.[42]

If you do these things, you will be displaying true aptitudes for growth and effective attitudes for success. Get excited about the adventure your life can be.

PART 2
BUILDING A SUPPORT NETWORK

Chapter 14

THE GIFT OF SUPPORT

> All praise to the God and Father of our Master, Jesus the Messiah! Father of all mercy! God of all healing counsel! He comes alongside us when we go through hard times, and before you know it, he brings us alongside someone else who is going through hard times so that we can be there for that person just as God was there for us.
>
> (2 Cor. 1:3–4 MESSAGE)

IT IS A simple fact that you can't give away what you don't have. To be a supportive person you must first receive the perfect love and support only God has to offer. Praise Him in gratitude that He would stoop from His lofty heights to love every human being He created—each of us. He desires a relationship with you. He wants to help you. He wants to be merciful to you. He wants to make available to you His healing counsel. When you reach out to God through prayer, all this and more is attainable. Pray, read His Word, and sing Him a song of adulation.

God doesn't want the relationship to stop there, however. He wants you to imitate His love and give it away. He created you to share His love and support with others you encounter on life's journey. You are to act as His conduit, to be His agent to reach out and share His love with others.

John Townsend, in his book *Loving People*, put it this way: "The debt we have to love, and the command to love each other, is so central that the Bible calls it 'the royal law'—that is, the king of all laws."[1]

As James expressed it, "You do well when you complete the Royal Rule of the Scriptures: 'Love others as you love yourself'" (James 2:8 MESSAGE).

Two or more players are involved in this Royal Rule: you and other people. The glorious thing about loving others is they usually love you in return. However, even if someone doesn't respond lovingly right away, with some tender care that person may come around. Even if the person never reciprocates your attempts to connect, God is pleased that you tried and you are a better person for it.

Other people in your life can be a real joy and bring such encouragement. In truth, relationships are the ultimate facet to life. Other things will pass away but the love and caring we share with one another continues. Therefore, being good to others and receiving that good in return should be your absolute priority.

We were created to be social beings. Going it alone is rough. It is also very unwise. Being without support can lead to loneliness, depression, sickness and despair. God hard-wired you to love and to be loved by others. He demonstrated this phenomenon at the very beginning of our world when He gave Adam the gift of Eve.

Social support buffers you against the effects of stress. Friends can give you feedback and affirmation. They can help with your emotional stability through trust, caring, and nurture. They can help you with advice and suggestions. Finally, they can help you through acts of service and needed aid.[2]

We were made to serve together, work together, live together, celebrate one another's joys, and comfort one another in our sorrows.[3] A cornucopia of rewards spills over when we intimately share our lives with others. These include: a diminished effect of diseases, improvement of stress-related health problems, a decrease in the intensity of pain, an increased sense of self-worth, a decrease in helplessness and depression, and greater happiness and optimism.

Finally, relationships enhance feelings of joy, emotional resilience, and vigor.[4]

Chris Widener wrote an article entitled "Put Some Z.I.P. in Your Relationships." He points out that when relationships are at their best, Z.I.P. is present. "Z" stands for bringing Zest to your encounters. "I" stands for cultivating Intimacy in your interactions, and "P" stands for developing Purpose in your affiliations.[5]

It is fun to be with a zestful person. Exuberance often seems to rub off on others. If you have lost the zip in a relationship, try reintroducing the activities that glued you together in the first place.[6] It is worth the effort to make those special little gestures that can mean so much.

Are you cultivating intimacy in your relationships? Being intimate means taking your connection to a deeper level. Every relationship can move to a level that is satisfying and meaningful for both parties. We were made to have intimacy in our lives. It involves opening up to others. To be emotionally healthy we must know and be known by others. We must be willing to be vulnerable at our core.[7]

There is one important caveat to consider. Developing intimacy in a relationship takes place over time. It is important that you gradually get to know the other person well enough to decide he or she is trustworthy and safe. Certainly be willing to affiliate with everyone and reach out a hand of companionship, but choose your intimates carefully.

Relationships at their best have a common purpose, vision, and mission. This means that the people in the relationship want to accomplish something for each other but also for a greater good. Setting common goals with others is a great way to strengthen your bond. By putting some Z.I.P. in your friendships, you will, as Widener says, "see them strengthen in ways you never imagined!"[8]

Being able to manage ourselves and our relationships with others demonstrates emotional intelligence (EQ). Emotion is pure energy. Learning to harness that energy in a positive way ignites you to conquer untapped resources within yourself and others.[9]

APTITUDES FOR GROWTH; ATTITUDES FOR SUCCESS

The EQ framework is comprised of five aptitudes. The first is self-awareness and control. This is demonstrated when you function knowing yourself well enough to predict your reactions to situations. You act from your values and core beliefs. You are the master of your emotions.[10] The second aptitude is empathy. This is the ability to perceive how others are feeling from their viewpoint while remaining wholly apart.[11] This means that your thoughts and feelings do not become enmeshed with the other person's thoughts and feelings. If that were to happen, you would not be objective enough to be helpful to the other person.

The third aptitude is social expertness. It is the ability to build genuine relationships that allow caring, support, and concern to reign supreme in the friendship. The fourth aptitude, personal influence, is the ability to inspire others as well as to confront issues that could derail a relationship. The final aptitude is mastery of vision. It entails being aware of your own personal philosophy and being true to that—being genuinely yourself. It is being brave enough to articulate the passion, direction, and vision to get you where you want to go.[12]

Being able to articulate who you are and what you want is the gift of good communication. It is a simple concept, but it can also be one of the most complex of human endeavors. Basic strategies include being clear about what you want and don't want. Be specific rather than general. Don't assume you know what another person is feeling. Prevent and resolve one issue at a time. Be aware that timing is everything. When you have issues, argue ideas, not people. Set boundaries, and respect those of others. Make "I" statements rather than demeaning the other person with "you" statements.[13] For example, it is better to say, "I feel upset when you come home late" rather than, "You are terrible for coming home late."

Interacting socially is healthy and can increase your sense of joy and completeness. "Psychology research documents very few necessary or sufficient conditions for anything, but it looks like good social relationships may be a necessary condition for extreme happiness," said Christopher Peterson in *A Primer in Positive Psychology*.[14]

THE GIFT OF SUPPORT

Think of everything you would want in a friend and then try to be that for others. Be grateful for the special attitudes and aptitudes each of your friends has to offer. Maintain friendships with the people most supportive of you. This person may not be the most physically attractive, wealthiest, or brightest. However, if he or she truly cares about you, he or she will grow to be beautiful in your eyes and heart.

Examine your personal strengths and think about how you might best support others. Perhaps you can be a healing comfort to people who are going through something you have had to face in your own life. Perhaps you are good at cheering people up and getting them to laugh. Whatever you give of yourself in love will come back to you a thousand-fold.

Love is the highest of endeavors. Loving well and deeply is what makes us feel truly alive. Become a person who genuinely cares for others. Immerse yourself in the process of learning to love people authentically in ways that matter to them. Yes, it will benefit them. But it will also change you for the better.[15]

"Experiencing and giving love are signs of life to us—that we are here, that God is real, and that our lives matter," Townsend said.[16] So how is love effectively infused into your life? It can be learned. It is all about seeking and doing the best for other people. You can make acting in such a way as a core value by which you live your life.

This seeking and doing the best for others is simple but not easy. It is something that can grow through time and practice. You must keep practicing if you are to become your best self. This is only possible when you are a connected branch to the vine of Jesus Christ.

Like Jesus, we must love everyone, even the unlovely. We must care about each person based on the fact that he or she is a creation of God, not on how lovable he or she seems on the surface. In fact, when you love the unlovely, you are demonstrating love at its best. We must remember that we are all hopeless sinners without the grace of what Jesus did for us on the cross. Hence, as Townsend said, "No one deserves love, but everyone needs love."[17]

APTITUDES FOR GROWTH; ATTITUDES FOR SUCCESS

It is becoming clear just how important connecting with other human beings really is. The elements involved in connecting include your feelings, your dreams and desires, your fears and failures, your past, the other person, and your knowledge and experience of God in your life. "When you reach out and connect, you bring someone out of isolation, loneliness, fear, or detachment and into the world of relationship," Townsend said.[18]

Etta and Jerry are experts on giving the gift of support. They live near their son, Eric, and his wife, Anna. Eric has muscular dystrophy and Anna has bipolar disorder. Etta and Jerry are always doing things to make the kids' lives easier. They don't mind running to the store when Anna is down. They provide a lot of meals to make life easier. They are always available by phone and will be at Eric and Anna's house in five minutes if needed. Jerry works out with Eric three times a day with physical therapy, plus helps him with grooming and activities of daily living. Etta is always happy to listen to Anna's problems and patiently support her.

In addition, Etta and Jerry have two grandchildren that are the apples of their eyes. Etta watched Sasha when she was a baby and they became extremely close. Jerry played games with Sasha and kept her entertained. Sasha is now in the fourth grade and still completely attached to Etta and Jerry. She is an athlete and they would not think of missing one of her games. She comes over to their house to stay and play as much as possible. In fact, she camped out at her grandparents' home for the five last days of summer before school started.

Sasha has a little sister named Delia. She is one and a half years old and just as bright and sharp as her sister. With Jerry now retired, Etta can use his help as they watch Delia every day while her mom works. These people are unbelievable with the kids! They drop everything and play with Sasha and Delia the entire time they are around. They are the best entertainers in town. They are loving, caring supporters and their love holds the family together in a beautiful bond.

The simple truth is that you were created as a social being and you will never be able to flourish without deep and purposeful relationships in your life. You need other people. That need is a strength, not a weakness. It is only after that basic need has been satisfied in your life that you are able to help others satisfy their needs. It is impossible to be empathic with others if no one has ever been empathic with you.

Seek out people who will help you fulfill emotional need. Find someone who will validate and understand your feelings as you are experiencing them. All of us need to be understood. We also need to be able to receive care when it is offered. When you find time to both give and partake of support, you will find yourself growing and finding deep and satisfying meaning in your life. Resolve to nurture long-term commitments with your friends. You may never know until you get to heaven how much you helped another human being by reaching out in love.

When you profoundly care about another person, you will have the strength to confront that person when necessary. Be sure, however, that you approach the issue calmly and with love, not angrily or judgmentally. That is a lot to live up to, isn't it?

You will fail at times. It is inevitable, given our fallen natures. That's when a relationship needs to be very strong—so we can confess our faults to one another. We need to acknowledge our fundamental brokenness. As we share the naked truth about ourselves to another, or vice versa, healing can occur.

Part of the reality of life is that ultimately people must be free. You have to be courageous enough to be OK with the fact that someone may not be OK with you. That's when letting go in love is the kindest thing you can do. Life is not fair. That is why you must conduct yourself and your relationships in light of God's grace on you and every person in the world. You must trust God enough to let Him "help you let go of what you cannot keep."[19]

Whether it is time to express our need for affection or to abstain from doing so must be approached with prayer and God's guidance. Whichever is appropriate is the most loving. Truly loving behavior can change the world more than any other force.

Certainly by now it must be apparent that you need to interact with others if you are to be happy and healthy. Eminent positive psychologist Christopher Peterson said he could summarize positive psychology in three words: "Other people matter."[20]

Growth is fostered in the context of relationships. There is much need in your friendships, family, community, and the world for your loving presence. Remember, as Townsend said, "You cannot overestimate the value God places on love."[21]

CHAPTER 15

FRIENDSHIP: PEOPLE NEED PEOPLE

A friend loves at all times.

(Prov. 17:17 NKJV)

So this is my prayer: that your love will flourish and that you will not only love much but well. Learn to love appropriately. You need to use your head and test your feelings so that your love is sincere and intelligent, not sentimental gush. Live a lover's life, circumspect and exemplary, a life Jesus will be proud of: bountiful in fruits from the soul, making Jesus Christ attractive to all, getting everyone involved in the glory and praise of God.

(Phil.1:9–11 MESSAGE)

DO YOU REMEMBER the old classic hymn "What a Friend We Have in Jesus"? Jesus is our ultimate example of what it means to be a friend. He certainly fits the definition given in Proverbs 17:17—He loves us at all times. He loves everybody at all times. His nature is love, like that of His Father's.

Obviously, you and I cannot live up to Jesus' perfection in our endeavors to be a good friend. Paul, however, gave us a helpful blueprint to follow in the first chapter of Philippians. He wrote that love should flourish.

This is an interesting choice of words because one of positive psychology's major themes has to do with flourishing. It is associated with emotional vitality. People flourish when they are functioning positively in the private and social realms of their lives. "Far from being supermen or superwomen, flourishing individuals are truly living rather than merely existing," said Corey Keyes and Jonathan Haidt in *Flourishing: Positive Psychology and the Life Well-Lived*.[1]

To reap the full benefits of your journey through life, you need to be involved in all sorts of relationships. To be robust in health you need involvement in deep intimacy with a mature person who is able to give and receive love in a positive way. One true, good friend is to be highly valued.

One person's impact on a life can be immense. That is why there is a great need for mentoring of all kinds. You can form a bond with an older person who has wisdom from having lived a full life. You can also bond with a young person in need of direction.

You can invest in some people even if they really cannot reciprocate. You never know how a seed you planted might manifest.

To be at your best, you need a social network of all kinds of constructive affiliations. Reach out to people and find commonalities. We were not designed to be solitary islands. Just as a rope is made more effective by the interweaving of cords, so multiple cords of friendship give you a more vigorous mind and body.

Researchers are investigating the biochemical basis of love. They are paying special attention to the hormone-like substance oxytocin that the brain releases in response to social contact. "The fact that our biological bodies are designed to draw us to one another is a strong argument that social relationships are neither arbitrary nor merely convenient ways to obtain other things that matter—food, sex, power, whatever. Our biology teaches us that relationships in and of themselves matter," said Christopher Peterson in *A Primer in Positive Psychology*.[2]

God designed you to participate in friendships. When you are with good friends, you generally feel more self-assured. It is a pleasure to share their company. You might not always understand each other, but you are able to accept and appreciate one another just as you are.

Affinity, respect, and trust create the foundation upon which you can build a kinship. In a relationship between full-grown people, each person is allowed the space to change and develop. Each person is free to make his or her own decisions, and autonomy and mistakes are tolerated. Together, the two can overcome difficulties.

When you are in a close and good relationship, you know your confidentiality will be protected. Friendship is all about listening and sharing with one another. Friends celebrate each other's victories together and cry together over defeats.

A friend "lets you freely express your feelings and emotions without judging, teasing, or criticizing," said Mary Ellen Copeland in "Making and Keeping Friends: A Self-Help Guide."[3] Having the openness and flexibility to allow each other to feel what either is feeling in a safe and supportive environment is a priceless commodity, as is just being able to vent or toss around ideas about possible approaches to situations.

Giving advice is permissible in friendships as long as it is requested. Being a true friend means being there in the tough times and helping the other person through difficulties and challenges. Each of you should be able to reciprocate by giving help to each other as it is needed.

Copeland said it very nicely in her guide to making and keeping friends. A friend "accepts your self-defined limitations and helps you to remove them."[4] Wow, this friendship is powerful stuff! It is a necessary ingredient if you are to become all you were meant to be and to do with your life what you were meant to do.

Copeland explained that "friendship is a continuing source of bonding, releasing, and creating,"[5] both within yourself and with the other person. It can be, at its best, a dynamic and synergistic interchange that widens the scope of all involved.

Support and love are great aspects to friendship. It is joyous and intrinsically rewarding to express mutual admiration through greeting cards, gifts, hugs, and any other way we can demonstrate our caring.

Friendships can grow to a maximum when all involved are independent and self-sufficient. Being needy or co-dependent is not the best way to conduct a relationship. People who have these tendencies need experiences of being loved unconditionally to overcome their emotional handicaps. That way, the person can internalize the caring feelings given and can begin to reciprocate as well as become more capable of standing on his or her own two feet.

Friendships provide great support in crisis, but most of the time the relationship should be upbeat and warm. It is important to plan fun events together. Then, when the storms of life engulf you, you will not be alone.

Some factors can get in the way of a successful friendship. They are illness, distance, stress, overwork, fear, financial difficulties, and differences in expectations or extreme differences in taste.[6] However, if the participants are strong enough to continue engaging in the relationship and seeing it through, friendships can deepen by going through the crucible and coming out the other side together. Such relationships can become thriving friendships because of the ability of those involved to reach into themselves for the best inside while reaching out to the other for the best inside him or her.

As a Christian, you are to reach out and be a friend to everyone, just as Jesus is. Make having a relationship with Jesus Christ a very attractive option to everyone you encounter. As Philippians 1:9–11 teaches, an important part of your purpose is to get everyone involved in the glory and praise of God. How can you get everyone involved unless you take the time to have relationships with those who need Christ in their lives? "We are designed to enjoy an intimate relationship with God and are called by Christ into healthy relationship with others," says Jeff Wickwire in *Friendships: Avoiding the Ones that Hurt, Finding the Ones that Heal*.[7]

In his book on friendships, Wickwire describes "cleavers" as "those rare individuals who are there for the long haul, who do not find the exit door when you are down, shoot at you from the shadows when you have fallen hard, or inwardly rejoice at your misfortunes."[8] He goes on to say, "Those who cleave in love and loyalty carry a piece of God."[9]

Micah 6:8 admonishes, "He's already made it plain how to live, what to do, what God is looking for in men and women. It's quite simple: Do what is fair and just to your neighbor, be compassionate and loyal in your love, and don't take yourself too seriously—take God seriously" (MESSAGE).

John Winthrop and his fellows set out to survive in the harsh New World of the Massachusetts Bay Colony in 1630. He encouraged all to follow the counsel of Micah "to do justly, to love mercy and to walk humbly with our God." He added, "We must delight in each other ... rejoice together, mourn together, labor, and suffer together."[10]

Do you know God will treat you the way you treat others? Max Lucado said in one of his e-newsletters, "Are you aware that this is what you are saying to your Father? Give me what I give them. Grant me the same peace I grant others. Let me enjoy the same tolerance I offer."[11]

Referring back to this chapter's opening counsel from Philippians 1:9–11, you are to "live a lover's life, circumspect and exemplary." Don't you want to live your life by displaying the fruits of the Spirit in a way that would make Jesus proud of you?

Part of being circumspect means using caution in approaching relationships. As 1 Corinthians 15:33 explains, "Bad company corrupts good character" (NIV). Sometimes when you are at a lonely juncture of your life, you are more susceptible to the temptation to get involved with improper kinds of friends. "A wrong relationship is the enemy's smoothest point of entry into the life of the godly," Wickwire said.[12]

Red flags can signal a corrupting relationship. If you have to compromise your morals, watch out. If the relationship takes away from your relationship with God, beware. Finally, if friends and loved ones are warning you about a relationship, take heed.

Let's talk a little bit about people Wickwire labeled as "deceivers" and "leavers." We use the expression "the Judas kiss" to reflect betrayal and deception in a close relationship. After Judas sold out on Jesus and arrived with the guard to arrest Him, Judas greeted Jesus with a kiss. (See Mark 14:45.)

Judas Iscariot was one of Jesus' handpicked disciples. They walked from town to town together, ate together, and shared life experiences, but through it all Judas was plotting Jesus' death. He betrayed Jesus for thirty pieces of silver.

Has a deceiver given you "the Judas kiss" while pretending to be your friend? Wickwire said, "It is high-octane betrayal of the devastating kind when we lead someone's heart down the road of false promises and counterfeit feelings. The impact of this kind of deception on our well-being spikes the far end of the emotional Richter scale. Barring an inner healing from God, it carries the potential of life-long wounding."[13]

He continued, "In the presence of deep wounding, the choice is ours. We can choose to live in disillusionment, accepting the message of the wound, or move on to what God has planned."[14] Remember this: God saw what was done to you. Leave the justice to Him. Make a decision to forgive and move forward, and dare to risk friendship again. Jesus calls you to "fear not." He will never leave you.

Be assured that once you have invited Jesus into your life, the Holy Spirit will come to you and remain with you. This is not always true in our relationships with other people. For various reasons, there are times when "friends" desert friends. When things get too hard to take, some people make a fast getaway.

Perhaps part of the problem with leavers is they are so involved in themselves that they don't have the internal resources to help a friend who is in deep pain. Our culture and the media tend to lead people in a direction of thinking more and more about themselves and what they can do and possess rather than about caring about others. Wickwire said this creates a recipe for disaster. He goes on to explain, "A friendship is all about sharing, giving and sacrificing for the other. It is give and take, bend and bow, flex and flow. When selfish people are required to stretch, forgive or sacrifice, when their style is cramped and they become inconvenienced, they will leave in search of a less demanding pastures."[15]

It doesn't have to be that way in a relationship. Jesus showed us the perfect example of friendship. He made Himself a servant. Our glorious, majestic Lord bowed down to wash His disciples' feet to make the point that we should put other people's needs above our own. This is not easy, especially in today's culture. But when you think of what Christ did on the cross because He wanted to be our True Friend, you can force yourself to be more like Him and look for meaningful ways to serve others.

With optimism and hope, you can help in your own way to create a society that reflects Christian values. The challenge lies in changing your priorities. Positive psychology suggests, said Seligman, "A resurgence of traditional religion, volunteerism, or philanthropy would facilitate this change, so long as people do not ask what is in it for them."[16]

Western culture has often placed thoughts over feelings, but "the actual data of positive psychology imply just the opposite. Again and again, the heart trumps the head. We do not have friends and spouses because we 'think' they will benefit us. We have friends and spouses because we love them," Peterson said.[17]

Jesus said it is more blessed to give than receive. Scientific data indicates that giving support is more advantageous than getting it. Peterson explained, "In other words, it is not an equitable relationship that is rewarding but rather one in which a person can provide love and support, whether or not the score card comes out even."[18]

The fully engaged life of securely attached adults is about finding meaning and purpose through pouring one's life out for others. You can do this through parenting, mentoring, or helping elderly relatives. In addition, however, you need good friends. "Companionate love is the unshakable affection shared by two people whose lives have become intertwined," Peterson said.[19]

My adopted grandfather, James Lester, and I have been friends since the day I was born. He gave me my first toy, and took me to my first circus, my first rodeo, my first hunting and fishing expeditions, and my first baseball game. He always made time for me.

From the time I was three years old he would take me with him to Greenup, Kentucky, to visit his mom and brother. We always stayed a few days and had a great time. We could talk about anything and never missed an opportunity for fun and laughter.

In my college years I became quite opinionated. We would meet weekly for lunch and never fail to get into a big argument. But we loved each other and would not have thought of missing our lunch date. Sometimes we look back on those days of useless bickering and laugh. The thing was, we were together—the best of friends.

I became very ill at one point in my life. He was available to me anytime I called. At a minute's notice, I would call feeling poorly and he would drive from his home in Kentucky to Indiana to pick me up and take me for a long ride. Once when I was despondent I sat on a park bench and cried. He simply sat beside me and cried too.

James Lester is now eighty-five years old. He lives happily in an assisted living center and we talk daily. We love to reminisce about all the good times, all the years of smiles and laughter. People need people. My life could have never been complete or as special if I had not spent so much of it with my dear, dear friend.

That loveable old bear, Winnie the Pooh put it this way: "If you live to be a hundred, I want to live to be a hundred minus one day so I never have to live without you."

Interestingly, children as young as three or four years of age start using the word "friend" to refer to special peers in their lives.[20] As children grow older, they need to have close relationships with other people if they are to live "the good life." Other aspects of the good life include gratitude for the past and hope for the future. Also important are the opportunity to use talents and strengths in fulfilling pursuits.[21] (The next two chapters will elaborate on this.)

Positive psychologist Chris Peterson said, "Let me for the time-being forget utopia, and ask why we can't all just get along. It has been said that the primary lesson of the twentieth century is that there is no them, just us. The challenge of the twenty-first century is therefore to ask how we can all be us."[22]

I believe we should look to our ultimate source, the Bible, for direction. We find this direction in Hebrews 10:24–25: "Let's see how inventive we can be in encouraging love and helping out, not avoiding worshiping together as some do but spurring each other on, especially as we see the big Day approaching" (MESSAGE).

FRIENDSHIP: PEOPLE NEED PEOPLE

We do not know when, but we know that the big Day will arrive when Christ will return and take us up into the sky to be with Him in heaven. As his dear friends, He has assured us He has dwelling places ready for our arrival. In the meantime, let us solemnly take up the cross of reaching out to as many people as possible with the Good News that Christ will forgive us of our sins, cleanse us, and save us if we will only ask. While we work diligently to fulfill the Great Commission, let us remember that as Sefra Kobrin Pitzele wrote in *One More Day: Daily Meditations for People with Chronic Illness*, "we should cherish friendships and protect them as we would a newborn infant."[23]

PART 3
DISCOVERING AND EMBRACING YOUR CALLING

CHAPTER 16

DARING TO HONOR YOUR DEEPEST DESIRES

> So, my dear brothers, since future victory is sure, be strong and steady, always abounding in the Lord's work, for you know that nothing you do for the Lord is ever wasted as it would be if there were no resurrection.
>
> (1 Cor. 15:58)

IF RELATIONSHIPS ARE vital to a fulfilling life, meaningful work follows closely behind. For work to be satisfying and rewarding it has to be more than just a job; it must be a calling. You deserve to spend your time and energy doing the job for which God has equipped you. You have attributes and attitudes no one else has now or ever will have. When you were born, God created you with your own fingerprint and your own assignment. Over the years He has molded and fashioned you to be in just the right place at the right time to accomplish the work He has consecrated.

In 1 Corinthians Paul admonished us to be always abounding in the Lord's work. That sounds exciting, doesn't it? It is such an honor that the Lord would give each of us a special task to accomplish. He has included us in His creative endeavors. Each of us has a little part of the whole to contribute. How astounding that the work you and I do on this earth is vital to the unfolding of the universe as God has ordained it!

APTITUDES FOR GROWTH; ATTITUDES FOR SUCCESS

What does it mean to abound in our work for God? It means we are to be zestful and enthusiastic about our mission. It means we should wake up excited about the challenges that lie ahead. We can persevere in our work and diligently reach for the eternal prize that awaits us if we fully surrender our efforts to the Lord. By doing so, we have the honor of being partners with God in His beautiful plan. That plan is more glorious and more enthralling than we will ever be able to comprehend on this side of forever.

The Ultimate Designer has planted a seed in your heart that will come to fruition as you obey Him. He has placed your deepest desires for your special calling inside your spirit. In your innermost being, you and God have the same yearnings. The Father knows what is best for you and what vocation will make you happy. All you have to do is fully turn your life over to Him and then watch Him makes things happen!

Amazingly, we Christians know how the story is going to end. We will have absolute victory if only we will hearken to His still, small voice and never ever give up. No matter what happens to us, we know our risen Lord is coming back to gather us to Himself someday. Yes, He who arose on the third day is walking alongside us today. He takes notice of every unselfish work we do. If we do what He bids, we will reap a great reward.

Many rewards come to us in this present life, too, if we live in tune with what God has orchestrated. Dare to honor your deepest desires and fulfill your mission with a flourish. You have only one life, so make it the best it can be. This will satisfy you and glorify God.

Doesn't it make you tingle inside to think that you have an important part to play in how everything will culminate in the future? Doesn't that thought motivate you to try your very best in your given vocation? You can accomplish that goal by using your distinct strengths.

"Working in a way that takes advantage of our unique talents, abilities and interests means working with our strengths. Many people spend their whole lives working against their strengths—doing work not really suited to their innate abilities. The key is to find

DARING TO HONOR YOUR DEEPEST DESIRES

the work you were born to do—the work that takes full advantage of your special talents, interests and abilities," said Laurence Boldt in *How to Find the Work You Love*.[1]

It is sad to think of people clocking in and out of a job just to get a paycheck. They struggle and strain in a labor that does not recognize their potential. Determine not to be such a person. "To fail to express your own talents is not only to deny your individuality, but also to withhold from the world the special gifts that you possess," Boldt said.[2]

Don't worry that it might be selfish to follow a career path that is exciting and dynamic to you. Your zeal will make you more effective in your job and more helpful to all with whom you come into contact. According to Boldt, "To the extent that your work takes into account the needs of the world, it will be meaningful; to the extent that through it you express your unique talents, it will be joyful."[3]

Once you discover what your gifts and passions are, it is your duty to serve with excellence and diligence. You will be fulfilled only if you give everything you have inside you for the greater good. This will greatly benefit you, society, and God Himself. In fact, it will further the Lord's work.

There comes a point in life when a person truly becomes an adult. I believe that happens when the person understands for the first time that it truly is more blessed (and fulfilling) to give than to receive. This philosophy will shine through people who have matured to the point they truly care about others' welfare. In fact, such people make this desire to serve others a top priority.

"Somewhere along the line, we may have gotten the idea that life is for getting. We think that if we could just get more money or approval, more fame or love, everything would be terrific. As corny as it may sound, giving really is what it is all about. Tapping into your desire to give is the key to unlocking your own sense of purpose and to releasing your talents. It is the key, in other words, to finding the work you love," Boldt said.[4]

When you use your strengths over and over again, they will be sharpened to perfection. Marcus Buckingham and Donald Clifton, the authors of *Now, Discover Your Strengths,* define a strength as "consistent near perfect performance in an activity."[5]

There are three basic principles of living a strong life. First, for an activity to be a strength you must be able to do it with consistency. It must be a predictable part of your performance that you can replicate again and again. It would be something from which you derive intrinsic satisfaction. Second, you do not have to have strength in every aspect of your role to excel. Excellent performers are not usually well rounded but they are sharp. Third, thrivers find ways to manage their weaknesses, thereby freeing them up to hone their strengths to a sharper point.[6]

"Shift your focus. Suspend whatever interest you may have in weakness and instead explore the intricate detail of your strengths," say Buckingham and Clifton.[7] If you purchase a copy of *Now, Discover Your Strengths* you will receive a code. You can log on to the Internet and go to strengthsfinder.com. When you insert your ID code you can take an assessment that will give you a profile of your top five strengths.[8] The Gallup International Research and Education Center created this tool.

The StrengthFinder is composed of thirty-four themes. Some examples include communication, focus, input, learner, and woo. People strong in communication would entice people to listen to them by using word pictures to pique people's interest and inspire them to act.[9] If you have focus you have a clear destination.[10] If you are high in input you are inquisitive and like to collect things. Some people will collect words, others butterflies.[11] If you are a learner, you are energized by the steady and deliberate journey from ignorance to competence.[12] A person with woo enjoys the challenge of meeting new people and getting them to like them.[13]

I hope this brief overview of a few themes inspires you to find out what yours are. Once you know your strengths, you must decide how to put them into play in a way that gives you the greatest advantage. You do this by sculpting out a niche for yourself in which you feel fulfilled. This is how you will thrive and flourish.

Sadly, according to Gallup research, only 20 percent of employees working in large surveyed organizations felt they used their strengths daily. Surprisingly, the longer employees are with an organization and the higher they climb on the traditional career ladder, the less likely they are to strongly agree that they are playing to their strengths.[14]

This can be explained by two flawed assumptions operating in many organizations, say Buckingham and Clifton: "1. Each person can learn to be competent in almost anything. 2. Each person's greatest room for growth is in his or her areas of greatest weakness."[15]

These incorrect assumptions should be supplanted by the two assumptions that guide the world's best managers. They say: "1. Each person's talents are enduring and unique. 2. Each person's greatest room for growth is in the areas of his or her greatest strength."[16]

Take for example the life of wealthy investor Warren Buffet. His down-home style and simple tastes for Dairy Queen over fine restaurants belies the fact that he is one of the richest men in the world. Speaking to a group of students, he said, "If there is any difference between you and me, it may simply be that I get up every day and have a chance to do what I love to do, every day. If you want to learn anything from me, this is the best advice I can give you."[17] He reckons his success is due to his gift for carving out a role that plays to his unique strengths.

"Like the rest of us," say Buckingham and Clifton, "he responds to the world around him in distinct ways. The way he handles risk, the way he connects with other people, the way he makes his decisions, the way he derives satisfaction—none of these is random."[18] All of these attributes make up a stable pattern that family and friends have seen in him since his childhood.

"What makes Buffet special," they say, "is what he did with this pattern. First, he became aware of it. Many of us don't seem able to take even this step. Second, and most significant, he chose not to focus on reinforcing its weaker threads. Instead, he did the exact opposite: He identified its strongest threads, wove in education and experience, and built them into the dominating strengths we see today."[19]

Buffet has figured out something you can replicate. Begin by looking inside yourself to identify your strongest threads. Sharpen those talents with learning and practice. Then either find or create a role that uses those strengths every single day. When you do these things, you will grow in productivity, fulfillment, and success.[20]

"Sadly we too often put concerns about financial security ahead of our creative passion. Many people discover when they shake off their fears about money and commit themselves to doing work they truly love, they begin to experience a prosperity greater than they have ever known before," Boldt said.[21]

My husband is a *Star Wars* aficionado. He has seen it over fifty times. In fact, he created Super 8 movies in high school with similar themes. One of them won fifth place in a *Star Wars* fan club creativity contest. He believes a man named Ben Burtt dared to honor his deepest desires and so received a fantastic opportunity. Burtt had just graduated from the University of Southern California when George Lucas, who had graduated from USC earlier, hired him to do sound effects for *Star Wars*. By pursuing what really interested him, he became quite successful.

Have the courage to pursue a vocation that excites you. This will allow you to harness your specific aptitudes and attitudes to add to others' lives. By setting off confidently in this direction you will attract the knowledge, relationships, skills, and resources you need to succeed. As you step out in this way, don't be surprised if you get a sense that a loving and caring God is guiding your every step.

God knows you have the innate potential to make a great contribution to the world. That contribution can come in many different forms and fashions. Consider, for example, the work of Cole Porter.

Porter created many successful productions enjoyed by millions. His strength was the ability to chisel out the perfect lyric. Writing believable characters and plots, however, was not his forte. He took an aggressive and risky strategy that worked around his weaknesses, according to Buckingham and Clifton. "He bet that if he kept polishing his strengths as a songwriter, very soon the audience simply wouldn't care that his plots were weak and his characters stereotypical. His strengths would blind people to his weaknesses. Today, many would say that his strategy paid off. When you can write words and melodies as scintillating and sophisticated as his, it is almost irrelevant who is singing them or why."[22]

Maybe you are thinking you just don't have the abilities of a Warren Buffet or a Cole Porter. Could it be you have never figured out how to go inward to the fathomless part of you where your core talents meet with your deepest desires? Do you instead focus on useless worries or fantasies of what could go wrong? Do you always take the attitude that the worst possible scenario will be the one that comes true? If you are thinking in this distorted manner, how do you ever hope to tap into your God-given creativity?

"People wonder why they are so 'uncreative,' why it is that their own souls are not possessed with the fire of creative inspiration they have seen in the lives of others," Boldt said. "Human beings are naturally creative; yet to expect our imaginations to be constructively engaged while they are busy recycling a monotonous and wearisome round of worries and fantasies is surely asking too much."[23]

We live in a fast-paced world with pressures and deadlines and sometimes we get so busy putting out fires that we fail to realize we never wanted to be a fireman in the first place. Bombarded by media conveying violence and mindlessness, we begin to internalize fear and doubt. It is easy, then, for the mind to become worried about anything and everything.

"If my imagination is preoccupied with worries and silly fantasies," Boldt said, "how can I ever hear the voice of my true self calling me to a life of creative adventure? How can I ever know the kind of desire or creative passion that transcends fear? One whose soul is active is free to let her imagination wander in a creative quest. She is free to seek a vision of her destiny and, having found it, free to fix her attention on the creative visions she has seen."[24]

There is only one sure way to transcend the paralysis of fear and reach our full potential. That way is to turn our hearts and wills completely over to the care of Jesus Christ. He will protect us from all dangers. He can heal us from wounds and scars and the voices telling us we can never have what we want, that we are just not good enough. That is a lie! Jesus went to the cross for that very reason—so we might be saved, washed in His blood, and gain a new start. With Him at our side, we can begin to understand our place in God's family. It is a beloved place. It is a beautiful place. It is a safe place.

It is just such a place we can reach by trusting all our cares to Him. Then He will take us by the hand and lead us to fulfill every long-lost dream we have. For it is Jesus Himself who put the seed of those deep desires into our DNA.

A successful example of this is illustrated in *Now, Discover Your Strengths*. Pam D. is described as a director of health and human services for a very large county with a huge budget: "To succeed in this role you might think that Pam would need strengths such as a gift for thinking strategically or, at the very least, for a detailed analysis and planning. But although she understands the importance of both, neither comes close to the top of her strengths' list. In fact, two of the strongest threads in her pattern are a need to inject drama and passion into her employees and an impatience for action."[25]

Can you begin to have the courage to realize that you can build a successful career around your specific aptitudes and attitudes? You do not have to pigeonhole yourself into a job that brings you no pleasure of fulfillment. You, like Pam D., can succeed. How does she do it?

The book continues: "Her modus operandi is, first, to identify achievable goals where action can be taken today, and act; second, to seek opportunities to paint a picture for her thousands of employees of the overarching purpose of their work; and third, to give the formal strategic planning process to an outside consultant.... So far things are working beautifully. She has advanced on all fronts. She has succeeded in winning important service contracts away from the private sector. And she is having a blast."[26]

You, too, can find your personal calling and have a blast while making it happen. According to Boldt, "To creatively engage your life's work, you must not only believe in the human potential, you must also believe in yourself ... believing in yourself is called having 'high self-esteem' ... [which] can be defined by two little words: *I can*. As a practical matter, improving your self-esteem means expanding the scope and difficulty of activities to which you respond with the confident words 'I can.' I can create a way. I can learn. I can manage. I can communicate. I can concentrate. I can persist. I can be victorious."[27]

Victory is yours when you put your hand in Jesus' hand and say, "Today, with His help, I can!" Always remember to emphasize *His* help. Apart from Him, we can do nothing. In fact, God might be delaying His timing in giving you your breakthrough because you are not ready to handle it properly.

A problem can accompany success: the tendency to forget the source and purpose of the success. Success can sabotage the memories of the successful. As Max Lucado warns, "Kings of the mountain forget who carried them up the trail."[28]

He continues, "Success begets amnesia. Doesn't have to, however. God offers spiritual ginseng to help your memory. His prescription is simply, 'Know the purpose of success.' Why did God help you succeed? So you can make Him known. Why are you good at what you do? For your comfort? For your retirement? For your self-esteem? No. Deem these as bonuses, not as the reason. Why are you good at what you do? For God's sake. Your success is not about what you do. It's all about Him—His present and future glory."[29]

Make a lifelong commitment to your Maker. Trust His steady voice to lead you to fulfill His greatest desires for your life. Honor those desires. The contributions you made to the kingdom while serving here on earth will, in the end, be your greatest treasure.

CHAPTER 17

COMMITTING YOURSELF TO YOUR LIFE'S WORK

> For we are God's fellow workers; you are God's field, you are God's building. According to the grace of God which was given to me, as a wise master builder I have laid the foundation, and another builds on it. But let each one take heed how he builds on it. For no other foundation can anyone lay than that which is laid, which is Jesus Christ.
>
> (1 Cor. 3:9–11 NKJV)

ISN'T IT GRAND to realize God would elevate you and me to the status of fellow workers? This significant thought should motivate us to be utterly committed to the work to which God has called us.

Think about it—by His grace you have been given a spectacular type of talent with which to serve in your own special way. Now it is your turn to take the reins. The time is right to give all that you are. Use the totality of who you are to carry out your mandate. Lend every aspect of your life to this great and noble cause.

As you build, make sure Jesus is your sure foundation. Without His power and love you would be unable to construct anything of merit. It is His creative nature working though you that brings meaning and success to your endeavors. But this transformation can occur only if you approach your life's work with an attitude of excellence.

Your attitude has a tremendous effect on the magnitude of meaning and success God brings your way. "There are three ways to overhaul your attitude: 1. concentrate on your strengths; 2. don't try to be perfect; 3. stop negative mind-feeding," Helen Johnson says in *How Do I Love Me?*.[1]

Do you realize the best way to turn your attitude around is to focus on your strengths? "If you look at yourself and see what is right instead of what is wrong, that is the true mark of a healthy person," Johnson says.[2] It is not advisable to continually focus on your inadequacies. To forever view your weaknesses critically is both demoralizing and a waste of time. It is crucial to remember that everyone has limitations.

Ice skater Kristi Yamaguchi is a great example of overcoming limitations. She was born with clubfeet. She had to wear special shoes for many years. Johnson tells us: "By age six, the ice had become her second home and she has reached the top of the ladder in skating."[3]

Sandra Day O'Connor graduated with Great Distinction from Stanford but no one would hire a "lady lawyer." She was offered a legal secretary position. "But her attitude, determination, persistence, and intelligence led her to the height of her profession," Johnson says.[4] She went on to become a Supreme Court justice.

There are two types of people who have "anti-strength" attitudes that deter them from recognizing and using their strengths. These groups are the "deniers" and the "critical comparers." Deniers are unwilling to recognize or use their gifts. Once deniers realize they should gratefully nurture and exercise their skills and begin to do so, others around them validate the value of this new way of being.[5]

Critical comparers insist on comparing themselves to those who are better than they.[6] This is a foolish waste of time because God made each of us as unique as our fingerprints and loves each of us as we are. Isn't that a lovely thought? Hold on to it. Make it your own.

If you are a critical comparer, don't be so critical if you do not reach your top level every time. "This flagellating of oneself takes energy, energy that could be used for approving of their strengths. It exerts terrible pressure and can be a form of self-torture. This is no way to develop your potential," Johnson says.[7]

Choose to become neither a denier nor a critical comparer but an appreciator. "You can be the best you can be; nobody else can do that," she says. "The way to self-esteem is not to compare yourself to the experts in every area but to develop the potential that is yours alone. Your attitude will be: 'I'm going to give to the world the best me I can be!' And then appreciate your successes.... Find the things that you do well (compared to you) and build on these strengths. You have many talents and abilities; just start appreciating them."[8]

One way to appreciate yourself is to list the successes you have had in your life and then identify the strengths it took to accomplish these successes. Another is to get into the habit of giving yourself mental strokes each time you do something well. Also, at the end of the day, recall what you feel good about having done.[9]

Now let's talk about perfectionism. It can lead to procrastination and even paralysis. If you get caught in this trap, you begin to ruminate over past mistakes and constrict your activities and relationships. No matter what you do or do not do you will invariably make mistakes. Learn to accept yourself unconditionally as a worthy human being, regardless—no strings attached.[10]

We have talked about the importance of fully embracing your strengths as well as avoiding perfectionism. The third element in having a positive attitude is to stop negative mind-feeding. "By that," Johnson says, "I mean eliminate the catastrophic, illogical, self-defeating, negative thoughts you have about yourself."[11]

Learn how to do thought stopping. One of the fathers of behavior therapy, South African psychiatrist Joseph Wolpe helped people cure obsessive and unproductive perceptions through thought stopping. From his work, four steps emerged to help anyone develop a better attitude. Johnson describes them in her book: "1. Recognize that you are indulging in negative mind-feeding. 2. Ask yourself if that kind of talk is really productive for you. 3. Stop the counterproductive self-talk. 4. Replace it with reassuring or self-accepting statements."[12]

Do you think you could learn to be kinder to yourself? "One secret of gaining self-esteem is simply to make the decision to talk to yourself in the same way you would talk to a beloved friend who was upset," Johnson says.[13] Doing so can help you drop a lot of useless baggage and reach out for your full potential in the dawning days ahead.

Now that you have your attitude in check, let's talk about some practical steps you can take in seeking out your calling. To do this, you must set aside the strategies of the traditional job-hunt. I urge you instead to embrace what Richard Bolles, author of *What Color Is Your Parachute?*, terms the life-changing job hunt. Unlike the traditional desire to put bread on the table and get a job as quickly as possible, the life-changing method helps to infuse a mission into your life.[14]

To do the hunt right takes time and effort. You will need to do homework and research, and learn to make contacts to find your new career. Rather than looking for which places have job vacancies, find places you would like to work whether or not there are current vacancies. Find a place that appeals to you, where you believe you could grow. Then all you have to do is simply talk the company into creating a job there to match your skills and passions. "This intuitional search," Bolles says, "will require face-to-face meetings and learning about [yourself]. [You] will travel down a new path and at last, go after [your] dreams."[15]

The great advantage of the life-changing job-hunt is it prods you to do a lot of thinking. You need to think about who you are, what you want out of life, what you have to give to the world and what you want to accomplish with your life while you are here on earth. This process has the possibility of changing your life completely.[16]

When we search for a "dream job" we are seeking happiness. We want serenity in our work and our lives. This can occur when, as mentioned earlier, we have the right attitude. "Your attitude is the first and last thing everyone notices about you," Bolles says. "It creates the texture of your life. It has been said, 'What you have

COMMITTING YOURSELF TO YOUR LIFE'S WORK

is God's gift to you. How you use it is your gift to God.' It is also your gift to all those around you."[17]

Just as I noted in chapter 16, success comes from approaching any job with the attitude that it can be transformed. Think of Warren Buffet and how he became successful by majoring on his unique strengths. He had the guts and attitude to make a place for himself that was intrinsically rewarding. You, too, can have guts and a good attitude.

First of all, ponder what your strong transferable skills are. Then think about fields that fascinate you. Make a mental picture of your new career. Interview people, and share your picture. Note the responses. Figure out a way to talk to people who are already doing the kind of work you want to do.

Research organizations. Ask yourself what their biggest problems are. Figure out a way to help with those difficulties. Armed with research and tentative solutions, approach the person who has the power to actually give you a job. Use contacts to get you into that person's presence.[18] Then sit down with your potential boss and impress the heck out of him or her.

This life-changing job hunt asks you to step out and take big risks. The most important advice for you to remember is that the only thing that can make you lose the game is to lose your self-confidence. Know the odds you are working against so you can realistically appraise your progress. If one strategy doesn't work, realize you are free to try another strategy.[19]

Bolles encourages us with this: "Hold on to all of your dream. Most people don't find their heart's desire because they decide to pursue just half their dream—and consequently they hunt for it with only half their heart. If you decide to pursue your whole dream, your best dream, the one you would die to do, I guarantee you will hunt for it with all your heart. It is this passion which often is the difference between successful career-changers and unsuccessful ones."[20]

I have a friend named Anne who decided to follow her passion rather than retire. She is exceptionally skilled in math, and she loves

APTITUDES FOR GROWTH; ATTITUDES FOR SUCCESS

kids. She kicked around a lot of different job possibilities. All had some elements she liked, but somehow none of them seemed to fit.

When she was asked to tutor her granddaughter in geometry, she jumped at the chance to spend time with the youngster. My friend's tutoring helped so much that the girl's report card moved up two grades. Both were thrilled.

Anne noticed something. She enjoyed preparing for the lessons as much as delivering the lessons themselves. Her talents allowed her to move into a state of flow when she worked on the complex problems. She was so absorbed that the time just flew by without her losing concentration.

Her college degree in mathematics was quite helpful to her. Since she had somehow missed geometry, she bought the textbook used at her granddaughter's school and began to go through it systematically. In helping the girl, Anne had found what she loved to do: figure out knotty math problems and teach kids how to do the same.

She then had to make a decision. Did she want to work with a tutoring agency in the area? After thinking through her strengths and preferences, she decided to start her own business from home. In addition, she called around and found out what tutors were charging. She decided to charge the minimum-going rate so her work could be a calling. She would help children with difficulties in math and make it affordable for the parents struggling financially in a difficult economy.

Anne then decided to wait several months to start her business so she could systematically and thoroughly go through the geometry book used at her granddaughter's school. By doing so she would know what she was talking about. The icing on the cake is that word is spreading among the parents at Anne's granddaughter's school about Anne's excellent tutoring skills. Hence, she has not even needed to do any marketing to launch her new venture. People call her. She truly is an example of how to create a job one loves.

Sometimes we think we need big solutions to problems when small steps can carry a person huge distances. We need to leave the past behind and jump into an exciting life of living out our dream—whatever our special dream might be. Surely that dream includes Jesus. Well, guess what? He is in need of workers. Read Matthew 9:35–38:

> Jesus traveled around through all the cities and villages of that area, teaching in the Jewish synagogues and announcing the Good News about the Kingdom. And wherever he went he healed people of every sort of illness. And what pity he felt for the crowds that came, because their problems were so great and they didn't know what to do or where to go for help. They were like sheep without a shepherd. "The harvest is so great, and the workers are so few," he told his disciples, "so pray to the one in charge of the harvesting, and ask him to recruit more workers for his harvest fields."

Consider yourself recruited!

PART 4

EMPOWERED BY OUR TRIUNE GOD

CHAPTER 18

THE HOLY SPIRIT: SOURCE OF SELF-CONTROL

> But when the Holy Spirit controls our lives he will produce this kind of fruit in us: love, joy, peace, patience, kindness, goodness, faithfulness, gentleness and self control.
>
> (Gal. 5:22–23)

THESE VERSES FROM Galatians have always been among my favorites. When I first came across these beautiful words, I wistfully dreamed of someday possessing each attribute. The words sounded lovely and desirable, but far off from where I was. Oh, how I wanted to be loving, joyful, peaceful, patient, kind, good, faithful, gentle, and self-controlled!

I went wrong for many, many years because I tried to be "good enough" in my own power. I desired to be a faithful Christian, but there were times when I despaired of ever being a person I could respect.

Finally one day I realized I had been ignoring the most important part of those verses. They did not say, "One day you will wake up and be able to bear this fruit." Not at all! The verses very clearly said that when the Holy Spirit controls our lives, He produces this wonderful fruit within us.

This fruit is fully available to me as a great sinner if only I believe in Jesus Christ as my Savior. I am never going to be "good enough." That is why Jesus went to the cross—to pay my ransom. I can look in the mirror and respect myself not because of my own merits, but because Christ cancelled the debt of my sins when He died and rose again. After He ascended, He sent the Comforter, the Holy Spirit, to dwell in us and make us all that we should be.

Zechariah 4:6 says, "'Not by might, nor by power, but by My Spirit,' says the Lord of hosts" (NKJV). Give yourself fully to God and you will begin the greatest adventure you have ever had.

Over time as I have studied the Word, I have joyfully embraced the truth that I need to put my trust in God's capabilities rather than my own. He is the only one who is perfect. I can make good grades in school and volunteer time to help others, but unless I lay down the control of my life to the Holy Spirit, there will be no spark of inspiration, no sign of true life.

It is possible to get off the rollercoaster of pride and shame. Obsessing over the record of how we have performed is foolhardy. When we have done well, successfully using a God-given gift adroitly, do we give all the praise and credit to the Creator, or do we have a tendency to puff up in pride, thinking better of ourselves than we ought? Conversely, when we look back at our mistakes and failures, do we become so ashamed that paralysis and breakdown follow, or do we accept the sweet forgiveness Christ is always waiting to give us?

We can avoid the two poles of pride and shame not by relying on the self but by relying on Jesus and all He is capable of doing in our lives. He said, "Without Me you can do nothing" (John 15:5 NKJV). "Letting go and letting God" is not just some trite cliché—it is shorthand for a way of living that brings peace, contentment, and balance into our lives.

In Galatians 5:16–17 the apostle Paul exhorted, "I advise you to obey only the Holy Spirit's instructions. He will tell you where to go and what to do, and then you won't always be doing the wrong things your evil nature wants you to. For we naturally love to do evil things that are just the opposite from the things that the Holy Spirit

THE HOLY SPIRIT: SOURCE OF SELF-CONTROL

tells us to do; and the good things we want to do when the Spirit has his way with us are just the opposite of our natural desires."

We do not achieve self-control by gritting our teeth and forcing progress. Each of the positive attributes, such as self-control, is a fruit. Fruit takes time to develop. An apple tree does not instantly produce apples. As seasons pass, the tree grows and fruit occurs naturally. That is because God created a living, growing world. The supernatural Creator is so glorious that He fashioned our earth with natural processes by which trees bear fruit and the seasons change from winter to summer. We, too, can bear fruit during the seasons of our lives if we will give His Holy Spirit complete freedom to work within us. After all, He designed us. He alone holds the perfect instruction manual for bringing to fruition all He desires our lives to be.

One small increment at a time, our self-control will mature as we continue to follow God's guidance. It is the Holy Spirit's job to produce the fruit of self-control in our lives. It is our job to stay dependent on the Holy Spirit:

> Do you want more and more of God's kindness and peace? Then learn to know him better and better. For as you know him better, he will give you, through his great power, everything you need for living a truly good life. He even shares his own glory and his own goodness with us. And by that same mighty power he has given us all the other rich and wonderful blessings he promised; for instance, the promise to save us from the lust and rottenness all around us and to give us his own character. But to obtain these gifts, you need more than faith; you must also work hard to be good, and even that is not enough. For then you must learn to know God better and discover what he wants you to do. Next, learn to put aside your own desires [self-control] so that you will become patient and godly, gladly letting God have his way with you. This will make possible the next step, which is for you to enjoy other people and to like them, and finally you will grow to love them deeply.
>
> (2 Peter 1:2–7)

We achieve self-control by getting closer and closer to God. If we seek Him, we will find Him. One step at a time, He will give us His character. This includes self-control.

Many practical ideas abound on how to work toward greater self-control. It can be helpful to set a simple but regular schedule with achievable goals that increase gradually in difficulty. Creating an exercise plan and eating healthfully are some of the best ways to take control of your life. In addition, journaling is one of the greatest gifts you can give yourself—you get to sort out your issues with greater clarity, which can increase your sense of peacefulness and positive self-esteem.

We need to refresh our spiritual selves at regular and frequent intervals. Search the Bible on various topics that are relevant to your current situation. You can use a concordance to look up the word that describes the area with which you are struggling (i.e., faith, joy, self-control, etc.). In the concordance, you will find a list of all the verses in the Bible that refer to that topic.

When you find verses that speak to you, write them down and turn to them daily. Work toward memorizing those verses. Speak them aloud. You will be amazed in times of trouble how the memorized verses will bubble up in your mind, giving you the ability to deal with tough situations more effectively.

As you gain greater control over yourself, you can think ahead to prevent problems. Avoiding thoughts, feelings, and situations that upset you can improve the level of calm with which you operate throughout your daily life. Some typical problem areas might be mismanaging money, acting out in anger or violence, unbalanced eating habits, shopaholic practices, indiscriminate sex, quitting jobs or school, and/or making poor decisions without thinking things through.

We want to control our impulses rather than letting them control us. We must deal with our feelings effectively to avoid frustration, anger, abusiveness, aggression, explosiveness, and unpredictable behavior.

Take a personal inventory. Do you look before you leap? Is impatience an issue for you? How do you react when drivers cut

THE HOLY SPIRIT: SOURCE OF SELF-CONTROL

you off? Do you have a reputation for being a hothead? Have you thrown objects out of a sense of frustration? Have you struck someone in anger?

How can you proceed effectively when you are overwhelmed by emotion?

Instead of letting the stress of intense feelings overwhelm and control you, move into the coping and problem-solving mode. Putting your problems on paper is very helpful in clarifying the situation in which you find yourself. Write down the problem and brainstorm as many solutions as possible.

Develop some scripts for tough times. Sometimes it can be helpful to buy some time in order to regain your composure when emotions are running wild. You can always respond to a stressful situation by saying, "I'd like some time to think about that," or, "I'm not in a good place to respond right now."

One of the secrets of people who exhibit a lot of self-control is the ability to distract oneself away from the frustrating situation. If you can distract yourself for twenty minutes, the part of your brain called the amygdala will work to get you back to a balanced state of equilibrium. Another good strategy is to make an effort to be as objective as possible about the situation.

Objectivity is not influenced by emotions, but rather bases judgment on fact and the reality of the situation. It is basing responses on facts and not on feelings. When tensions are running high, you can help stop yourself from being flooded or overwhelmed by your emotions by training yourself to be an objective observer. Objective observing is simply watching your overwhelming feelings as if you were watching someone in a movie in the particular situation.

James 1:19–20 advises: "Dear brothers, don't forget that it is best to listen much, speak little and not become angry, for anger doesn't make us good, as God demands that we must be."

Sometimes we can enhance our understanding by exploring various interpretations to a verse of scripture. Take Proverbs 12:16, for example. The *Living Bible* translation reads, "A fool is quick-tempered; a wise man stays cool when insulted." The King James version reads, "A fool's wrath is presently known; but a prudent man covereth shame." The *Amplified Bible* reads, "A fool's wrath is quickly and openly known, but a prudent man ignores an insult."

Notice how richly you can understand the verse by comparing translations. All of them refer to a fool. One version calls the fool quick-tempered, while the other two versions speak of the fool's wrath. One version says wrath is presently known while the other says it is quickly and openly known. Then the verses talk about a wise man or a prudent man. This man stays cool when insulted, according to one version, while the other versions say he covers shame or ignores an insult. Notice how the different wordings give us greater insight into this proverb and expand our understanding of self-control.

Peter talked about self-control as an element existing within a larger progression. Let's examine the New King James version of 2 Peter 1:5–11 (it is interesting to compare this scripture from the New King James to the same verse quoted in part earlier in this chapter from the *Living Bible*):

> But also for this very reason, giving all diligence, add to your faith virtue, to virtue knowledge, to knowledge self-control, to self-control perseverance, to perseverance godliness, to godliness brotherly kindness, and to brotherly kindness love. For if these things are yours and abound you will be neither barren nor unfruitful in the knowledge of our Lord Jesus Christ. For he who lacks these things is shortsighted, even to blindness, and has forgotten that he was cleansed from his old sins. Therefore, brethren, be even more diligent to make your call and election sure, for if you do these things you will never stumble; for so an entrance will be supplied to you abundantly into the everlasting kingdom of our Lord and Savior Jesus Christ.

The word *virtue* is often associated with Christ's character. We cannot in ourselves produce virtue. Instead, we must choose to obey the virtuous promptings of the Holy Spirit who lives within us. Practical wisdom is found in learning God's truth in the Scriptures and incorporating that learning into our everyday lives.

THE HOLY SPIRIT: SOURCE OF SELF-CONTROL

Self-control is the ability to take mastery over what formerly mastered us. Empowered with God's truth, we can develop perseverance. If we persevere, we will learn to fight discouragement or the temptation to quit. The secret of perseverance comes with comprehending the fact that all circumstances come from the hand of a loving Father who is in control of everything.

I grew up in Ebenezer Baptist Church. There were many older people who had a profound effect on my development. I have so many pleasant memories of climbing trees on Bode and Marion Love's farm with the stone house they had built themselves. I think of the gracious and intelligent Eloise Spencer who once gave me five dollars after I had put my whole childhood allowance of that amount into the offering. She said, "I want to teach you that when you give, you receive."

But by far my most poignant memory is of visiting Bob Downey as he was dying. I was a teenager riding by his house on a bike when I thought to stop in and see Bob because I had heard at church that he was not doing well at all. His wife, Louella, was not home but the lady taking care of him ushered me to his room. I have never experienced anything like what I saw before or since. He was not upset or disgruntled in any way. He was fully in control of himself. He was so near death he was actually glowing. I sat beside his bed and patted his hand. He looked up at me and mouthed, "I love you."

I did not stay long but the experience had a profound impact. It was as though the Holy Spirit was shining through him. As I thought back on it later, it almost seemed as though he was already halfway into heaven when I saw him. There is not a doubt in my mind that he is rejoicing with the Father today.

It is vital for us to be continually aware of God's presence in our lives. Every aspect of our lives is transformed when we place our lives in His hands, living not for ourselves, but for Him. This is godliness.

Brotherly kindness is closely related to godliness. If we are truly in tune with God, we will realize that love is the ultimate aim. Yes, we must love God with all our might, but we must also love other people as we love ourselves.

First John 4:20 says, "If someone says 'I love God,' and hates his brother, he is a liar" (NKJV). Self-control is developed as we practice patience and forgiveness with people. People, after all, are God's most beloved creation. We can love each person when we realize he or she is made in God's image.

Jesus taught us in John 15:12–17 that love involves serving one another, sharing with one another, and praying for one another. God's kind of love originates in His loving us first. God is love incarnate. We can love because we are from God and because He loved us first. Being a faithful Christian means we love each person with whom we come in contact. Further, it is seeking that person's good, even if we seem to gain nothing for ourselves.

With our hearts in harmony with God's way, we will bear much fruit. We will live the productive lives God foreordained us to lead. Self-control, then, is recognizing the eternal spiritual realities rather than getting caught up in earthly or material values. It is looking beyond this present life to the things of God, and remembering always the wonderful cleansing that inevitably results when we turn our lives completely over to the Holy Spirit.

Billy Graham completed a systematic study of what the Bible teaches about the person and work of the Holy Spirit. In his book *The Holy Spirit: Activating God's Power in Your Life,* Graham begins by pointing out that when Jesus left His followers, He gave them a promise. Jesus said, "Nevertheless I tell you the truth. It is to your advantage that I go away; for if I do not go away, the Helper will not come to you; but if I depart, I will send Him to you" (John 16:5–7 NKJV).

This promise was fulfilled at Pentecost. There was a rushing wind, and tongues of fire rested on each person. They all began to speak with other tongues. Acts 2:4 says "the Spirit gave them utterance" (NKJV).

Before the day of Pentecost, believers were instructed to ask God to give them the Holy Spirit. After the Pentecost, Peter told Christians to repent and receive the gift of the Holy Spirit (Acts 2:38). Graham says, "This is the good news: we are no longer living in a time of promise, but in the days of fulfillment."[1]

THE HOLY SPIRIT: SOURCE OF SELF-CONTROL

We know from the Bible that the Holy Spirit is not a force but a Person with intellect, emotions, and will. From various passages of Scripture in the New Testament, we learn that He speaks, intercedes, testifies, leads, commands, guides, and appoints, and He can be lied to, insulted, blasphemed, and grieved.[2]

The Bible also makes it clear that the Holy Spirit is God Himself. As God, He is all-knowing, everywhere present, and all-powerful. He is eternal—there was never a time when He did not exist.

One of the most magnificent things the Holy Spirit does is lift the veil that Satan puts over our minds. If we read and study the Word, the Holy Spirit illuminates our minds so we can understand the things of God.[3]

God Himself, in the person of the Holy Spirit, dwells within our very bodies. How reverently, then, we should care for our earthly bodies, as they are the Holy Spirit's temples.

The Holy Spirit also inspired the Scriptures. He guided the men who wrote the Bible. The Bible is the most important book ever written. It is the constant foundation for faith, conduct, and inspiration from which we should drink daily. We learn to abide in the Spirit through personal daily contact with the Word. The Word is alive and active. It has the power to change our lives dramatically.

The Bible tells us that when a person comes to Christ, the Holy Spirit has been deeply involved. The new Christian receives salvation and is "born again." Just as we have been born physically, we can be born again spiritually. First Peter 1:23 says, "For you have been born again not of seed which is perishable but imperishable, that is, through the living and enduring word of God" (NASB).

So why do we need spiritual rebirth? Graham points out that man's moral capacities lag far behind his technological advancements. Science and technology cannot change man's basic nature. Neither can economic restructuring. No amount of self-improvement or wishful thinking can make us "good enough." God, and only God, created us. He alone is able to recreate us. He does this the moment we give our lives to Christ. Jesus said, "Therefore, if anyone is in Christ, he is a new creature; old things have passed away; behold, all things have become new" (2 Cor. 5:17 NKJV).

Oh, so marvelous and mysterious is this process! The Holy Spirit can make all things new in our lives. He can regenerate us. He can renew our minds. He can help us let the past go and move forward toward eternity with joy and thanksgiving.

Hebrews 9:14 says, "How much more shall the blood of Christ, who through the eternal Spirit offered Himself without spot to God, cleanse your conscience from dead works to serve the living God?" (NKJV).

Graham notes, "God the Holy Spirit can take the humblest preaching or the feeblest words of our witness to Christ, and transform them by His power into a convicting word in the lives of others."[4]

God the Holy Spirit can equip and enable us to make a difference in this world. In fact, every believer has been given at least one gift from the Holy Spirit. We must not fail to recognize, cultivate, and fully use the gifts God has given us. You have strengths the world desperately needs. Yes, you! Study, think, and pray about the positive attributes and attitudes the Holy Spirit has placed in you. One sign of a strength is that you really enjoy using it, that when you are using this gift things just seem to flow. Time passes and you hardly notice because you are so enjoying being involved in the activity.

Usually we get into flow when the task is neither too boring nor too difficult. If we can get into the correct alignment for a task that is both doable and challenging, we can enjoy the process in the same way an Olympic athlete approaches her training. Csikszentmihalyi wrote a groundbreaking book on this topic in 1990 entitled *Flow: The Psychology of Optimal Experience.*[5]

When we are born again, incalculably significant results flow into our lives. But understand the Holy Spirit will not strive with man forever. If you do not turn your life over to Christ, there is danger you will go beyond the point of no return. Your heart can become so hardened by sin that you are unable to hear the Spirit's voice. I pray you never allow this to happen to you. Be very sober in your understanding of refusing Christ. Turn to Him and make Him your life. He is the only true source of life. Repent and leave your sins behind.

THE HOLY SPIRIT: SOURCE OF SELF-CONTROL

When you choose to accept Jesus Christ as your personal Savior, your new birth will bring about big changes in your life. Your relationships with God, your family, your neighbors, and yourself will improve as you live the obedient believer's life. The Holy Spirit will reshape and remold you so your disposition, affections, aims, principles, and dimensions are transformed.[6] It is only through the Holy Spirit's power that you can reach your full potential.

No matter what Satan tries to accuse you of, he cannot overcome the power of the written Word of God, nor stop the Spirit's quiet work on your heart. Miraculously, the Holy Spirit seals you as a believer so nothing can touch you. You are separated and set apart as belonging to the Lord.

More thrilling even than that, when the Holy Spirit enters your life, He lives with you in fellowship. He gives you a sample here on Earth of what you will inherit when you get to heaven.

The Holy Spirit, then, seals you with His presence. God gives you security and declares His ownership over you. The Holy Spirit's presence in your life is the pledge that God will fulfill all He has promised you in His Word. The Holy Spirit also witnesses within you, assuring you of the reality that Jesus Christ has saved you.

As the Holy Spirit begins to work with you, He sensitizes your conscience to the sin in your life. You awaken and begin to desire to be free and clean from sin before God. Everything about life has changed.

As your relationship with God deepens, the Holy Spirit makes you keenly aware of your heart's evil desires. This conviction is necessary to convince you of the complete need for Christ in your life. If you put your mind on Christ and work to obey the Holy Spirit, He brings your body back from the deadness of sin into life. If you are a Christian, the Holy Spirit will give you life and peace.

The Devil, however, is an implacable enemy. He continually tries to get you into a struggle with temptation. Fortunately, 1 John 4:4 teaches us, "Greater is He who is in you than he who is in the world." There will be a struggle to go back to your old tendencies but you can claim victory in Christ by the power of His Holy Spirit that lives within you (see Rom. 8:4).

Paul said nothing good dwelt in his flesh. This old nature will assert itself unless you make the decision to surrender your mind and body to the Holy Spirit every moment of every day. When you discover this for yourself and you decide to yield to the Holy Spirit's dictates, you can experience victory, spiritual maturity, love, joy, and peace as well as all the other fruits.

Paul discovered how to yield. It is the secret of presenting all your members and faculties as a living sacrifice, holy devoted and well pleasing to God, which is your reasonable service and spiritual worship (see Rom. 12:1). If you desire to have the Holy Spirit within you, you will not refuse to meet the conditions necessary for His indwelling. Then His presence will produce within you the overflowing rivers of blessings and abundant life. Through the Holy Spirit God will give you a supernatural strength equal to the tasks He has planned for you to achieve.

We are filled with the Holy Spirit for an important purpose—to spread God's Word and glorify Christ. The Holy Spirit does not draw attention to Himself, but to Christ. The test to affirm that the Holy Spirit is alive and active in you is if people see that Christ is becoming more and more evident in your life.

Be honest with yourself, however, if you desire the Holy Spirit's power. Make sure you can follow through and use that power. Do not ask for might in prayer unless you are going to pray. Do not ask for strength to witness unless you are going to witness. Do not ask for holiness unless you are attempting to live a holy life. Do not ask for the power to serve unless you are going to serve. Do not ask for grace in suffering unless you are willing to take up your cross.

Have you ever really told God that you want to fulfill His will, whatever that might be? Have you desired for God to take possession of your life absolutely and completely? Give your Lord and Master your entire life without reservation.

In Revelation 3:19–20, He said, "Therefore be zealous and repent. Behold, I stand at the door and knock. If anyone hears My voice and opens the door, I will come in to him and dine with him, and he with Me" (NKJV).

THE HOLY SPIRIT: SOURCE OF SELF-CONTROL

Graham says in his book, "Personally I find it helpful to begin each day by silently committing that day into God's hands. I thank Him that I belong to Him, and I thank Him that He knows what the day holds for me. I ask Him to take my life that day and use it for His glory. I ask Him to cleanse me from anything that would hinder His work in my life. And then I step out in faith, knowing that His Holy Spirit is filling me continually as I trust in Him and obey His Word."[7]

Prayer allows you to tap into God's power. Surrender yourself totally to God through a continuing conversation with Him. Then the Holy Spirit's wonder-working power will make your life and witness an overwhelming force. There you will find purity, safety, and certainty.

Be careful not to extinguish the Spirit's love as He seeks to carry out His purpose for your life. You can quench the Spirit if you fail to pray, witness, or read God's Word. Stir up your soul to use the grace that reigns within you.

An anonymous source wrote, "Resist not His incoming; grieve not His indwelling; quench not His outgoing. Open to Him as the Incomer; please Him as the Indweller; obey Him as the Outgoer in His testimony of the things concerning Christ, whether through yourself or others."

Did you know God expects you to be fruitful? Jesus compared our relationship with Him to the branches of a vine. He is the vine. You are a branch. Abide in Him and let Him abide in you. In this way, you can have an intimate relationship with Christ. Nothing should come between the two of you.

V.R. Edman said in his book *They Found the Secret*: "Such indeed is the abiding life that draws its sustenance and strength from the Vine. By the refreshing and reviving flow of the Holy Spirit through that life there is prayer that prevails, preaching that is powerful, love that is contagious, joy that overflows, and peace that passes understanding. It is the adoration that is stillness to know God for one's self. It is the obedience that does the Savior's bidding in the light of the Word. It is the fruitfulness that arises spontaneously from abiding in the Vine."[8]

Are you as inspired by these words as I am? They make me realize just how glorious the rewards are for living life in harmony with the Holy Spirit. I want to be grafted into all he is talking about—prevailing prayer, powerful preaching, contagious love, overflowing joy, and an incomprehensible peace that only the triune God can provide.

Unfortunately, we have an adversary who wants with all his might to stop us from realizing all of the God-given promises that are ours to claim. Graham says, "We must constantly be aware that Satan can take any human effort and twist it to serve his own purposes, but he cannot touch the spirit that is covered by the blood of Christ and rooted deep in the Holy Spirit."[9]

Oh, how we must sing praises to God for the Spirit's protection! He shields us from Satan's darts and allows us to live safely under the strongest of supernatural protection. Though the Devil may try to assault us in any way he can, we can grow in faith and in the ability to stand victoriously through our bond with the indwelling Holy Spirit.

Charles Stanley said in *Living in the Power of the Holy Spirit*, "The more mature we are in our faith and the more intimate our relationship with our heavenly Father, the more dependent we must be on the Holy Spirit."[10]

He also said, "We must choose to be filled with the Holy Spirit each and every day. Every day, ask the Holy Spirit to fill your life anew with His life-giving, joy-producing, comforting, guiding, renewing presence. Every day, ask the Holy Spirit to fill you anew with His love, His peace, His truth. Every day, ask the Holy Spirit to fill you to overflowing with His compassion for others…. Being filled with the Holy Spirit is something we must seek every day of our lives."[11]

His mercies are new every day, but we must seek Him every day for a fresh indwelling and strengthening. It is by His strength within us that we are able to display self-control.

As we come to the end of this chapter, let's think just for a moment more about what self-control really is.

THE HOLY SPIRIT: SOURCE OF SELF-CONTROL

Self-control is the ability to "anticipate future contingencies and to reflect on one's capability to cope with them. These capacities for forethought and self-reflection underpin a most central aspect of personality functioning, namely, people's ability's to exert intentional influence over, or to 'self-regulate' their experiences and actions. The capacity for self-regulation rests on a number of distinct component processes. These include the abilities to evaluate one's action in relation to internalized standards of performance, to plan and to set goals for the future, to assess one's personal efficacy for upcoming challenges, and to motivate one's action through affective self-evaluation," say Caprara and Cervone in *A Psychology of Human Strengths; Fundamental Questions and Future Directions for a Positive Psychology*.[12]

Self-control is a strength and virtue worth pursuing. It is an aptitude that will help you grow and an attitude that will lead you to success. Once self-control becomes more viable in your life, you'll start to realize how good it feels, which will train your mind into wanting to use it more and more.

Demonstrating self-control is a lifelong process that takes daily practice. It is an empowering process that can make your life more fulfilling. It can equip you to thrive and flourish.

As Stanley said in his book, "Only God knows the full agenda He has established for you. And only God knows the richness of the rewards that He has set aside for you both now and in eternity."[13]

CHAPTER 19

JESUS: HOPE IN A MANGER, HOPE ON A CROSS

Christ in your hearts is your only hope of glory.

(Col. 1:27)

DO YOU HAVE a positive expectation about your future? Do you anticipate what is to come with pleasure and confidence? If your answer is a resounding yes, you are one of the blessed people who possess the character strength of hope.

Some of us are not so fortunate. This life can be a trial. Past hurts and rejections can scar us emotionally and make us fearful and worried about what will happen next. However, God doesn't want us to live discouraged, defeated, and hopeless. That kind of life is filled with negative strongholds that need to be demolished.

God has a good plan for your life. Your task is to push beyond the fear, pain, and doubt and grasp hope with open hands and an open heart. Fill that heart with the person of Jesus Christ. He is ultimately our only hope. Only by living in Him can we reach a state of glory where we can live out the loving, faithful, and vibrant future He has planned for us.

Hope can transform your life. It can help you wake up in the morning singing the praises of the Creator. Can you envision yourself warbling a robust rendition of *Something Good Is Going to Happen* every morning in the shower? Would you be willing to try it?

God inhabits His praises, you know. That's why hope is so intertwined with giving God praise. When you praise Him for what He is doing in your life, He wants to give you even more. That is the hope of glory that can be yours if you will believe that blessings are on their way to you from a loving and caring Father.

Embracing hope means letting go of the hurts in the past and believing that God can transform every aspect of your life if you surrender completely to His sovereign will. In your own power, you can do nothing. However, with Christ in your heart nothing can stop you!

"He Who began a good work in you will continue until the day of Jesus Christ [right up to the time of His return], developing [that good work] and perfecting and bringing it to full completion in you" (Phil. 1:6 AMP).

What a promise lies within those words! When you gave your life to Jesus, He began a good work in you. He is in the ongoing process of developing and perfecting that work until He makes you into all He wants you to be. If you submit to His will, you can enjoy inner transformation through the Holy Spirit until finally you grow into the image of Christ Himself.

Only an awesome God could do something so spectacular. Isn't it amazing the care and concern He gives to each of us, though we are lowly sinners? It flows from His being out of love for us. He is love. He cannot act any other way. You can be secure in His love for you. You can make that truth the foundation of your life.

"Because we are followers of Christ, our confidence in unstable times lies in an unchanging God who provides steady anchors of faith and assurance," said Charles Stanley in *Living the Extraordinary Life*.[1]

Through faith in Christ, we have access to God's favor. We can stand firmly and safely on that grace God so generously provides. Romans 5:2 exhorts: "Let us rejoice and exult in our hope of experiencing and enjoying the glory of God" (AMP).

JESUS: HOPE IN A MANGER, HOPE ON A CROSS

You can be changed from glory to glory if you trust the triune God to create peace and joy within your heart. If you have accepted Jesus as your Savior, you can know with complete certainty that you are headed for the unspeakable glory of living in heaven eternally. It is hard to comprehend such an amazing fact, but the truth is that someday you will see Jesus face to face. Sweet ecstasy!

It is only through what Christ has done that we are able someday to go to heaven. This is the biggest thrill of all—Jesus paid our sin debt on the cross and was resurrected on the third day. No other religion can claim that its leader did something so miraculous.

But there is more Good News. If you cooperate with God, He will begin your transformation from glory to glory while you still live on earth in this life. You can grow closer and closer to Jesus by praising Him, reading about Him in His Word, and praying to Him about your needs and most heartfelt dreams. You can experience that transformation now.

You have much to be hopeful for in both the next life and this one. Believe that your future can be different from your broken past. Place all the bits and pieces into His competent hands. "Such hope never disappoints or deludes or shames us, for God's love has been poured out in our hearts through the Holy Spirit Who has been given to us" (Rom. 5:5 AMP).

God's love never ends or changes. He offers you hope at every turn if you only will trust and obey Him. With His help, you can reach the goals that contain your deepest hopes and aspirations. Though you feel insecure and fearful at times, God offers you a fulfilled and blessed life. When you surrender to Him, He does for you what you cannot do for yourself. He offers you peace, power, and wholeness.

His power dwells within you. "God created each one of us in the brilliant image of His Son, Jesus Christ," Stanley said, "and His power exists within us; we have only to move out of the way and let our Master bring it forth."[2]

The degree of success you will have in becoming Christ-like depends on where you put your focus. Does breakthrough come when you fix your mind on the things of this world? Certainly not!

Does peace enter your heart when you are needy and clingy toward others rather than depending on the only firm foundation, Jesus Christ? The answer is absolutely no. Does fixing your mind on yourself and all your problems or even on all your little successes bring joy? Again, no! There is only one way to live successfully. That way is a life focused above all else on our Savior.

Join now with Paul in saying, "I have been crucified with Christ [in Him I have shared His crucifixion]; it is no longer I who live, but Christ (the Messiah) lives in me; and the life I now live in the body I live by faith in (by adherence to and reliance on and complete trust in) the Son of God, Who loved me and gave Himself up for me" (Gal. 2:20 AMP).

Jesus is our hope. He has plans for us. These plans are positive and truly give us a future and a hope (see Jer. 29:11). Jesus, Lord of lords, acquiesced to come to planet Earth and be born in a lowly manger so you and I would have a future and a hope. He perspired great drops of blood and hung on a cross so we could possess that future and that hope. What amazing love! What miraculous saving grace!

And because He was willing to carry out this great sacrifice, you and I can be completely and utterly changed and made whole. When you sincerely give your life to Christ, what you have done in the past becomes irrelevant. "If anyone is in Christ, he is a new creature; the old things passed away; behold, new things have come" (2 Cor. 5:17 NASB).

This truth can be hard to grasp. Sometimes we have the tendency to examine and reexamine our filthy rags of sin, shame, and hurt. We mourn our great inadequacy. This is where focus becomes so critical. Are you going to continue to focus on all the guilt and shame of your past or are you going to gaze into the face of the One who loves you unconditionally?

If you are willing to believe it and receive it, the sins of all your yesterdays are gone. If you have asked for forgiveness, whatever you did is thrown into the sea of forgetfulness. God no longer can remember those sins. All He can see is the beautiful indwelling of the Holy Spirit He sent to abide in your heart.

JESUS: HOPE IN A MANGER, HOPE ON A CROSS

When you become fully aware the Holy Spirit lives in you, you can grasp the truth that you are a totally new creation. You possess the righteousness of God through Christ Jesus. Don't turn back and try to make sense of the miasma and heartaches you brought upon yourself. Choose life! Choose healing. Acknowledge Christ's presence in you now and trust that He holds your future in His loving hands.

When you understand and completely claim the depth of love He has for you and what an important purpose He has planned for your life, you will have the strength to completely trust Christ to make His home inside you. He promised, "Behold, I stand at the door, and knock: if any man hear my voice, and open the door, I will come in to him, and will sup with him, and he with me" (Rev. 3:20 KJV).

As you become conformed to His image, you will begin to live out your divine purpose—to give away His love to the world. Throughout the Gospels Jesus gave away His love to anyone who desired it. We, no less, must take up our cross and love a world in which hurting and suffering people need a caring heart's healing attention. You can be that heart—the heart through which the love of Jesus beats.

We do not become complete through obeying rules and regulations. We are saved only by believing in Jesus Christ. But a wondrous transition takes place when we fully believe—we become partakers of His divine nature. This miraculous fact means the old sin nature is unplugged and becomes inactive. Then, paradoxically, the moral laws we could not in and of ourselves meet now become doable because the Holy Spirit reigns completely within.

You do not have to depend completely on your own aptitudes and attitudes. It is Christ in you who accomplishes things (see Phil. 4:13). Apart from Christ, you can do nothing (see John 15:5). When you allow Christ's mind to further and further penetrate your own, your attitude will become one of absolute confidence in Him. When you display that kind of fruit, God soon will respond by showing you how to apply your gifts.

APTITUDES FOR GROWTH; ATTITUDES FOR SUCCESS

Galatians 5:22–23 clearly identifies the fruit you will display if you are one with the mind of Christ: "But the fruit of the Spirit is love, joy, peace, longsuffering, kindness, goodness, faithfulness, gentleness, self-control" (NKJV). These are areas of growth that you could work on for the rest of your earthly life. With time and practice you can help to drop them inside the deepest recesses of your soul.

As you earnestly work on developing your fruit, Jesus will help you discern what your gifts are and how to apply them to bring profit to the body of Christ and also to unbelievers. A diversity of gifts is given to believers just as the human body has a diversity of parts. We have eyes, ears, arms, legs, and brains, yet they all are a part of one body. There is unity among the parts.

There is also unity among the diversity of gifts the Creator endows to His followers. Paul put it this way: "There are diversities of gifts, but the same Spirit. There are differences of ministries, but the same Lord" (1 Cor. 12:4–5 NKJV).

It is by our Lord's graciousness that you are able to display your fruit and your gifts. But you have to exercise your hope muscles that through faith you can have the expectation that you can contribute something of value through the power of the Holy Spirit dwelling within.

In order to contribute you must have honorable goals. Hope is the catalyst that assures you your God-given goals are achievable. You must believe that God has planted determination inside you so you can achieve your goals and your purpose. You must also clasp on to the assurance that you can make plans and successfully achieve them because of the Almighty's beneficent generosity. And so, you can pursue your goals with zest and a peaceful heart realizing God will always make a way where there is no way.

Augusta had always dreamed of a career in the opera. She had trained for it and it was her life passion. A throat operation, however, put her dreams of being a star to an end. But Augusta was resilient. After an initial grieving period, Augusta decided to get training at a local technical school as a licensed practical nurse. She began to work as a nurse and as she did she took classes until she became an RN. After this accomplishment she became a traveling nurse and worked all over the United States for three- to five-month increments at places such as Stanford and Los Angeles. Just recently she obtained a post teaching beginning students how to become LPNs. Augusta is now quite happy with her life and thankful for the way everything turned out. She had the hope that if things didn't turn out the way she had planned that life might hold something even better in store.

Hope, like zest, gratitude and love, is a character strength robustly associated with life satisfaction.[3] Satisfaction is not found in fleeting pleasures or self-absorption but in earnestly aspiring to be used by God. There are many rewards for living such a life.

Deuteronomy 33:25 explains the concept of the rewards of living an obedient life: "Your castles and strongholds shall have bars of iron and bronze, and as your day, so shall your strength, your rest and security, be" (AMP).

The Devil is our adversary, and he is very real. That is why we need to protect ourselves by denying him entrance into our minds and hearts. We must use attributes such as hope to protect our dwellings, as if secured by bars of iron and bronze. Then we can feel strong, calm, and protected.

Ephesians 6:13–18 tells just how to achieve this protection: "So use every piece of God's armor to resist the enemy whenever he attacks, and when it is all over, you will still be standing up. But to do this, you will need the strong belt of truth and the breastplate of God's approval. Wear shoes that are able to speed you on as you preach the Good News of peace with God. In every battle you will need faith as your shield to stop the fiery arrows aimed at you by Satan. And you will need the helmet of salvation and the sword of the Spirit—which is the Word of God. Pray all the time. Ask God for anything in line with the Holy Spirit's wishes. Plead with him, reminding him of your needs, and keep praying earnestly for all Christians everywhere."

If you are to live with the hope of Christ in this dark and fallen world, you must use the complete array of God's armor to protect you. The strong belt of truth can be placed around you as you spiritually grasp that which is ultimately good, beautiful, and true. The breastplate of God's approval is placed on you as you obey all He imparts to you and love Him with all your heart.

You can lace up your shoes of peace by sharing the Good News with others. Hold up the shield of faith so you can repel Satan's poisoned arrows as he aims to destroy your mortal soul. You are gifted with your helmet when you receive salvation by believing Jesus Christ died for your sins and rose again victorious.

Finally, confidently wield your sword of the Spirit, God's Word. As you meditate on Bible verses that bring you comfort and hope, you will find yourself becoming stronger, happier, and more in control of your own life. Paradoxically, when you turn your entire self over to Jesus, He helps you by giving you the fruit of self-control. This invigorates you to feel good about yourself and the work you are doing.

Hope is a beautiful thing. It allows you to look to the future with a positive expectation. You can trust that God has a good plan for your life. When you get in line with His will, you will be on an anointed adventure of growth and enjoyment. Hope gives you the heart to recognize your aptitudes and attitudes and the strength to use them totally in the service of the Person of Jesus Christ.

CHAPTER 20

GOD: AN EVERLASTING LOVE

Finally, brethren, farewell. Become complete. Be of good comfort, be of one mind, live in peace: and the God of love and peace will be with you.

(2 Cor. 13:11 NKJV)

YOU HAVE PERSEVERED in completing this book. (Nehemiah would be proud of you.) We have examined the strengths of great Bible characters. I hope you have gained a greater knowledge and appreciation of your own strengths. It is my wish that you have learned how to move beyond surviving to a state of thriving. I pray you have grasped the great adventure that awaits you as you grow your relationship with God.

We have discussed the importance of social support, of living in community. You can think outside the box and be creative with your friendships and mentoring. Anything that works for you is good, whether that means attending a church group, connecting over lunch, conversing by phone, or exchanging e-mail messages. The main thing is that you connect deeply with a core group of fellow Christians.

This book also encouraged you to ponder your calling and purpose in God's plan for you. If you make the effort to persevere until you have found the work you truly love, you will be rewarded with a lifetime of meaning and joy.

Finally, I pray you have been empowered to think of all the glorious benefits of having an intimate relationship with the triune God. This last chapter can help you draw closer to God the Father. We can explore all the gifts and favor He is waiting to shower on you if you only will give Him first place in your heart.

We have viewed all of these ideas through the lens of positive psychology. Positive psychology is a recent branch of psychology that scientifically studies the virtues and strengths that enable individuals and communities to thrive.[1] It entails looking back on your life with overriding feelings of well-being and satisfaction. It is about embracing joy, flow, and happiness in the present. It is, as well, about looking toward your future with optimism, hope, and faith.[2]

All the strengths and virtues that individuals and communities need are accessible through one source: a loving God. First and foremost, we need a God who loves us. It is amazing and miraculous to realize there is a Great Designer of everything and He embodies love. It was in love that He created us.

How amazing that God would care enough about us, as insignificant as we are, to consider us His beloved children. We have the privilege of calling Him "Abba," which translates as "Daddy."

God cares about us with a great passion. He knows the number of hairs on your head, and He knew you before you were being formed in your mother's womb.

God has a good plan for your life if you will only listen to the still, small voice. When you believe Jesus died for your sins and you trust in Him as your Savior, the Holy Spirit will dwell within you. You are an empty vessel until God pours His very self into you and gives you eternal life.

You never can do anything that will make God withdraw His love from you. He patiently awaits the return of each prodigal son. The prodigal represents all of us at one time or another. He wants to welcome you into His loving arms and be involved in every aspect of your life if only you will throw open the doors of your heart to Him.

In *Knit Together*, Debbie Macomber put it this way: "He wants our time. He wants our love, and He wants our hearts. He wants our best in everything we do, but, bottom line, He wants our availability."[3] She also said He wants to show us our passions and our calling so we can pursue those things with gusto! He created us to dream big and follow those dreams. We need to follow our dreams and our purpose because that brings God much glory.[4] He created us for success, and we should enjoy each little success as we make our journey toward eternity with Him.

And so we must put Him first in our lives. We must place Him at the pinnacle of our devotion. We must give Him our allegiance before we give it to our family, friends, or vocation. He wants to be number one in our lives and He deserves to be. He is the only one who truly can fill our souls with peace and love. Every moment you spend with God is the greatest gift you can give yourself. It will also help you with other people because His loves spills out to others when you are filled with Him to overflowing.

One of the primary ways to connect with God is through His Word. The Bible can help us to be hopeful and optimistic. Reading it can plant seeds from God within us so we might ignite our strengths and values to bring honor and reverence to His name.

Our Creator crafted you for worship. Worship is the time spent talking with and listening to our Lord. Worship is primarily a response to God. He always desires to initiate a relationship with you. He reached out to all humankind in love and grace when He sent Jesus into our world to save us. "When we worship God we recognize who He is and what He does; we honor Him," Macomber said.[5]

In the intimacy of talking with Him, do not share only your heart; give your whole day to Him. Ask Him what He wants you to do and how you can best use the time He has given you.

Prayer is a discipline necessary for effective worship. When you pray on a regular basis to the Father, it can become a spiritual muscle memory just like the muscle memory created once you learn to ride a bicycle.[6]

APTITUDES FOR GROWTH; ATTITUDES FOR SUCCESS

Prayer energizes your faith to dream dreams and take risks. It helps you learn to trust in God and wait on His timing. It can unleash an all-consuming love for the Maker. Let yourself be driven to the Word by your need to hear from God. Through prayer, God can give you specific direction for now and for the future. Prayer releases God's supernatural power in your life by kindling the Holy Spirit within you.

Prayer entails several elements. You can glorify God by adoring and reverencing Him. You can praise God in gratitude for all that is good in your life. You can pray for the needs of friends and family. You can intercede for strangers in other parts of the world who are hurting. You can ask God to be with our government officials. Finally, you can pray for direction for your own life. Ask Him to bless you with ideas on how to live. Ask for the knowledge and wisdom to carry out your special calling. He will answer.

It is important to spend time every day with God. I suggest you start with a small goal. Take the time to read a little of the Word. Obtain a good Christian book. Write a small prayer list and voice it aloud to Him every day. As you get into the process, you probably will be energized to increase the amount of time you spend in these inspiring activities.

Such activities point you in an outward looking direction. When you are fed spiritually then it is your turn to go out and feed others. It doesn't have to be some great and fantastic act to show someone you care.

Recently, a woman at my mother's church gave several women some very nice watches to give away as they felt led to do so. The watches were placed in lovely gift bags with a card from the church telling the recipient that Jesus loved her.

The church's senior citizens periodically take trips to Butler State Park in Kentucky for a lovely buffet overlooking the park. They finish by visiting a nearby discount mall for bargains. Stella was on such an excursion when she decided to give a watch to a clerk at the discount mall. She did not think too much about it.

Several months passed and the group took another trip to the park and outlet mall. Jeri, another member of the church, happened

GOD: AN EVERLASTING LOVE

to talk with the clerk at the discount mall to whom Stella had given the watch. The clerk recognized the church's name and started to cry. She explained, "I had really been needing a watch but I didn't tell anyone but God. I never even mentioned it to my husband. Then this lady from your church came in here and gave me this watch. Isn't it the most beautiful thing you have ever seen?"

We never know this side of heaven what reverberations and impact a simple loving act might have on the people we encounter in our day-to-day lives.

Loving other people is one of the most important endeavors you will ever undertake. We are told in the Great Commission, "Therefore go and make disciples of all nations, baptizing them in the name of the Father and of the Son and of the Holy Spirit, and teaching them to obey everything I have commanded you. And surely I am with you always, to the very end of the age" (Matt. 28:19–20 NIV).

We were hardwired by humans to love and be loved. This is a natural outflow from following the Greatest Commandment of all. The commandment Jesus called the most important one was to love God:

> A teacher of the law asked Jesus, "Of all the commandments, which is the most important?"
>
> "The most important one," answered Jesus, "is this: 'Hear, O Israel, the Lord our God, the Lord is one. Love the Lord your God with all your heart and with all your soul and with all your mind and with all your strength.'"
>
> (Mark 12:28–30 NIV)

Yes, loving God is the most fantastic thing we can ever do. However, our most fervent devotion pales when we consider how deep, wide, and great God's love is for us. He is the alpha and omega, the beginning and the end. His love for us will never end.

Notice that Jesus said the Lord is one. God is one and at the same time triune. If you believe in His Son, Jesus Christ, you will be saved. He is preparing a home for you in heaven. If Jesus has saved you, the Holy Spirit resides in your heart; He will dwell there always.

There is no sting to death when we think of how magnificent it will be to love God face to face. We will be like Him, and we will see Him as He is. This everlasting love story will continue throughout all eternity. Praise the Lord for His most excellent benevolence and mercy upon us.

ENDNOTES

Chapter 1

[1] Authentic Happiness website, ed. Martin Seligman (Pennsylvania: University of Pennsylvania, 2006), www.authentichappiness.com (accessed September 11, 2008).
[2] Claudia Wallace, "The New Science of Happiness," *Time*, January 2005, A6.
[3] International Positive Psychology Association website, pres. Ed Diener (Pennsylvania: University of Pennsylvania, 2007), www.ippanetwork.org (accessed September 11, 2008).
[4] Martin Seligman and Mihaly Csikszentmihalyi, "Positive Psychology: An Introduction," *American Psychologist* 55, no. 1 (2000): 5.
[5] Ibid., 6.
[6] Shane Lopez, "The Emergence of Positive Psychology: The Building of a Field of Dreams," *APAGS Newsletter* 12, no.2 (2000).
[7] Ibid.
[8] Ibid.
[9] Martin Seligman, *Learned Optimism* (New York: Pocket Books, 1990), 10.
[10] Ibid., 8–10.

[11]*Google,* s.v. "Learned Helplessness," www.noogenesis.com/malama/discouragement/helplessness.html (accessed September 11, 2008).

[12]Paul Pearsall, *The Beethoven Factor: The New Positive Psychology of Hardiness, Happiness, Healing, and Hope* (Canada: Hampton Roads, 2003), xi.

[13]Ibid.

[14]Wallace, A6.

[15]Martin Seligman, *Authentic Happiness: Using the New Positive Psychology to Realize Your Potential for Lasting Fulfillment* (New York: Free Press, 2002), xiv.

[16]Wallace, A6.

[17]*Google,* s.v. "Quotes by Joseph Campbell," www.goodreads.com/author/quotes/20105Joseph_Campbell.html (accessed April 9, 2010).

Chapter 2

[1]Rick Renner, *Sparkling Gems from the Greek* (Tulsa, OK: Teach All Nations, 2003), 65.

[2]Joel Osteen, *Become a Better You,* as excerpted in *Enjoying Everyday Life Magazine,* January 2008, 24.

[3]Kenneth Pargament and Annette Mahoney, "Spirituality: Discovering and Conserving the Sacred," in *Handbook of Positive Psychology,* ed. C.R. Snyder and Shane Lopez, 646–659 (USA, Oxford University Press, 2002), 646–7.

[4]Christopher Peterson and Nansook Park, "Classification and Measurement of Character Strengths: Implications for Practice," in *Positive Psychology in Practice,* ed. P. Alex Linley and Stephen Joseph, 433–446 (USA, Wiley, 2004), 438.

[5]Ibid.

[6]Pargament, 646.

[7]Pargament, 647.

[8]Ibid., 648.

[9]Ibid., 648.

[10] William Bennett, *The Book of Virtues* (New York: Simon and Schuster, 1993), 741.
[11] David Meyers, "Human Connections and the Good Life: Balancing Individuality and Community in Public Policy," in *Positive Psychology in Practice*, 641–657 (see note 5), 642.
[12] Pargament, 648.
[13] Ibid., 650.
[14] Ibid., 651.
[15] Ibid., 651.
[16] Ibid., 653.
[17] Ibid., 655.
[18] Ibid., 655.
[19] R. Coles, *The Spiritual Lives of Children* (Boston: Houghton Mifflin, 1990), 141–2.
[20] Emily Dickenson, "I Never Saw a Moor," in *The Book of Virtues* (see note 11), 753.
[21] Pargament, 654.

Chapter 3

[1] Lisa Aspinwall and Ursula Staudinger, "A Psychology of Human Strengths; Some Central Issues of an Emerging Field," in *A Psychology of Human Strengths: Fundamental Questions and Future Directions for a Positive Psychology*, ed. Lisa Aspinwall and Ursula Staudnigner, 9–22 (Washington D.C., APA, 2003), 16.
[2] Ibid.
[3] Charles Carver and Michael Scheier, "Three Human Strengths" in *A Psychology of Human Strengths; Fundamental Questions and Future Directions for a Positive Psychology*, 87–102 (see note 1), 89.
[4] Penelope Green, "This Is Your Brain on Happiness," *The Oprah Magazine*, 9, no.3 (2008), 230.
[5] Gabrielle Leblanc, "5 Things Happy People Do," 233–235 (see note 4), 234.
[6] Ibid.
[7] Ibid., 235.
[8] Ibid., 235.

[9]Ibid., 235.

[10]C.W. Metcalf and Roma Felible, *Lighten Up: Survival Skills for People Under Pressure* (Cambridge, Mass.: Perseus Books, 1992), 6–7.

[11]*Google*, s.v. "Red Skelton quotes," thinkexist.com/quotation/live_by_this_credo-have_a_little_laugh_at_life/338308.html (accessed April 9, 2010).

[12]Martin Seligman, *Learned Optimism* (New York: Pocket Books, 1990), 10.

[13]Ibid., 16.

[14]Ibid., 208.

[15]Ibid., 173.

[16]Daniel Gilbert, *Stumbling on Happiness* (New York: Alfred A. Knopf, 2006), 162.

[17]William James, *The Varieties of Religious Experience* (New York: New American Library, 1958), 107.

[18]*Google* s.v. "Dietrich Bonhoeffer quotes," http://thinkexist.com/quotes/dietrich_bonhoeffer/2.html (Accessed April 9, 2010).

Chapter 4

[1]Martin Seligman, *Authentic Happiness: Using the New Positive Psychology to Realize Your Potential for Lasting Fulfillment* (New York: Free Press, 2002) 75.

[2]Ibid., 78.

[3]*Archaeological Study Bible, New International Version.* (Michigan: Zondervan, 2005), 67.

[4]Ibid., 3.

[5]Joyce Meyer, "Following Forgiveness Instead of Emotions," *Enjoying Everyday Living* 22, no. 5 (2008), 1.

[6]Ibid., 5.

[7]Ibid., 1.

[8]Ibid., 7.

[9]Ibid., 7.

[10]Joyce Meyer, *Conflict-free Living* (U.S.A.: Charisma House, 2008), 97.

ENDNOTES

[11] Ibid., 108.
[12] Frank Fincham and Todd Kashdan, "Facilitating Forgiveness: Developing Group and Community Interventions," in *Positive Psychology in Practice*, ed. P. Alex Linley and Stephen Joseph, 433-446 (USA, Wiley, 2004), 617.
[13] Ibid., 618.
[14] Ibid., 619.
[15] Ibid., 619–20.
[16] Ibid., 621–22.
[17] Ibid., 623.
[18] Ibid., 623.
[19] Ibid., 629.
[20] Ibid., 631.

Chapter 5

[1] Aristotle, *Nicomachean Ethics* as quoted in William Bennett, *The Book of Virtues* (New York: Simon and Schuster, 1993), 441.
[2] Beth Moore, *A Heart Like His: Intimate Reflections on the Life of David* (Nashville: Broadman and Holman, 2003), 11.
[3] Christopher Peterson and Nansook Park, "Classification and Measurement of Character Strengths: Implications for Practice," in *Positive Psychology in Practice*, ed. P. Alex Linley and Stephen Joseph, 433–446 (USA, Wiley, 2004), 437.
[4] Moore, 53.
[5] Peterson, 437.
[6] Moore, 59.
[7] Peterson, 437.
[8] Moore, 65.
[9] Ibid., 64.
[10] Dieter Frey, Eva Jonas, and Tobias Greitemeyer, "Intervention as a Major Tool of a Psychology of Human Strengths: Examples from Organizational Change and Innovation," in *A Psychology of Human Strengths: Fundamental Questions and Future Directions for a Positive Psychology*, ed. Lisa Aspinwall and Ursula Staudinger,

149–64 (Washington D.C., American Psychological Assocation, 2003), 158.

[11] Ibid, 156.
[12] Moore, 81.
[13] Ibid., 103.
[14] Ibid., 169.
[15] Ibid., 108.
[16] Ibid., 109.
[17] Ibid., 114.
[18] Ibid., 120.
[19] Ibid., 122.
[20] Ibid., 170.
[21] Ibid., 177.
[22] Ibid., 178.
[23] Martin Seligman and Christopher Peterson, "Positive Clinical Psychology," in *A Psychology of Human Strengths,* 305–317 (see note 6), 314.
[24] Moore, 199.
[25] Ibid., 206.
[26] Ibid., 214.
[27] Ibid., 224.
[28] Ibid., 256.
[29] Martin Seligman, *Authentic Happiness: Using the New Positive Psychology to Realize Your Potential for Lasting Fulfillment* (New York: Free Press, 2002), 145.
[30] Dan Baker and Cathy Greenberg, *What Happy Women Know: How New Findings in Positive Psychology Can Change Women's Lives for the Better* (USA: Rodale), 38–42.
[31] Seligman, *Authentic Happiness,* 146.
[32] Ibid., 147.
[33] "'Hurricane' Antigua Was a Pioneer for the Globetrotters," *The Cat's Pause,* August 2009, 5.
[34] "Remarkable Career Truly a Long Shot," *The Cat's Pause,* August 2009, 19.
[35] Tal Ben-Shahar, *Happier: Learn the Secrets to Daily Joy and Lasting Fulfillment* (New York: McGraw Hill, 2007), 100–101.

Chapter 6

[1] Martin Seligman, *Authentic Happiness: Using the New Positive Psychology to Realize Your Potential for Lasting Fulfillment* (New York: Free Press, 2002), 146.
[2] Martin Seligman, *Learned Optimism* (New York: Pocket Books, 1990), 101.
[3] Ibid.
[4] John Maxwell, *The 21 Indispensable Qualities of a Leader: Becoming the Person Others Will Want to Follow* (Nashville: Thomas Nelson, 1999), xi.
[5] Seligman, *Authentic Happiness*, 182.
[6] Jeanne Nakamura and Mihaly Csikszentmihalyi, "The Concept of Flow," in *Handbook of Positive Psychology*, ed. C.R. Snyder and Shane Lopez, 89–105 (USA, Oxford, 2002), 95–6.
[7] Charles Swindoll, *Hand Me Another Brick* (New York: Bantam Books, 1986), 17.
[8] Ibid., 13.
[9] Ibid., 9.
[10] Robert Emmons, "Personal Goals, Life Meaning, and Virtue: Wellspring of a Positive Life," in *Flourishing: Positive Psychology and the Life Well-Lived*, ed. Corey Keyes and Jonathan Haidt, 105–128 (Washington DC, APA, 2003) 123.
[11] Swindoll, 20.
[12] Ibid., 26.
[13] Ibid., 29.
[14] Ibid., 33.
[15] Seligman, *Learned Optimism*, 255.
[16] Seligman, *Authentic Happiness*, 246.
[17] Swindoll, 3.
[18] Vic Johnson, "Simply Solving the Puzzle," *Your Achievement Ezine* 327 (2007) www.ezine@yoursuccessstore.com (accessed September 5, 2007).
[19] Seligman, *Learned Optimism*, 104.
[20] Swindoll, 84.
[21] Ibid., 107.
[22] Ibid., 106.

[23] Martin Seligman, "Positive Psychology, Positive Prevention, and Positive Therapy," in *Handbook of Positive Psychology*, 3–9 (see note 6), 3.

[24] Swindoll, p.113.

[25] Nakamura, 93.

[26] Ken Blanchard and Phil Hodges, *The Servant Leader: Transforming Your Heart, Head, Hands and Habits* (Nashville: Countryman, 2003) 49.

[27] Charles Carver and Michael Scheier, "Three Human Strengths" in *A Psychology of Human Strengths: Fundamental Questions and Future Directions for a Positive Psychology* ed. Lisa Aspinwall and Ursula Staudinger, 87–102 (Washington DC, APA, 2003) 88.

[28] Ibid., 89.

[29] Joyce Meyer, *A Leader in the Making: Essentials to Being a Leader After God's Own Heart* (Tulsa: Harrison House, 2001), 245.

Chapter 7

[1] Mark Brazee, *31 Days of Healing* (Tulsa: Harrison House, 2003), 25.

[2] Ibid.

[3] Ibid., 26–27.

[4] Stephen Arterburn and David Stoop, eds., *The Life Recovery Bible* (Wheaton, Illinois: Tyndale, 1992), 591.

[5] Billy Graham, *The Holy Spirit: Activating God's Power in Your Life* (Nashville: Word Publishing), 259.

[6] Arterburn, 564.

[7] Wikipedia on the World Wide Web, (2008).

[8] Ibid.

[9] Ibid.

[10] Ibid.

[11] Jim Rohn, Patience, *Jim Rohn's Weekly E-zine* (accessed June 30, 2008).

[12] Mihaly Csikszentmihalyi and Jeanne Nakamura, "The Concept of Flow," in *Handbook of Positive Psychology*, eds., C.R. Snyder and Shane Lopez, 89–105 (USA: Oxford University Press, 2002) 95.

[13] Ibid.

[14] Ibid.
[15] Dan Baker and Cathy Greenburg, *What Happy Women Know* (USA: Rodale, 2007), xiii.
[16] Robert Emmons, "Personal Goals, Life Meaning, and Virtue: Wellsprings of a Positive Life," in *Flourishing: Positive Psychology and the Life Well-Lived*, eds., Corey Keyes and Jonathan Haidt, 105–128 (Washington D.C.: APA, 2003) 121.
[17] Ibid., 121–22.
[18] Charles Carver and Michael Scheier, "Three Human Strengths," in *A Psychology of Human Strengths: Fundamental Questions and Future Directions for a Positive Psychology*, eds., Lisa Aspinwall and Ursula Staudinger, 87–102 (Washington D.C.: APA, 2003) 88.
[19] Ibid., 89.
[20] Rick Renner, *Sparkling Gems from the Greek* (Tulsa: Teach All Nations, 2003) 641.

Chapter 8

[1] Jenifer Westphal quoted in Dan Baker and Cathy Greenburg, *What Happy Women Know* (USA: Rodale, 2007) 225.
[2] Ute Kunzmann, "Approaches to a Good Life: The Emotional-Motivational Side to Wisdom," in *Positive Psychology in Practice*, eds. P. Alex Lindley and Stephen Joseph, 504–517 (USA, Wiley, 2004) 504.
[3] Ibid., 511.
[4] Steven Scott, *The Richest Man Who Ever Lived: King Solomon's Secrets to Success, Wealth, and Happiness* (USA, Waterbrook Press, 2006) 2.
[5] Paul Baltes, Judith Gluck, and Ute Kunzmann, "Wisdom: Its Structure and Function in Regulating Successful Life Span Development," in *Handbook of Positive Psychology*, eds. C.R. Snyder and Shane Lopez, 327–347 (New York: Oxford Univeristy Press, 2002) 331.
[6] Ibid., 330, Table 24.
[7] Scott, 12.
[8] Ibid., 53.

[9]Ibid., 251.
[10]Ibid., 264.
[11]John Maxwell, "Lessons from Basketball's Greatest Coach," *Eric Musselman's Basketball Notebook*, emuss.blogspot.com (accessed July 29, 2008).

Chapter 9

[1]Dan Baker and Cathy Greenberg, *What Happy Women Know: How New Findings in Positive Psychology Can Change Women's Lives for the Better* (New York: Rodale, 2007), 13.
[2]Nancy Eisenberg and Vivian Ota Wang, "Toward a Positive Psychology: Social Developmental and Cultural Contributions," in *A Psychology of Human Strengths: Fundamental Questions and Future Directions for a Positive Psychology*, eds. Lisa Aspinwall and Ursula Staudnigner, 117–129 (Washington D.C., APA, 2003), 123.
[3]L. Quisumbing, "A Framework for Teacher Education Programmes in Asia and the Pacific," in *Korean Nation Commission for UNESCO's Education for International Understanding and Peace in Asia and the Pacific*, 108–120 (Bangkok, Thailand: UNESCO Principal Regional Office for Asia and the Pacific, 1999), 110–111.
[4]Google S.V. "Leo the Great Quotes and Quotations," http://www.famousquotesandauthors.com/authors/leo_the_great_quotes.html (Accessed April 24, 2010).

Chapter 10

[1]Edwin Locke, "Setting Goals for Life and Happiness," in *Handbook of Positive Psychology*, eds. C.R. Snyder and Shane Lopez, 299–312 (New York: Oxford, 2002), 305.
[2]Christopher Peterson and Nansook Park, "Classification and Measurement of Character Strengths: Implications for Practice," in *Positive Psychology in Practice* eds. P. Alex Linley and Stephen Joseph, 433–446 (USA: Wiley, 2004), 437.

ENDNOTES

[3]Martin Seligman, *Authentic Happiness: Using the New Positive Psychology to Realize Your Potential for Lasting Fulfillment* (New York: Free Press. 2002), 13.

Chapter 11

[1]Emmit Miller in M.J. Ryan, *Attitudes of Gratitude: How to Give and Receive Joy Every Day of Your Life* (New York: MFJ Books, 1999), 73.
[2]Giacomo Bono, Robert Emmons, and Michael McCullough, "Gratitude in Practice and the Practice of Gratitude," in *Positive Psychology in Practice*, eds P. Alex Linley and Stephen Joseph, 464–481 (USA: Wiley, 2004), 464.
[3]Ryan, 5.
[4]*Google* s.v. "Meister Eckart Quotes," http://www.brainyquote.com/quotes/authors/m/meister_eckhart.html (Accessed April 15, 2010).
[5]Chris Widener, "Attitudes of Successful Learners," *Chris Widener's Ezine*, Issue no. 83. Accessed March 26, 2008.
[6]Bono, 477.

Chapter 12

[1]Martin Seligman, *Authentic Happiness: Using the New Positive Psychology to Realize Your Potential for Lasting Fulfillment* (New York: Free Press, 2002), 13.
[2]Ibid., 43.
[3]Ibid., 35.
[4]Ibid., 41.
[5]Ibid., 59.

Chapter 13

[1]Bill Bright, *5 Steps to Christian Growth* (Peachtree City, Georgia: Campus Crusade for Christ, 2007) 16.
[2]Ibid., 17.
[3]Ibid., 20.

[4]Ibid., 28.
[5]Ibid., 41, 43.
[6]John Maxwell, *Your Roadmap for Success: You Can Get There from Here* (Nashville: Thomas Nelson, 2002) vii, 1, 5.
[7]Ibid., 11.
[8]Corey Keyes, "Promoting and Protecting Mental Health as Flourishing," *American Psychologist* 62, no. 2 (2007) 95.
[9]Corey Keyes, "Mental Illness and/or Mental Health? Investigating Axioms of the Complete State Model of Health," *Journal of Counseling and Clinical Psychology* 73 (2005) 541.
[10]Ibid.
[11]Ibid.
[12]Ibid.
[13]Ibid.
[14]Ibid.
[15]Ibid.
[16]Zig Ziglar, *Success for Dummies,* (New York: IDG books, 1998) 20.
[17]Ibid., 173.
[18]Ibid.
[19]Ibid., 174.
[20]Ibid., 81.
[21]Ibid., 299–304.
[22]George Vaillant, "Mental Health," *American Journal of Psychiatry* 160 (2003) 1377.
[23]Ibid.
[24]George Vaillant, "Love," *The Monthly Newsletter of the International Positive Psychology Association* 2, no. 2 (February 2009).
[25]Denis Waitley, "The Power of Positive Self-Expectancy: The Psychology of Winning," *Denis Waitley's Ezine* 123 (2009) www.ezine@deniswaitley.com (accessed February 11, 2009).
[26]Ibid.
[27]Barbara Fredrickson, e-mail interview by David Pollay, *The Monthly Newsletter of the International Positive Psychology Association* 2, no.2 (February 2009).
[28]Ibid.
[29]Maxwell, 18–19.

[30] Ibid., 34.
[31] Ibid., 36.
[32] Ibid., 48.
[33] Ibid., 104.
[34] Ibid., 80.
[35] Ibid., 120.
[36] Ibid., 121.
[37] Ibid., 156.
[38] Chris Peterson, *A Primer in Positive Psychology,* (USA: Oxford, 2006) 147–8.
[39] Ibid., 157.
[40] Ibid., 158–9.
[41] Ibid., 155.
[42] Maxwell, 39.

Chapter 14

[1] John Townsend, *Loving People: How to Love and Be Loved* (Nashville: Thomas Nelson, 2007), 195.
[2] Christopher Peterson, *A Primer in Positive Psychology* (USA: Oxford, 2006), 255.
[3] Debbie Macomber, *Knit Together* (New York: Faith Words, 2007), 213.
[4] Ibid., 199–200.
[5] Chris Widener, "Put Some Z.I.P. into Your Relationships," *Jim Rohn's Weekly Ezine* 483 (2009) www.ezine@jimrohn.com (accessed February 9, 2009).
[6] Ibid.
[7] Ibid.
[8] Ibid.
[9] Adele Lynn, *The Emotional Intelligence Activity Book* (New York: Amacom, 2002), 2–3.
[10] Ibid., 3.
[11] Ibid.
[12] Ibid., 4.

[13] Kathleen Crowley, *The Power of Procovery in Healing Mental Illness* (San Francisco: Kennedy Carlisle, 2000), 177–8.
[14] Peterson, 94.
[15] Townsend, 5.
[16] Ibid., 9.
[17] Ibid., 31.
[18] Ibid., 51.
[19] Ibid., 167.
[20] Peterson, 249.
[21] Townsend, 193.

Chapter 15

[1] Corey Keyes and Jonathan Haidt, "Introduction: Human Flourishing—The Study of That Which Makes Life Worthwhile," in *Flourishing: Positive Psychology and the Life Well-Lived*, ed. Corey Keyes and Jonathan Haidt, 3–12 (Washington D.C., APA, 2003), 6.
[2] Christopher Peterson, *A Primer in Positive Psychology* (USA: Oxford, 2006), 250.
[3] Mary Ellen Copeland, "Making and Keeping Friends: A Self-Help Guide," www.mentalhealth.samhsa.gov (accessed February 28, 2009).
[4] Ibid.
[5] Ibid.
[6] Ibid.
[7] Jeff Wickwire, *Friendships: Avoiding the Ones that Hurt, Finding the Ones that Heal* (Grand Rapids: Chosen, 2007), 15.
[8] Ibid., 166.
[9] Ibid., 167.
[10] Mike Huckabee, "What Really Matters," devotional@loi.org (accessed February 15, 2009).
[11] Max Lucado, "Treat Me as I Treat My Neighbor," email@maxlucado.com (accessed February 14, 2009).
[12] Wickwire, 40.
[13] Ibid., 72.

ENDNOTES

[14] Ibid., 83.
[15] Ibid., 123.
[16] Martin Seligman. "Why is there so much depression today? The waxing of the individual and the waning of the commons." *Invited lecture at the 96th Annual Convention of the American Psychological Association* (Atlanta).
[17] Peterson, 258.
[18] Ibid., 257.
[19] Ibid., 267.
[20] Ibid., 265.
[21] Ibid., 307–8.
[22] Ibid., 312.
[23] Sefra Kobrin Pitzele, *One More Day: Daily Meditations for People with Chronic Illness* (USA: Harper/Hazelden, 1988) Day January 26 of devotional.

Chapter 16

[1] Laurence Boldt, *How to Find the Work You Love* (USA: Penguin Compass, 2004), 8.
[2] Ibid.
[3] Ibid., 9.
[4] Ibid., 12.
[5] Marcus Buckingham and Donald Clifton, *Now, Discover Your Strengths* (New York: The Free Press, 2001), 25.
[6] Ibid., 26.
[7] Ibid., 3–4.
[8] Ibid., 79.
[9] Ibid., 90.
[10] Ibid., 99.
[11] Ibid., 105.
[12] Ibid., 107.
[13] Ibid., 116.
[14] Ibid., 6.
[15] Ibid., 7.
[16] Ibid., 8.

[17] Ibid., 19.
[18] Ibid., 21.
[19] Ibid.
[20] Ibid.
[21] Boldt, 20.
[22] Buckingham, 25, 27.
[23] Boldt, 42.
[24] Ibid., 43.
[25] Buckingham, 22.
[26] Ibid., 22.
[27] Boldt, 51.
[28] Max Lucado, My Success Is About Him, *The UpWords Weekly Email Devotional from Max Lucado.com* (accessed July 11, 2009).
[29] Ibid.

Chapter 17

[1] Helen Johnson, *How Do I Love Me?* (Salem Wisconsin: Sheffield Publishing, 1998), 27.
[2] Ibid.
[3] Ibid., 28.
[4] Ibid.
[5] Ibid., 28.
[6] Ibid., 29.
[7] Ibid.
[8] Ibid., 30.
[9] Ibid., 36, 38.
[10] Ibid., 48.
[11] Ibid., 59.
[12] Ibid., 62.
[13] Ibid., 58.
[14] Richard Bolles, *What Color Is Your Parachute?* (Berkeley, California: Ten Speed Press, 2004), 2.
[15] Ibid.
[16] Ibid., 12.
[17] Ibid., 145–6.

[18]Ibid., 155.
[19]Ibid., 39.
[20]Ibid., 186.

Chapter 18

[1]Billy Graham, *The Holy Spirit: Activating God's Power in Your Life* (Nashville: Word, 1988), xvi.
[2]Ibid., 4.
[3]Ibid., 5, 33.
[4]Ibid., 55.
[5]Mihaly Csikszentmihalyi, *Flow: The Psychology of Optimal Experience* (New York: Harper and Row, 1990).
[6]Graham, 61.
[7]Ibid., 151.
[8]V.R. Edman, *They Found the Secret* (Grand Rapids: Zondervan, 1960), 98.
[9]Graham, 267.
[10]Charles Stanley, *Living in the Power of the Holy Spirit* (USA: Nelson Books, 2005), ix.
[11]Ibid., 97.
[12]Gian Caprara and Daniel Cervone, "A Conception of Personality for a Psychology of Human Strengths: Personality as an Agentic, Self-Regulating System," in *A Psychology of Human Strengths; Fundamental Questions and Future Directions for a Positive Psychology*, eds. Lisa Aspinwall and Ursula Staudnigner, 61–74 (Washington D.C.: APA, 2003), 63–4.
[13]Stanley, 51.

Chapter 19

[1]Charles Stanley, *Living the Extraordinary Life* (USA: Nelson, 2005), xii.
[2]Ibid., 2.
[3]Christopher Peterson, *A Primer in Positive Psychology* (USA: Oxford, 2006), 154.

Chapter 20

[1] William Compton, *An Introduction to Positive Psychology* (Belmont, CA: Wadsworth, 2005), 1.

[2] Martin Seligman, "Positive Psychology, Positive Prevention, and Positive Therapy" in *Handbook of Positive Psychology*, ed. C.R. Snyder and Shane Lopez, 3–9 (USA, Oxford, 2002), 3.

[3] Debbie Macomber, *Knit Together: Discover God's Pattern for Your Life* (New York: Faith Words, 2007), 212.

[4] Ibid., 213.

[5] Ibid., 205.

[6] Ibid., 206.

WinePressPublishing
Your Book, Defined.
Since 1991.

To order additional copies of this book call:
1-877-421-READ (7323)
or please visit our website at
www.WinePressbooks.com

If you enjoyed this quality custom-published book,
drop by our website for more books and information.

www.winepresspublishing.com
"Your partner in custom publishing."

LaVergne, TN USA
11 November 2010
204550LV00003B/22/P